W9-BMO-850

OUR BELOVED SWEDEN

FOOD, FAITH, FLOWERS & FESTIVALS

JANET LETNES MARTIN and ILENE LETNES LORENZ

SENTEL PUBLISHING

HASTINGS, MN 55033

i

SENTEL PUBLISHING

PO BOX 551

HASTINGS, MN 55033

Copyright ©1996 by Janet Letnes Martin and Ilene Letnes Lorenz

All rights reserved. No part of this book may be reproduced or transmitted in any form or by any means, electronic or mechanical, or by any information storage or retrieval system, without written permission from the publisher.

Printed in the United States of America

Published by Sentel Publishing

PO Box 551, Hastings, MN 55033

Library of Congress Catalog Card Number 96-092173

ISBN 1-886627-02-9

First Printing

Editor: Suzann Nelson

Contributing Editors: Jennifer Green and Linda Lewis

Artists and Illustrators: (See Appendix B)

Layout: Lisa Beytien-Carlson and Paulstad Communications

Sentinel Printing, St. Cloud, MN

Sentel Publishing assumes no liability for any inaccuracies, and makes no warranties, either expressed or implied, for the recipes contained herein.

IN HONOR

OF THE

150th ANNIVERSARY

OF

MASS EMIGRATION

FROM

SWEDEN

TO THE

UNITED STATES

1846 - 1996

INTRODUCTION

Three years ago we wrote to over 1900 churches and organizations with Swedish-American ties, asking them to submit their Beloved Swedish Recipes, "Faith Stories," and Traditions. Even though we didn't hear back from all of them, we were totally overwhelmed by the response that we received. We thank you.

With everyone's effort and help, we were able to compile a beautiful book of wonderful old recipes, courageous and heart-warming faith stories, and memories of how Swedish traditions have been celebrated, preserved and promoted in the United States, both in the past and at the present time.

To really make this a book that will be cherished, usable and special, we enlisted the help of Ann L. Nilsson of Edina, MN to coordinate the Dala-painted dividers. These paintings were done by American Dala painters from across the United States.

Also, Avis Johnson of Minneapolis, MN – an artist who specializes in painting flowers – researched, and then pen-and-ink sketched the Provincial Flowers of Sweden. We think the Dala paintings and flower sketches add a lovely touch to this book. Lisa Beytien-Carlson drew the beautiful *Linnea* flower that graces the top of each recipe page.

However, before this could become a beautiful book, we had the horrendous task of selecting the recipes for the final version of this book. We received over 150 recipes for *bruna bönor*, rye bread and Swedish meatballs. Hundreds of others were duplicates. Many were not of Swedish origin, but all of them were wonderful. We thought it only fair that each church and organization that was gracious enough to submit recipes for this book should be acknowledged. However, since some churches sent only one recipe and others sent us their own cookbooks to pick and choose from, we had to cut and paste and do the best we could.

Some churches and organizations have several recipes printed in this final version. This is because these churches or organizations were the only ones that submitted a recipe for a particular dish that we thought should be included in a Swedish and Swedish-American cookbook. Sometimes we included several recipes for the same or similar dish. We thought this was important too because recipes were submitted from all over the United States from people whose customs and traditions came from different parts of Sweden. In this way, we hope readers may be able to find a recipe that was "just like the way Grandma made it "

The recipes were sent to us in all sizes, shapes and forms. Some were easy to figure out and others were nearly impossible to understand. Some had Swedish titles and others were in any number of dialects, and yet other titles were spelled phonetically.

Our editorial assistant, Suzann Nelson, has pored over many reference books and spent hundreds of hours deciphering Swedish-American spellings and Swedish dialects and rewriting the words and recipes in a uniform, standard way. We have earnestly tried to keep the "flavor of the recipes" without destroying their charm. Suzann edited them only to the extent that the final product would be easy to read, easy to understand and usable!

We have included some recipes that are not Swedish. Some originated in the other Scandinavian countries and some were American recipes "blended with an immigrant's touch." Sometimes, America as a "melting pot" has transferred to the "cooking pot," and some people submitted "Swedish" recipes that were really Finnish or Norwegian. This, too, reflects the process of immigration throughout successive generations. A Norwegian recipe becomes Norwegian-American and then is referred to as Scandinavian or Scandinavian-American, and a few generations later this same dish might be called "Swedish" because Grandma made it and her mother was from Sweden. All recipes included in this book are indeed Scandinavian-American, and yes, Grandma did prepare and serve them!

We think it is especially appropriate this year (1996), the 150th anniversary of the mass emigration from Sweden to the United States, that we document these beloved Swedish-American traditions and recipes which were passed down in the last century and a half. Also this year, Janet's church, Our Saviour's Lutheran Church of Hastings, MN is celebrating their 125th Anniversary. Like so many churches that celebrate "special anniversaries," they are remembering their Swedish heritage with special services.

The strength of the Swedish-American immigrants prevails today in Minnesota. Our Governor, Arnie Carlson; our University President, Nils Hasselmo; our well-known successful entrepreneur, Curt Carlson; and Herbert Chilstrom, the first bishop of the Evangelical Lutheran Church in America all are of Swedish heritage. More importantly, these same leaders are helping us preserve the Swedish-American heritage.

In Minnesota, we are also grateful for both the work of the American Swedish Institute and the volunteers at the *Gammelgården* Museum and to the other organizations and churches that keep our Swedish past alive.

In September 1996, Their Majesties King Carl XVI Gustaf and Queen Sylvia came to Minnesota to help us celebrate and remember the Swedish immigrants. We thank them for this and welcome them back.

We dedicate this book to the honor of our ancestors who came from Sweden with their hopes and dreams, and brought with them the Swedish ways that they cherished and hoped would be perpetuated. We, Janet and Ilene, sisters and co-authors of this book, are hopeful that these traditions, which originally were Swedish or Swedish-American will always be part of our American experience.

God Bless You.

TABLE of CONTENTS

DRYCKER

Här är det frun som regerar

Och härliga rätter serverar

Beverages

The Swedish love affair with coffee goes back to the 18th Century when it was first introduced into Sweden. Whether or not the recipe for egg coffee came to America from Sweden, we do not know. However, in homes, church basements and at coffee parties throughout the United States, egg coffee became the standard beverage—oftentimes diluted with cream and sugar. Some Swedish-Americans refer to it as their "Swedish Gasoline."

SWEDISH EGG COFFEE

"Swedish egg coffee is an economical treat for those who are patient. The reward is a mellow, less bitter brew that can be held longer on the beans although it does get darker with time. It takes about 15 minutes to make a batch. You can adjust the strength by the amount of beans used. The following is one of many recipes for egg coffee."

Select coarsely ground beans and use a tapered-body pot to aid settling. To make four cups of coffee, add about 4 1/2 cups of water. (Note the level for future use.) Bring the water to a full boil. Meanwhile put 6 slightly heaping "spoons" of coffee beans in a cup. Add about 1/2 cup of water to the beans. Now add a teaspoon of well-stirred egg and blend until all beans are wet.

When the water is boiling, turn off the heat. After pouring enough hot water into the cup of wet beans, set the pot on a cool burner. Take the lid off and pour in the wet beans. Stir to sink the beans and to allow the batch to settle. (The foam from stirred eggs placed in hot water will cause some beans to float.)

After 3 to 5 minutes, stir the batch again to equalize the color. This time the beans will settle. After 3 to 5 more minutes, the batch can be poured, but use a strainer. The coffee is still quite hot.

"To make a week's supply of egg mixture, stir the eggs well and add a few extra drops of water unless you have a small, covered container to help prevent water loss in the refrigerator."

*Swedish Council of St. Louis
St. Louis, MO*

1

SWEDISH EGG COFFEE

7 cups water
1 egg
2 tablespoons water
1/3 cup regular-grind coffee

Bring 7 cups of water to boiling in a heavy, enameled coffee pot. Meanwhile, in a small bowl, beat the egg with 2 tablespoons of water. Stir in the coffee. When the water boils, add the coffee-egg mixture and boil gently for 7 minutes. Remove from the heat and add 1/2 cup of cold water to settle the grounds.

Makes 10 servings.

First Evangelical Lutheran Church
Rockford, IL

NYPONTE
Rosehip Tea

3 tablespoons crushed, dried
    rosehips
1 1/2 cups water

Boil the water. Add the rosehips, boiling for 8 to 10 minutes. Strain the tea and serve.

Our Saviour's Lutheran Church
Hastings, MN

EGG COFFEE

4 *"measures"* of coffee
1/2 of a small, beaten egg
8 1/2 cups cold water

Mix the egg and coffee. Add this to the water and bring it to a boil. Stir occasionally. It needs watching as it boils over easily.

Take the pot off the heat and let it settle. To help it settle, pour in an additional 1/2 cup cold water. Use a strainer when serving if the grounds haven't sunk to the bottom. Simmer the coffee for stronger tasting coffee.

"Do not use an electric pot."

Evangelical Covenant Church
Helena, MT

APPLE TEA

Pare apples very thinly. Place in a hot oven until thoroughly dry. Store in airtight cans. *"To serve the tea, take out enough apples to make a good taste. It requires more than ordinary tea leaves."* Steep in a teapot as with other teas and serve with sugar and cream, if desired.

"Equally good as a cold drink."

First Covenant Church
Minneapolis, MN

The word "skål" goes back to the Viking Age when people drank their mead from a common drinking vessel or ale bowl.

Skoaling is similar to toasting, but there are definite rules associated with skoaling. The person who is skoaling looks the person he is toasting in the eyes, says "Skål" and both proceed to empty their small glasses of wine, schnapps, "akvavit" or punch in one swallow. Then the host looks at his guest directly in the eyes again, nods his head and puts his glass down.

"Akvavit," a potato liquor which in Latin means "water of life," is often served at "smörgåsbords" or formal parties. It is often used as a toasting beverage which is then chased with beer. There are also songs that people can sing before drinking "akvavit."

GRAPE JUICE

1 basket Concord grapes (or
    5 pounds wild grapes)
3 cups sugar
Water

Crush and cover the grapes with water. Boil until the seeds separate from the pulp. Strain. Add 3 cups of sugar. Measure the liquid and, if necessary, add water to make 4 even quarts. Boil for 5 minutes. Bottle and seal.

*First Covenant Church
Minneapolis, MN*

SWEDISH CHRISTMAS PUNCH

2 cups apple juice
2 tablespoons sugar
4 cloves
1 cup grape juice
1 stick cinnamon
1 orange peel, spiraled

In a saucepan combine the juices, sugar, a stick of cinnamon, cloves and an orange peel in a small cloth bag. Bring just to a boil.

Serve warm.

*Immanuel Lutheran Church
Akron, IA*

HOT "GLÖGG"

6 whole oranges
Whole cloves
4 quarts apple cider
3 cinnamon sticks

Stud each orange with 10 to
12 cloves. Place on a baking pan
and bake in a 300°F oven for
1 1/2 hours or until the juices
start to run. Transfer this to a
heatproof, two-gallon serving
bowl or copper pan. Add the hot
apple cider and the cinnamon
sticks.

First Covenant Church
Oakland, CA

SWEDISH "GLÖGG"

2 cups apple juice
1 cup grape juice
2 tablespoons sugar
1 stick cinnamon
4 cloves
Peel of 1 orange (peeling only; no
    white membrane)
1/3 cup raisins

Simmer 30 minutes.

Alma Lutheran Church
Mead, NE

JULGLÖGG

1 fifth of port wine
1 fifth of sherry wine
1 fifth of sauterne or Rhine wine
1 pint vodka
1 cup sugar
4 cinnamon sticks
1 teaspoon orange peel
1 teaspoon crushed cardamom
    seeds
1 teaspoon cloves
1 cup raisins
1 cup blanched almonds

Slightly crush the spices and put
them in a small white bag. Place
the bag in a large pan. Add the
sugar and wines and cook to a
simmer. Add the vodka. Do not
boil. Float the cinnamon sticks
and orange peel in the liquid.
Raisins and almonds may be
added to the *glögg* or served
from a serving cup.

Swedish Club of Metropolitan Detroit
Swedish Women's Organization
Farmington Hills, MI

GLÖGG

15 cardamom seeds
1 stick cinnamon
15 whole cloves
1 peeling of orange
1 1/2 cups raisins
15 to 20 blanched almonds

Put all the ingredients into a
large pan and cover it with
water. Bring this to a boil for
about 1/2 hour.

Syrup:
1 cup water
2 cups sugar

Put into a 2-quart pan and heat
to make the syrup.

Pour the syrup into the large
pan that has the spices. Bring to
a boil. Add 1/2 gallon of port
wine and bring to a boil again.
Add 3/4 pint of grain alcohol
(12 ounces of 100 proof). Heat to
simmering or until steam begins
to form. With the flame, burn off
the alcohol for one second.
"Taste to perfection."

Let this set for 24 hours. With a
cheesecloth, strain *glögg* into a
clean jug. Save the raisins and
almonds to serve with the drink.

Makes 1/2 gallon.

*Our Saviour's Lutheran Church
Lansing, IL*

ANDERS' LAPPLANDSGLÖGG

1 dark beer
10 ounces of sugar
1 bottle of port wine
1 bottle of red wine
4 ounces (100 grams) of
    blanched, whole almonds
2 handfuls of raisins
4 tablespoons of chopped,
    candied peel

Warm all the ingredients almost
to boiling. Let it stand for
several minutes before serving.

*First Lutheran Church
Genesco, IL*

SWEDISH "GLÖGG"

1 gallon dry red wine, port or
   Burgundy
1 pound raisins
15 almonds
3 sticks cinnamon
15 cardamom seeds
8 cloves
Orange or lemon peel, grated
4 cups sugar
1 quart bourbon

Scald the almonds to remove the
skins or use blanched almonds.
Soak the almonds with raisins,
the peel and spices (which can
be tied in a cheesecloth bag) in
wine, overnight or longer.

Bring this mixture to a boil.
While simmering, add the sugar.
Simmer for 20 minutes and let it
cool. Remove the spices and add
the bourbon.

When serving, place a few
raisins and an almond in each
cup. This is usually served hot.

Ascension Lutheran Church
San Diego, CA

JULGLÖGG
Christmas Wine

1 gallon of Mogan David wine
2 cups brandy
1 cup rum
1 bag spices
2 cups sugar
2 cups water

Spices:
1 cup raisins
6 whole almonds
14 cardamom seeds
6 whole cloves
4 sticks cinnamon
Peel from 1/2 orange, quartered

Tie the spices in a thin gauze or
cheesecloth bag.

In a small pot, boil the water
and add the spices. Boil for
15 minutes. Pour the wine into
an 8-quart kettle. Heat, but do
not boil it. Add the brandy, rum,
bag of spices and water to the
wine.

Caramelize the sugar in a large
frying pan without burning the
sugar. When it's done, pour this
into the wine mixture heating it
until the sugar is melted. Do not
boil. *"More sugar can be added,
but don't make it sweet."*

Calvary Lutheran Church
Rapid River, MI

LEMON-FLAVORED MEAD

2 large lemons
1/2 cup plus 5 teaspoons white
 sugar
1/2 cup brown sugar
5 quarts of boiling water
1/8 teaspoon active dry yeast
Raisins

Peel and slice the lemons. In a large bowl, combine the lemon, 1/2 cup white sugar and 1/2 cup brown sugar. Pour the boiling water over the fruit and sugars and then add the yeast.

To bottle, use 5 one-quart bottles with tight covers. Put 1 teaspoon of sugar and a few raisins in the bottom of each bottle. Pour the strained liquid into the bottles. Close the bottles tightly and store them at room temperature for 2 to 3 days or until the raisins rise to the surface.

Chill the sealed bottles until serving time.

Salem Evangelical Lutheran Church
Duluth, MN

SWEDISH "MUMMA"

1 12-ounce bottle of Pilsner beer
1 12-ounce bottle of Christmas
 ale (or dark beer)
3 to 4 tablespoons of gin

Chill the beers. Immediately before serving, mix the beers and gin together in a cold container.

"This is a very traditional Swedish drink."

Our Saviour's Lutheran Church
Hastings, MN

ÄGGTODDY
Egg Toddy

Mix in a tall iced-tea glass:
1 raw egg yolk
1 to 2 tablespoons sugar
1 jigger brandy (or sherry)
Boiling water

Stir the yolk and sugar to a foamy white consistency. Gradually stir in the brandy (sherry) and slowly add as much boiling water as you like.

"The finished brew is to be consumed in sips. Just as 'glögg' fits with Christmas and large groups of people, egg toddy suggests spring, intimacy and leisure."

First Lutheran Church
Genesco, IL

STOCKHOLM TODDY

2 cubes of sugar
1/2 cocktail glass of brandy
1/2 cocktail glass of port wine
4 dashes of raspberry syrup
1 slice of lemon

Dissolve two sugar cubes in a tumbler. Add the remaining ingredients and fill the tumbler with boiling water.

First Lutheran Church
Genesco, IL

SALLADER, GRÖNSAKER & SOPPOR

Salads, Vegetables & Soups

Very few salad recipes were brought over by the Swedish immigrants as salads were not a "typical" Scandinavian dish until the American influence of recent decades.

The salads that were brought over were often as much a fish or vegetable dish as a salad. The recipes were based on foods more readily available to the Swedish people such as salmon, herring, other fish, beets and apples.

SILLSALLAD
Herring Salad

4 cups cooked, twisted macaroni
1 cup herring, finely chopped
1 onion, finely chopped
2 tablespoons white vinegar
1 tablespoon olive oil
Dash pepper
1 chopped red beet
1 jar pimentos

Mix all together and then add the dressing:
1/2 cup mayonnaise
1 cup sour cream
2 1/2 teaspoons curry powder

Trinity Lutheran Church
Axtell, NE

"BIRTHDAY PARTY"
SILLSALLAD

Water-draw three herring, clean and place in cold water. Skin and cube. Place 5 cups of cubed, boiled potatoes (*"preferably new potatoes with their skins"*) in a bowl with 2 cubed boiled beets, 3 cubed tart apples, 2 cups chopped boiled veal, 1 small onion, 1 stalk chopped celery and 1 "sweet cucumber."

Just before serving, add the dressing:
2 hard-boiled eggs, grated
1 teaspoon dry mustard
Salt and pepper, as desired
1/2 cup salad oil
1 tablespoon sugar
2 raw egg yolks

Beat all together and let it stand to blend flavors. Toss the salad and decorate it with grated hard-boiled eggs, paprika and parsley.

Maria Lutheran Church
Kennedy, MN

SILLSALLAD
Herring Salad

1 salt herring (about 1 pound)
1 1/2 cups diced, boiled
    potatoes
1 1/2 cups diced, pickled beets
1/3 cup diced, pickled
    cucumber
1/2 cup diced apple
1/4 cup chopped onion
1/2 cup heavy cream (optional)

Dressing:
1/4 cup vinegar
2 tablespoons sugar
Dash of pepper

Garnish:
Hard-boiled eggs
Parsley

Fillet the fish and soak it overnight in cold water in a cool place, preferably in a refrigerator.

Remove the small bones and skin. Rinse, drain and dice the herring.

Carefully mix all the salad ingredients in a large bowl. Shake the ingredients for the dressing and let the mixture stand a few minutes before pouring it over the chopped salad mixture. Blend gently.

If desired, 1/2 cup whipped cream may be added.

Pack into a glass bowl or mold which has been rinsed in cold water. Chill in the refrigerator.

*Messiah Evangelical Lutheran Church
Bay City, MI*

HERRING SALAD

Mix together:
1 jar whole, pickled beets;
    drained and cut into quarters
1/3 cup beet juice
1 jar (12 ounces) herring fillets
    in wine sauce, drained
2 large potatoes; peeled, diced
    and cooked
1 red apple, unpeeled and diced
1 cup cucumber, scored and
    diced
1 cup red onion, coarsely
    chopped
1/2 teaspoon whole allspice,
    crushed
1/2 cup sugar
1/4 teaspoon black pepper,
    coarsely ground
1/2 teaspoon mustard seed

Chop hard-cooked egg to garnish the salad and serve with sour cream. Refrigerate 4 to 6 hours.

*Bethlehem Lutheran Church
Cherokee, IA*

10

SWEDISH SALMON MOLD

1 tablespoon gelatin
1 tablespoon cold water
1/2 cup boiling water
1 No.2 can salmon; drained, boned and flaked
1 cup mayonnaise
1/2 cup diced celery

Combine the gelatin and cold water. Add the boiling water and stir until well-dissolved. When cold and syrupy, add the salmon, mayonnaise and celery. Mix well. Place the mixture in a mold. Chill until firm.

Unmold on crisp salad greens. Slice and serve.

Prince of Peace Evangelical Lutheran Church
Grandview, MO

SALMON MOUSSE

2 large cans salmon
1/4 cup fish stock from canned salmon
2 packages Knox gelatin
2 teaspoons capers
2 green onions, chopped
Juice of 1/2 lemon
8 drops of hot pepper sauce
1 tablespoon fresh dill, chopped finely
1 3/4 cups sour cream

Warm the stock. Add the gelatin to the stock. Stir until dissolved. Place the remaining ingredients (except the sour cream) in a large bowl, and add the gelatin mixture. Beat at a high speed. Blend in the sour cream. Pour into an oiled mold.

Chill for several hours or overnight before unmolding.

Swedish Club of Metropolitan Detroit
Swedish Women's Organization
Farmington Hills, MI

11

RÖDBETASALLAD
Beet Salad

1 can of beets, cooked and
cubed finely. *"However, beets
fresh from the garden are
much better."*

Cut 1 small onion and add:
3/4 cup sugar (more if you like)
1/2 cup vinegar
Pinch of salt and pepper
1/3 cup whipping cream
1/4 teaspoon cinnamon
1/8 teaspoon cloves
1/4 teaspoon ginger
3 pieces of herring or *sill*
   (optional)

Let the salad stand several
hours before serving.

*Bethlehem Lutheran Church
Cherokee, IA*

RÖDBETASALLAD
Cabbage and Beet Salad

2 cups raw, shredded beets
2 cups shredded cabbage
2 cups grated carrots
French dressing
1 head lettuce

Wash and chill the vegetables.
Marinate the vegetables in
French dressing.

Arrange the marinated
vegetables on lettuce leaves
individually. Serve with desired
dressing.

*The Southern Florida Associate of the
American-Scandinavian Foundation
Florida*

SWEDISH CABBAGE SALAD

1 head cabbage, chopped finely
1 tablespoon salt
2 cups vinegar
2 cups sugar
1/2 cup water
1 green pepper
7 celery stalks
1 teaspoon celery seed
1 teaspoon mustard seed

Place the chopped cabbage in a flat pan and sprinkle with the salt. Let it stand for 2 hours.

Boil the sugar, vinegar and water for 1 minute and then cool. Squeeze all the juice from the cabbage. Cut the pepper and celery finely. Add the mustard seed and celery seed. Pour the liquid over all and put it in the refrigerator. Let it stand overnight.

"This will keep for several weeks."

*Trinity Lutheran Church
Gresham, OR*

SWEDISH SLAW

Shred a head of cabbage and some carrots. Add diced celery and green pepper, if desired. Add salt and pepper, to taste.

To make the dressing, combine:
1/2 cup cider vinegar
1 cup sugar
1/2 cup water
1 teaspoon dry mustard

Bring the dressing ingredients to a boil and cool. When the dressing has cooled, pour the boiled mixture over the vegetables and refrigerate.

"This will keep for several days in the refrigerator."

*Bethel Lutheran Church
Danville, IL*

CUCUMBERS IN DILL SAUCE

3 cups thinly sliced, unpeeled
  cucumbers (approximately
  3 small cucumbers)
2 tablespoons tarragon vinegar
1 tablespoon water
1/2 teaspoon salt
Dash of pepper
1 tablespoon sugar
1 cup Miracle Whip salad
  dressing
1 small onion, thinly sliced
1/4 teaspoon dried dill weed

Stir together all of the
ingredients except the
cucumbers. Fold in the
cucumbers. Cover and chill at
least 2 hours.

Swedish Council of St. Louis
St. Louis, MO

SWEDISH CUCUMBERS

2 cucumbers
Salt
1 cup white vinegar
1/3 cup sugar
2 bay leaves
6 whole allspice
Coarse-ground black pepper
Chopped parsley

Pare and slice the cucumbers
very thinly. Sprinkle them with
salt. Cover and put a weight on
the vegetables for an hour. Pour
off the juice.

Mix the vinegar, sugar and
seasonings. Pour over the
cucumbers.

Sprinkle with parsley before
serving.

Bethany Lutheran Church
Crystal Lake, IL

POTATISSALLAD
Potato Salad

6 to 8 medium-sized, boiled
    potatoes, cold
2 tablespoons white vinegar
5 or 6 tablespoons olive or salad
    oil
1 teaspoon salt
Pinch of white pepper
2 tablespoons chopped, sweet
    onion
2 tablespoons chopped parsley
2 tablespoons chopped chives
1/2 cup pickled beets (optional)

Cool and dice the potatoes. Mix
the vinegar, oil, salt and pepper.
Pour this mixture over the diced
potatoes in a salad bowl.
Arrange the onion, parsley, beets
and chives in rows on the top.

Keep in a cool place 1 to
2 hours. Stir once or twice
before serving. Serve with cold
meats.

Powell Valley Covenant Church
Gresham, OR

MAMMA'S POTATO SALAD DRESSING

5 eggs
1 1/2 teaspoons salt
Dash pepper
5 tablespoons sugar
4 tablespoons vinegar
3 tablespoons prepared mustard
4 tablespoons margarine

Beat the eggs in a heavy
saucepan. Add the remainder of
the above ingredients. Cook over
a low heat whisking or beating
constantly until it thickens. Do
not overcook. Remove from the
heat and pour it into a bowl.
Cool.

When it has cooled, add:
5 tablespoons mayonnaise
1/2 pint whipping cream

Add the mayonnaise and cream
to the cooled salad dressing,
blending thoroughly. If the
mixture is too thick, it can be
thinned with a little milk.

Siloa Lutheran Church
Morris Run, PA

ONION SALAD

Pour 1/4 cup vinegar into 1/2 pint of half and half (half cream and half milk). Beat in 1/2 cup of sugar. After the cream is whipped, add 2 heaping teaspoons of prepared mustard, 1/4 teaspoon salt and two or three finely sliced onions. Mix thoroughly.

"This was a secret recipe of a Swedish smörgåsbord restaurant in Seattle which many people enjoyed some 50 years ago."

Magnolia Lutheran Church
Seattle, WA

SCANDINAVIAN VEGETABLE SALAD

2 cans tiny peas, drained
1 can French-style green beans, drained
1 can shoe-peg corn, drained
1 small jar pimento, chopped and drained
1 small onion, chopped
1 or 2 stalks celery, chopped

Mix together:
1 1/2 cups sugar
1 cup vinegar
2 tablespoons water
1/2 cup oil
1 teaspoon paprika

Heat to dissolve the sugar. Cool this and add it to the vegetables. Chill for 24 hours. Keeps well if refrigerated.

Evangelical Lutheran Church
Clay Center, KS

SWEDISH-STYLE VEGETABLES

6 tomatoes
3 boiled potatoes
2 small cooked beets
1 cup cooked peas or lima beans
1 head lettuce or endive
2 hard-boiled eggs

Wash the lettuce and slice the potatoes and beets. Cut the eggs in halves, crosswise. Press the yolks through a coarse sieve and slice the whites into delicate rings.

Arrange the lettuce or endive on a platter. Place the sliced tomatoes in the center, and cover with the boiled dressing. Over the tomatoes, but not concealing them, place the potatoes that have been dipped in the dressing. Arrange the beet slices next and then the peas or beans mixed with a little of the dressing. Sprinkle the sieved egg yolk over the whole dish and garnish the edges with the rings of egg whites.

Boiled Dressing:
1/2 teaspoon salt
1 teaspoon mustard
2 tablespoons sugar
1 tablespoon flour
1 egg
3/4 cup milk
1/4 cup vinegar

Mix the dry ingredients thoroughly. Add the slightly beaten egg and milk. When it begins to thicken, add the vinegar stirring constantly. Boil until thick.

First Covenant Church
Minneapolis, MN

ÄPPELSALLAD
Apple Salad

4 good tart apples
3/4 cup cream
1 to 3 tablespoons lemon juice
1 to 3 teaspoons sugar

Peel, shred or grate the apples coarsely. Mix the cream with the lemon juice and sugar. (The amounts depend on the tartness of the apples). Pour the sauce over the apples. Toss lightly and chill.

Serve cold. Sprinkle with nuts or paprika. Serve for a *smörgåsbord* or with pork dishes. Makes 4 servings.

Swedish Council of St. Louis
St. Louis, MO

"Bruna Bönor" is a very traditional Swedish dish. It is considered "authentically Swedish." Recipes for brown beans were brought to the United States by Swedish immigrants and this dish was served in many Swedish-American homes.

BRUNA BÖNOR
Brown Beans

1 28-ounce package Swedish
    brown beans

Soak overnight. Boil for 1 hour and then add 1/2 teaspoon soda. Boil for another 20 minutes. Pour off all the liquid.

Add the remaining ingredients:
1 cup brown sugar
1/4 pound margarine
1/2 cup molasses
1 tablespoon vinegar
Salt and pepper

Cook until tender or about 2 1/2 to 3 hours.

"Grandma Yellow Label molasses has a good flavor for the beans."

*Elim Lutheran Church
Marquette, KS*

SVENSKA BRUNA BÖNOR
Swedish Brown Beans

1 pound Swedish brown beans
1/4 cup vinegar
1 cup brown sugar
1 teaspoon salt (or more to taste)
3 tablespoons molasses
1 to 2 teaspoons cornstarch
    (depending upon the amount
    of liquid left when beans are
    cooked)

Wash the beans. Cover with cold water and allow to soak overnight. Bring to a boil and simmer until tender, 3 to 4 hours or more. Add more hot water if necessary. When tender, add the salt, vinegar, sugar and molasses. Thicken with cornstarch that has been mixed with cold water. You may add a dash of nutmeg and/or 1 or 2 tablespoons of butter. Add bacon pieces and bake at 325°F for 45 to 60 minutes more.

*First Lutheran Church
Granville, IL*

18

BRUNA BÖNOR
Brown Beans

Soak 1 pound of brown beans overnight. Then cover them with cold water and cook for 2 hours or until creamy and soft.

Add :
3/4 cup sugar
5 tablespoons vinegar
3 tablespoons butter

Emanuel Lutheran Church
Bradford, PA

SWEDISH BROWN BEANS

2 cups Swedish brown beans
5 cups water
1 stick cinnamon
1 1/2 teaspoons salt
1/2 cup brown sugar
1/4 cup vinegar

Wash the beans and soak them overnight in water. Drain. Add the salt and cinnamon to 5 cups of water in a kettle. Cook until the beans are done. Then add the brown sugar and vinegar. Simmer about 15 to 30 minutes.

"Swedish brown beans are difficult to find. Gurney's Seed Co. at Yankton, SD has the seed so people can raise their own."

Elim Covenant Church
Stockholm, SD

SÖTSUR BRUNA BÖNOR
Sweet and Sour Brown Beans

Soak overnight:
1 cup Swedish brown beans
3 1/2 cups cold water

Add:
1 teaspoon salt
1 stick cinnamon
Cook slowly until the beans are done.

Add:
1 tablespoon vinegar
1/2 cup sugar

Stir in:
1/3 cup cornstarch mixed with
    1/2 cup cold water

Cook until clear or about 5 minutes.

Zion Lutheran Church
Marinette, WI

KOKT RÖDKÅL
Boiled Red Cabbage

2 large heads red cabbage,
    shredded or cubed
2 to 4 tablespoons butter
1 to 3 tablespoons molasses
2 to 3 apples, peeled and sliced
1 onion, grated
Juice of one lemon
1/2 cup red wine or vinegar
Salt

Melt the butter in a Dutch oven.
Add the shredded cabbage and
molasses. Brown over a slow
fire, stirring constantly. Add the
apples, onion, lemon juice, wine
and salt. Simmer covered 1 to
1 1/2 hours, stirring
occasionally.

Season to taste and serve with
roast goose. Serves 8 to 10.

First Lutheran Church
Genesco, IL

RÖDKÅL
Red Cabbage

1 medium head red cabbage
1 rounded tablespoon butter
1/2 cup vinegar, lemon or pickle
    juice
1 teaspoon salt
1/4 cup sugar
1/4 cup currant jelly

Remove the inner stem and
outer leaves and shred the
cabbage finely. Melt the butter in
a kettle. Add the cabbage, salt,
sugar and vinegar. (Sweet pickle
juice or lemon juice may be used
instead of vinegar). Cook gently
until tender.

Season to taste with additional
salt, sugar or vinegar. Add the
jelly near the end of the cooking
time.

Concordia Lutheran Church
Kingsburg, CA

TOMATO-CABBAGE CASSEROLE

5 cups shredded cabbage
1 cup canned tomatoes, drained
1/2 cup of the drained tomato juice
1/4 cup chopped onion
1/2 cup crushed soda crackers
1 1/2 teaspoons salt
1/8 teaspoon pepper
1/2 cup grated American cheese

Steam the cabbage in a covered pan with a small amount of water until tender, yet crisp. Drain, if necessary. In a 1-quart buttered casserole dish, arrange the cabbage in layers with the tomatoes, onion, and crackers. Season the layers with salt and pepper.

Bake covered at 350°F for 30 minutes. Remove the cover and bake for 10 more minutes. Top with cheese and bake uncovered 5 more minutes.

All Saints Lutheran Church
Darwin, MN

SCALLOPED CABBAGE

1 pound cabbage, coarsely shredded
1/8 cup salt
5 tablespoons butter
1 cup milk
2 quarts boiling water
1/4 cup sugar
3 tablespoons flour
1 cup buttered bread crumbs

Cook the cabbage in water seasoned with salt and sugar for 4 minutes. Do not overcook. Drain very well and place in a buttered 2-quart flat casserole. Make a cream sauce with butter, flour and milk. Pour this over the cabbage.

Sprinkle with buttered crumbs and bake at 325°F for 45 minutes. Serves 4 to 6.

Maria Lutheran Church
Kennedy, MN

BLOMKÅL MED SKALDJURSTUVNING
Creamed Cauliflower with Shellfish

(Metric Chart: Appendix C)

Cauliflower, about 1/2 kilogram

Cooking the cauliflower:
Remove the heaviest part of the stem and the thicker leaves. Rinse the rest under cold running water. Place it in water with vinegar and let it sit for a while to remove insects. (The cauliflower will also become whiter through this procedure.)

Rinse the cauliflower again. Place a cloth on the cauliflower, if it is steamed. (Again, this will make the cauliflower whiter.) Add salt after half of the cooking time. If cooked in water, the cooking time is 20 minutes. If steamed, the time will almost be doubled.

For the cream:
1 to 1 1/2 *matsked* butter
2 *matsked* flour
4 deciliters milk with liquid from the canned fish and from the boiled cauliflower, if available
Salt and white pepper
Sugar (optional)

Preparing the fish:
This dish may be made with any one of these; shrimp, lobster meat or crab.

150 to 200 grams of shrimp (Clean and rinse the shrimp, if needed. If the shrimp is large, cut it lengthwise.)
1/4 to 1/2 can of lobster meat
1/4 to 1/2 can of crab

Drain the crab and cut it into smaller pieces. You may choose to sauté the fish in butter.

For the sauce:
Melt the butter. Add the flour and simmer for a while. Add the liquid and let the sauce cook for 10 minutes. Add seasoning to taste.

Add the selected shellfish and cold butter. Remove from the heat immediately. Add a little coloring, except when using crab.

First Lutheran Church
Genesco, IL

BAKED CORN PUDDING

1 16-ounce can creamed-style
   corn
2 eggs, slightly beaten
1 tablespoon flour
3/4 cup milk (or evaporated
   milk)
1/2 stick melted margarine or
   butter
8 doubled soda crackers,
   crushed (save a few cracker
   crumbs to sprinkle over the
   top)
Pinch of sugar
Salt and pepper

Mix all the ingredients together
and pour into a greased, glass
casserole. Sprinkle some of the
crumbs over the top. Dot with
butter.

Bake uncovered at 350°F until
lightly browned, approximately
1 hour or until set.

Bethlehem Lutheran Church
Florence, WI

CORN PUDDING

1/4 cup butter
1/4 cup flour
2 teaspoons salt
2 tablespoons sugar
1 3/4 cups milk
3 eggs
3 cups corn (fresh or frozen)

Melt the butter in a saucepan.
Blend in the flour, salt and
sugar. Stir until smooth, but do
not brown. Add the milk and
cook until thick. Stir the corn
into the flour mixture. Add the
eggs, beaten until frothy.

Pour into a buttered, shallow
1 1/2-quart casserole. Set in a
pan filled with 1 inch of hot
water. Bake in a moderate oven
at 350°F until just set, about
45 minutes.

Yield: 6 to 8 servings.

Nathaniel Lutheran Church
Alcester, SD

SWEDISH-STYLE SPINACH

2 pounds spinach
1 cup cream sauce
1 tablespoon sugar
Salt and pepper

Wash the spinach and cook it for 10 minutes. Drain and chop it finely. Mix it with cream sauce.

Mission Covenant Church
Foster City, MI

SWEDISH CARROT PUDDING

2 eggs
2 tablespoons sugar
1 teaspoon salt
1 cup boiled rice (1/3 cup when
    uncooked)
1 1/2 cups milk
2 cups carrots, mashed

Beat the eggs. Add the sugar, salt and milk. Stir in the rice and carrots. Pour into a casserole.

Bake at 350°F for 30 to 35 minutes or until set. This recipe can easily be doubled.

Yield: 6 servings.

Bethel Lutheran Church
Willmar, MN

SWEDISH CARROT PUDDING

1 cup bread crumbs
3/4 cup melted butter
1 pint milk
Salt to taste
4 or 5 well-beaten eggs
3 cups boiled and grated carrots
Almond extract

Mix the bread crumbs, butter, salt, milk, eggs and almond extract. After the bread crumbs are thoroughly soaked, add the carrots. Pour into a buttered dish and bake in a moderate oven.

"The pudding may be turned out on a platter if the baking dish has been well-buttered.

"Fried carrots may be used for garnish."

First Covenant Church
Minneapolis, MN

SWEDISH CARROTS

30 carrots
4 tablespoons sugar
1 tablespoon salt
3/4 cup melted margarine
1 cup light cream
1 1/2 cups shredded cheese

Cook the carrots in water with the sugar and salt until tender. Layer the carrots in a shallow baking pan. Pour the cream and melted margarine over the carrots. Top with shredded cheese.

Bake in a moderate oven for 30 minutes.

Fremont Lutheran Church
Essex, IA

POTATISPUDDING
Potato Pudding

(Metric Chart: Appendix C)

1 1/2 liters potatoes
Water
Salt
2 *matsked* butter (1 *matsked* melted butter=15 grams)
2 eggs
1 to 2 *"kkp"* mjölk, (milk)
3 to 4 *matsked skorpmjöl*, (bread crumbs or rusks)

2 *matsked* syrup (1 *matsked* syrup=20 to 25 grams)
1/8 *tesked* ground nutmeg
1 *matsked* salt
1 *matsked* bread crumbs or rusks

For the mold:
1/2 *matsked* butter
1 *matsked* crumbs

Peel and cook the potatoes. Save the liquid. Add the butter to the potatoes and mash them with a fork. When the mashed potatoes are cold, add the yolks beaten together with the milk, crumbs, syrup and spices. (Egg whites should be beaten until soft peaks form.) Blend all the ingredients well with a fork.

Place the mixture in a greased form with crumbs sprinkled on the bottom. Before the pudding is placed in the oven, it should be stirred with a fork and a design made with the fork. Bread crumbs should be sprinkled on top.

The pudding is baked until golden brown and is served with meat or fish or alone with dill or parsley.

First Lutheran Church
Genesco, IL

"Potatoes were important crops. During the famine years, the Swedish King proclaimed that every family grow potatoes to help feed hungry people when the grain crops were so poor.

"New potatoes are a favorite when flavored with butter and snipped dill feathers."

Axtell Mission Covenant Church
Vermillion, KS

"SMÖRGÅSBORD" POTATOES

Use tiny new potatoes or regular-sized potatoes and scoop out potato balls with a melon ball cutter. Boil them in salted water for 15 to 20 minutes or until they are done. Drain well. Let them dry for a minute in a warm oven.

Put the potatoes in a hot serving dish. Pour melted butter over the potatoes and sprinkle chopped parsley over the melted butter.

Immanuel Lutheran Church
Holden, MA

SWEDISH POTATOES

12 good-sized potatoes
2 onions, diced
1 pound cheese; part American, part Cheddar
1 small jar pimento
1 green pepper
1/2 pound butter
8 tablespoons milk
Salt and pepper, to taste

Cook, cool, peel and dice the potatoes. Dice the rest of the ingredients. Melt together the butter and milk. Mix the potatoes, onions, cheese, pimentos and green pepper together. Pour the butter and milk mixture over all the ingredients. Add the seasonings.

Place in a large, flat cake pan. (Do not use a deep casserole).

Bake uncovered for 1 hour in a 350°F oven. Occasionally stir the potatoes during the baking period.

This makes 12 servings.

Augustana Lutheran Church
Grand Forks, ND

HASSELBACKSPOTATIS

"This recipe is the creation of a famous chef at the Grand Hotel in Stockholm whose name happened to be Hasselback."

6 medium baking potatoes
1/4 cup melted butter
1/4 cup grated Parmesan cheese
2 tablespoons dry bread crumbs
Paprika
Salt and pepper

Cut the potatoes, peeled or unpeeled, into 1/8 inch slices. Cut only 3/4 of the way through each potato. (To avoid cutting too deeply, place each potato on a large spoon before slicing. The concave bowl of the spoon prevents slicing too far.) Place them cut-side up in a greased, oblong baking dish. Brush with butter and sprinkle with salt and pepper. Cover and bake in a 375°F oven for 45 minutes, basting once or twice. Remove the cover. Mix the cheese and crumbs. Sprinkle this on the potatoes. Also, sprinkle with salt, pepper and paprika. Bake another 30 to 35 minutes or until the potatoes are tender on the inside and crispy brown on the outside.

Svenska Vänner
Jamestown, ND

HASSELBACKSPOTATIS

6 medium peeled potatoes
1/2 cup melted butter
1 1/4 teaspoons salt
2 tablespoons fine, dry bread crumbs
2 tablespoons freshly-grated Parmesan cheese

Preheat the oven to 425°F. With a sharp knife, partially slice through each potato at 1/4 inch intervals. The potato should remain intact. Arrange the potatoes, cut-side up, in a well-buttered, shallow baking pan. Brush each potato with about 2 teaspoons of the butter and sprinkle generously with the salt.

Bake the potatoes, uncovered, for 30 minutes. Sprinkle the crumbs evenly over the potatoes and drizzle them with the remaining butter. Bake for 20 minutes more and sprinkle with grated Parmesan cheese. Baste them with the drippings in the pan and bake them for 10 to 15 more minutes or until they are tender when a skewer is inserted near the bottom.

Yield: 6 servings.

Arlington Heights Lutheran Church
St. Paul, MN

STUVAD POTATIS
Swedish-Style Creamed Potatoes

1 1/2 tablespoons butter
1 1/2 tablespoons flour
1 3/4 cups light cream
6 medium boiled potatoes, sliced
    or diced
1 teaspoon salt
1/2 teaspoon white pepper
1 tablespoon chopped dill,
    chives or parsley

In a saucepan, heat the butter. Stir in the flour and add the cream. Cook for 5 minutes over a moderate heat. Stir constantly. Add the potatoes, salt and pepper. Heat thoroughly.

Garnish with chopped herbs.

Yield: 4 servings.

Swedish Council of St. Louis
St. Louis, MO

POTATO GRIT FROM THE PROVINCE OF "VÄSTERBOTTEN"

(See Appendixes C and D)

8 white "mealy" potatoes
1 small carrot
1 small leek
1 to 2 deciliters milk
2 deciliters whipping cream
3 deciliters *Västerbottensost* (or
    some other sharp, well-
    ripened cheese)
1 teaspoon salt
1/2 teaspoon black pepper

Peel and cut the potatoes and carrot very thinly and cut the leek into very thin pieces. Put this into a casserole.

Mix and simmer the salt, pepper, milk and half of the whipping cream for 6 to 7 minutes. Stir to avoid burning. Pour this mixture, along with half of the cheese and the remaining whipping cream, into the casserole dish. Sprinkle with the remaining cheese. Bake at 375°F for 30 minutes.

Serve cold. Makes 4 portions.

Linneas of Texas
Houston, TX

Because rutabagas and turnips taste alike, the words – rutabagas and turnips – are commonly used interchangeably. In some places in America, the rutabaga is called a Swedish turnip or a Russian turnip.

SVENSKA ROTMOS
Mashed Potatoes and Rutabaga

Boil 4 to 5 medium-sized potatoes and a medium-sized rutabaga until tender. Cut them up and drain. Add 1/4 cup warm milk, 1/3 cup butter, and salt and pepper to taste. Mash all together. If the mixture is too stiff, add a little more milk. Serve while hot.

Approximately 4 servings.

Bethlehem Lutheran Church
Florence, WI

RUTABAGA MOUSSE

Peel rutabagas and cut them into little pieces. Add a small amount of water and boil until mushy. Beat with an eggbeater until smooth. Cool. There should be 4 to 5 cups. Beat in 4 eggs, a scant 1/2 cup sugar, 1 1/4 cups milk, and salt and pepper to taste.

Bake in a greased 2-quart dish at 350°F for about 30 minutes.

"Test for doneness with a silver knife until it comes out clean. You can also cook these the day before."

First Evangelical Lutheran Church
Taylors Falls, MN

RUTABAGA PUDDING

2 medium-sized rutabagas
3 eggs
1/2 cup raisins
1 teaspoon salt
1/4 cup sugar
1 1/2 cups milk

Peel and cut up the two rutabagas. Cook and mash them until they are lump-free. Add 3 beaten eggs, the seasonings and the milk. Next, add the raisins and mix well.

Bake at 350°F in a 2-quart casserole for about 45 minutes or until set. Serves 8.

"The Swedes insist that the raisins take the burp out of rutabagas."

Trinity Lutheran Church
Lindstrom, MN

SWEDISH PARSNIP SOUFFLÉ

2 large carrots, shredded finely
2 pounds of parsnips, peeled
    and sliced
1/4 cup butter
1 tablespoon sugar
1 teaspoon salt
1 cup milk
4 eggs, divided
1/2 teaspoon ground nutmeg
1 tablespoon minced parsley

Cook the carrots for 5 minutes in a covered pan with a small amount of boiling, salted water. Drain and set aside. Cook the parsnips the same way using the same pan. Cook for 15 to 20 minutes or until tender. Drain the parsnips and mash them with butter, sugar and salt. Blend in the milk and the carrots.

In a separate bowl, beat the egg yolks and nutmeg together for about 5 minutes or until thick. Blend 1 cup of the parsnip mixture in with the egg yolks. Next add the rest of the mashed parsnips and carrots.

In a separate bowl, beat the egg whites until stiff peaks form. Fold into the combined mixtures.

Bake at 350°F for 50 to 55 minutes in a buttered, 2 1/2-quart soufflé dish. Sprinkle with parsley.

Yield: 6 to 8 servings.

Cadillac Area Scandinavian Society
Cadillac, MI

GRATINERADE TOMATER
Broiled Tomatoes

4 large tomatoes
1 clove garlic
1/4 teaspoon salt
Dash of pepper
1 tablespoon soft butter or
    margarine
1 tablespoon chopped parsley,
    dill, or chives

Slice off the tops of the tomatoes. Rub the surfaces with garlic and sprinkle with salt and pepper.

Mix the butter or margarine with chopped parsley and spread this over the tomatoes. Broil 4 to 5 inches from the heat for 5 minutes or until the tomatoes start to get soft.

Makes 4 servings.

Swedish Council of St. Louis
St. Louis, MO

Pea soup is considered one of the humble Swedish foods in the "husmanskost" (home-cooked or plain food) category. It is often eaten on Thursdays. This tradition goes back to pre-Reformation times when people fasted on Friday and ate this hearty meal on Thursday.

GUL ÄRTSOPPA
Yellow Pea Soup

1 pound yellow dried peas
10 to 14 ounces salt pork
8 or 9 cups water
1 yellow onion, peeled
1 teaspoon thyme
2 teaspoons marjoram
1 teaspoon salt
1/2 teaspoon black pepper
1 tart apple, peeled
Mustard to serve with the soup

Soak the peas in 2 quarts of water with 1 teaspoon salt. Pour off the water and put the peas in a large kettle. Pour in 8 to 9 cups of water and add the onion and apple which have been cut up in pieces. Add the spices and bring to a boil.

Cook 30 minutes before adding the pork. Simmer about 1 1/4 hours or until the peas are soft. (More spices may be added to taste.)

Remove the pork from the soup. Cut it into pieces and "serve it on the side." Also serve the soup with strong mustard, dark bread and cold butter.

"In Sweden, beer is the beverage of choice to accompany this soup. Yellow pea soup is traditionally eaten in Sweden every Thursday. It is served not only in homes but also in most restaurants, large company lunchrooms and at parties.

"Favorite desserts served with pea soup are either paper-thin Swedish pancakes topped with lingonberry jam, or cloudberries with whipped cream. These typical desserts are enjoyed by both young and old."

*Augustana Lutheran Church
St James, MN*

SWEDISH PEA SOUP

1 pound dried peas
1 ham bone with some meat, or
    smoked pork hocks
1 large carrot, grated
3 ribs celery, cut up small
1 medium onion, chopped
Seasoning to taste

Soak the peas in warm water overnight. The next day, add the ham bone and some more water (enough to make 3 quarts) to the peas. Simmer until the peas are soft. If whole peas are used, skim the shells off as they rise.

Add the vegetables and cook until done. Season to taste. Add more water if needed.

Gammelgården Volunteers
Scandia, MN

GUL ÄRTSOPPA
Yellow Pea Soup

(Metric Chart: Appendix C)

4 deciliters dried yellow peas
    (1 3/4 cups)
1 1/2 liters water (6 1/2 cups)
1 tablespoon salt
10 1/2 to 14 ounces of lightly
    salted side pork or 1 small
    pork shank
Water

1 pinch ginger, thyme or
    marjoram

Rinse the peas and soak them in cold water with salt for 10 to 12 hours. Drain. Add 1 liter water. Season with salt. Cover and cook rapidly for a few minutes. Skim off the shells floating on the surface.

Add the whole piece of pork or cut the pork into cubes and add them when the peas have cooked for 30 minutes. Let the soup simmer for 1 to 1 1/2 hours or until the peas and pork are tender. If too thick, add more water to the soup. Season with salt and ginger, thyme or marjoram.

Remove the pork. Either cut the pork into slices to serve separately or cut it into cubes to put back into the soup.

"Pea soup should be accompanied by a glass of warm punch, an idea from earlier times when the 'akvavit' produced in Europe had an unpleasant aftertaste of fusel oil that could be covered up by the addition of arrack."

American Swedish Historical Museum
Philadelphia, PA

BEEF AND FOWL BOUILLON

(Metric Chart: Appendix C)

"The cooking of all meat bouillon is, in principle, done the same way. The ingredients, however, vary somewhat and can even be prepared in different ways. It is through these variations that different flavors, consistencies and colors are achieved leading to the best possible taste and color."

Regular Beef Bouillon: *"Vanlig köttbuljong"*

2 kilograms beef ribs or neck, or 1 mature chicken
4 liters water
1/2 tablespoon salt

Cook the bouillon in beef or a mixture of beef and veal. For a clear bouillon, only beef is used. For consommé, a mature, browned chicken is added and the bouillon is cooked with *"rotsaker"*, root or tuber vegetables such as carrots and parsnips.

"The proportions between beef and vegetables have to be carefully measured so that the vegetables don't dominate the flavor, and so that one vegetable isn't too strong."

Vegetables for soups:
1 carrot (75 to 100 grams)
1/2 to 1 parsnip (100 grams)
1 leek (100 grams)
1 bit of root of *selleri* or celery (30 grams)
A few sprigs of parsley
1 small, yellow onion
1 clove

Rinse the beef in cold water. Remove the meat from the bones and cut it into small pieces. If the bones are large, cut them in half. Place the bones on the bottom of the pot and place the meat on top. Pour cold water over it and let this stand at room temperature for about 1 hour so that the meat can become saturated with water.

Cover the pot and put it on the stove over very low heat. Heat the mixture very slowly, skimming off the foam. Add a little salt. Let the mixture simmer again and skim off more foam. Add a little more salt. Let the mixture simmer for about 10 hours. Strain the bouillon. To make it clearer, strain it through muslin or other fine cloth. Place the broth in a cool place so the fat can become firm.

*First Lutheran Church
Genesco, IL*

33

TISDAGSSOPPA
Tuesday Soup

2 tablespoons barley
1 quart pork stock
2 carrots
1 parsnip
1 piece celery root
1 piece turnip
3 to 4 potatoes
Salt
White pepper
1 1/2 cups milk

Rinse the barley in cold water and cook it in the stock until the barley is cooked halfway. Clean the vegetables, cut them into cubes, and add them to the stock and barley. Cook until tender. Add the milk.

Season and serve immediately.

First Lutheran Church
Genesco, IL

FISH SOUP

(Metric Chart: Appendix C)

1 1/2 liters fish stock (1 liter =
    3 3/4 cups)
1 tablespoon butter
2 tablespoons flour
1 egg yolk

1 1/2 deciliters cream
    (1 1/2 deciliters = 1 regular
    coffee cup)
2 to 3 tablespoons chopped
    parsley
Salt and white pepper

Melt the butter. Add the flour and cook for a minute. Add the stock a small amount at a time. Stir and cook for a few minutes. Whip up the cream with the yolk and add this to the soup, stirring frequently. Turn the heat off and add the parsley. Salt and pepper, if necessary.

First Lutheran Church
Genesco, IL

FISH STOCK

5 pounds raw fish
1 quart water
1 medium onion
1 teaspoon pepper
1 teaspoon salt
1 clove

Boil the fish. Skim the water and add the seasonings. Cover and simmer for 25 minutes. Strain the stock.

Our Saviour's Lutheran Church
Hastings, MN

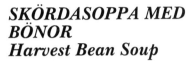

GRÖNSAKSSOPPA
Vegetable Soup

1/2 head cauliflower, cut into
   sections
1 cup peas, shelled
3 to 4 small carrots, sliced
5 to 6 cups water or beef stock
Salt
White pepper
1 tablespoon butter
2 tablespoons flour
1 egg yolk
1/3 cup heavy cream

Cook the vegetables in water or
beef stock until tender. Mix the
butter and flour together and
add these slowly to the soup.
Simmer about 10 minutes,
stirring with a wooden spoon
constantly. Beat the egg yolk
and heavy cream together in a
soup tureen. While continuing to
stir, pour the hot soup into the
tureen. Season and sprinkle
with chopped parsley.

First Lutheran Church
Genesco, IL

SKÖRDASOPPA MED BÖNOR
Harvest Bean Soup

In a 4-quart sauce pan, heat
1 quart of water and 1 package
of dry beans or mix several
kinds of dry beans, lentils etc.
Bring to a boil. Cover and boil
for 2 minutes. Remove the kettle
from the heat. Let the beans
soak for 1 hour. Drain.

Fry 1/4 pound of bacon until
crisp. Crumble the bacon and
discard all but 2 tablespoons of
the fat. Add 1 peeled and sliced
carrot, 1 medium chopped
onion, and 1 finely chopped
clove of garlic and cook them in
the 2 tablespoons of bacon fat
until tender. When tender, put
the vegetables into a large pan
and add 6 cups of water and
1 bay leaf. Cover and bring to a
boil over high heat.

Reduce the heat to low and
simmer for 1 1/2 hours. Add
salt and pepper to taste, and
remove the bay leaf before
serving.

Makes 8 cups.

Concordia Lutheran Church
Kingsburg, CA

SPENATSOPPA
Spinach Soup

(Metric Chart: Appendix C)

1 to 2 hectograms spinach
1 1/2 to 2 liters water
1 *matsked* salt
2 to 3 parsnips
1 leek
1 *matsked* butter
2 *matsked* flour
1/2 "*kkp*" cream
1 to 2 egg yolks
Salt
Sugar

The cleaned and sliced parsnips are boiled in salted water and puréed together with the liquid. Melt the butter in a saucepan and add the flour and stir. Add the puréed parsnips with its liquid.

Add the cleaned, rinsed and coarsely chopped spinach. Cook a few minutes and remove the spinach from the heat. (Salt and sugar are added to taste.)

"The soup is served immediately. Cauliflower flowerets could be used in place of the spinach. The cauliflower is then only cooked until it is soft. The cauliflower is not puréed."

First Lutheran Church
Genesco, IL

VITKÅLSSOPPA
White Cabbage Soup

1 small head of white cabbage
2 tablespoons fat or butter
3/4 tablespoon molasses or
    brown sugar
2 quarts pork or other stock
6 whole allspice
6 white peppercorns
Salt

Clean and cube the cabbage and brown it in the fat or butter. Add the molasses or brown sugar when the cabbage has slightly browned. Continue to brown it a few more minutes, stirring with a wooden spoon constantly. Bring the stock to the boiling point and add the cabbage. Season. Simmer the cabbage for 30 minutes.

Serve with sliced, small sausages or veal meatballs.

First Lutheran Church
Genesco, IL

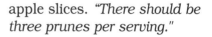

SVARTSOPPA
Black Soup

4 quarts soup stock
1 quart goose and hog blood,
    mixed
1 cup flour
2 tablespoons sugar
1 tablespoon vinegar
2 tablespoons syrup
1/2 cup red wine
1/2 cup sherry
1/4 cup cognac
1 teaspoon salt
1 teaspoon pepper
1 teaspoon ginger
1 teaspoon cinnamon
36 prunes, stewed
3 apples, sliced

Bring the soup stock to a boil
and then turn down the heat.
Mix the blood and flour together
and add this mixture slowly to
the soup stock stirring
constantly. Let the soup come to
a near boil. Take it off the heat
and add the rest of the
ingredients. Strain through a
sieve. *"Make the soup one day
prior to serving to allow the
spices to accent the soup."* When
heating the soup for serving, stir
constantly but do not boil.

Just before serving, add boiled
or stewed prunes and boiled

apple slices. *"There should be
three prunes per serving."*

*"This soup is made in celebration
of St. Martin's Day and is usually
served with roast goose."*

Superbly Swedish Recipes & Traditions
Penfield Press
Iowa City, IA

SVENSK POTATISSOPPA

(Metric Chart: Appendix C)

"1 liter potatis (potatoes)
2 liters buljong (bouillon)
1 knivsudd sellerifro (A *knivsudd*
    is an informal measurement
    translated into a 'pinch.' In
    this case, the recipe calls for a
    'pinch of celery seeds.')
1/2 matsked smör (butter)
1 matsked mjöl (flour)
2 äggulor (egg yolks)
Peppar and *salt,* to taste

*"Potatisen skalas, kokas i 1 liter
buljong tills den är mjuk. Smör
och mjöl sammanfräsas, puren
och resten av buljongen
påspädes. Soppan får koka
10 minuter; afsmakas. Äggularna
vispas upp i soppskålen och
soppan tillslås under
kraftigvispning."*

Mission Covenant Church
Foster City, MI

ÄNGAMAT
Soup From The Meadow

1 quart fresh vegetables such as
(carrots, cauliflower, sweet
peas, spinach, corn, etc.)
2 1/3 cups water
2 teaspoons salt
2 1/3 cups milk
2 tablespoons wheat flour
Freshly ground white pepper
1/2 cup whipping cream
1 egg yolk
Lots of chopped parsley

Cut the vegetables into strips or
small pieces. Boil the water with
the salt and place the vegetables
in the pot. Boil them until they
are somewhat soft, about 5 to
7 minutes. (They should still
have some crispness.) Remove
the vegetables with a ladle and
dish them into a serving bowl.
Save the boiled water.

Mix the wheat flour with a little
of the milk in a small bowl. Pour
the rest of the milk into the pot
with the liquid from the
vegetables and bring it to a boil.
Add the flour and milk mixture
and cook this for a couple of
minutes.

Beat in the egg yolk and the
whipping cream. Warm the

soup again, but don't allow it to
boil. Remove the pot from the
stove. Season with the freshly
ground white pepper to taste,
and pour the mixture over the
vegetables in the serving bowl.

Garnish with lots of parsley and
serve with hardtack sandwiches
and cheese.

*"The typical summer soup —
called 'ängamat'— has its origin
at this season and is a typical
soup at a time when everyone in
Sweden longs for fresh
vegetables. The name means
literally, 'food from the meadow',
that is to say, it is made with
those vegetables and greens one
picks in the field. When combined
with egg yolk and cream it is a
very nutritious food, good for
regaining strength after the long
winter."*

"Sweden & America"
Swedish Council of America
Eja Nilsson, Contributing Editor

BURNING BUSH SOUP

2 quarts nettles
2 cups water
1 1/2 tablespoons flour
1 1/4 quarts pork stock and
    water from nettles
1 tablespoon butter
Salt
White pepper

Wash the nettles well and drain.
Cook in slightly salted water for
10 minutes or until tender.
Strain, reserving the water. Chop
the nettles finely or pass
through a sieve. Melt the butter.
Add the flour and stir until well-
blended. Add the stock while
stirring, and simmer for
10 minutes. Add the nettle purée
and season.

Serve with poached eggs or with
hard-boiled eggs cut into halves
or sections.

Ann Nilsson
Dala Painter
Edina, MN

TOMATO DILL BISQUE
A Cold Soup

2 medium onions, chopped
1 clove garlic, sliced
2 tablespoons margarine
1/4 teaspoon salt
1/8 teaspoon pepper
4 large tomatoes (2 pounds),
    peeled and cubed
1/2 cup water
1 chicken bouillon cube
2 1/4 teaspoons fresh (or 3/4
    teaspoon dry) dill
1/2 cup mayonnaise

In a 2-quart pan, cook the onion
and garlic in margarine over low
heat for 3 minutes. Add the next
6 ingredients to the pan. Cover
and simmer it for 10 minutes.
Let it cool.

Place half the mixture at a time
in a blender. Blend until
uniform. Mix in the mayonnaise
and chill the soup overnight.

Serve cold. Makes 5 cups.

"Excellent for summertime."

Concordia Lutheran Church
Kingsburg, CA

**Note: Recipes for dessert soups (such as fruit soup and rosehip
soup) are found in the dessert section of this cookbook.**

SWEDISH DUMPLINGS FOR SOUP

4 tablespoons butter
1/2 cup water or broth
1/2 cup flour
1 teaspoon salt
2 eggs
1 teaspoon nutmeg

Bring the butter and water to a boil in a small saucepan. Add the flour and salt and stir until smooth. Cook over low heat, stirring until the mixture does not stick to the pan.

Remove from the heat and add the eggs one at a time. Add the nutmeg. Again, stir until well-blended over very low heat until the mixture does not stick to the pan.

Form into balls with a teaspoon and drop them into the soup or broth. Simmer these over low heat for 5 to 10 minutes.

If desired, sprinkle with nutmeg and chopped parsley.

Vasa Lutheran Church
Vasa Village
Welch, MN

SWEDISH DUMPLINGS

2 1/2 cups flour, sifted
4 teaspoons baking powder
1 teaspoon salt
7 tablespoons fat or shortening
2 tablespoons onion, grated
3 eggs
2/3 cup water

Sift the dry ingredients together. Cut in 2 tablespoons of the fat or shortening using 2 knives or a pastry blender. Add the grated onion.

Add the unbeaten eggs to the water and mix thoroughly. Stir the egg and water mixture into the dry ingredient/shortening mixture. Drop by tablespoons into 2 quarts of boiling water to which 1 teaspoon salt has been added. Cook for 15 minutes, uncovered.

Drain in a colander. Place the remaining fat or shortening in a frying pan. When melted, add the dumplings and fry until golden brown.

Makes 2 dozen dumplings.

Evangelical Covenant Church
International Falls, MN

BRÖD

Bread

Many of the Swedish immigrants brought their rye bread recipes with them to the United States. Rye bread—whether it is coarse, regular, flat or "knäckbröd"—is always thought of as "traditionally Swedish".

PIGAKAKA
Flat Rye Bread

2 1/2 cups milk
1/2 cup dark Karo syrup
3 tablespoons margarine
1 1/2 teaspoons of salt
2 cakes or envelopes of yeast
1 teaspoon anise or
    1 1/2 teaspoons fennel seeds
1 3/4 cups rye flour
3 1/2 cups white flour

Scald the milk and add the syrup and margarine. Then add the rest of the ingredients. Let the dough rise in a bowl until doubled in size.

Generously flour a pastry cloth. Roll the dough 1/4-inch thick, poke holes in it and place in pans. (The dough will be soft). Let it rise and bake for 15 minutes at 375°F.

The Dala Heritage Society
Mora, MN

SWEDISH RYE BREAD

5 cups lukewarm water
1 cake yeast
1 1/2 cups rye flour
1 cup whole wheat flour
1 1/2 cups brown sugar
2 tablespoons shortening
1/2 cup molasses
1 heaping tablespoon salt
1 teaspoon fennel seeds
1/2 teaspoon anise
1 teaspoon orange peel

Mix the yeast with the water and add the 2 flours. Then add enough white flour to make a soft dough and allow it to rise in a warm place for 1 hour. Add the brown sugar, molasses, salt, fennel, anise and orange peel. Add more white flour and knead until firm. Let it rise 1 hour again. Roll the dough into loaves and place them into greased pans. Let them rise 1/2 hour. Bake in a moderate oven for 1 hour. *"Brush the top of the loaves with butter to make them shine."*

Evangelical Covenant Church
Kingsburg, CA

SWEDISH RYE BREAD

Put 2 cakes of compressed yeast
(or 2 tablespoons of dry yeast)
and 1 teaspoon of sugar into
1 quart of warm water in a large
bowl. Let it stand for 10 minutes
and stir well.

Add:
1/2 cup molasses
1/2 cup brown sugar
4 teaspoons salt
1/2 cup melted shortening or
  vegetable oil
3 cups rye flour

Add 9 cups of white flour
gradually until the dough does
not stick to your hands when
kneading. Place in a greased
bowl, turning the dough so the
top is greased. Let it rise until it
is doubled in size. Cut into
4 pieces and make into 4 loaves.
Place in 4 greased 9-inch by
5-inch loaf pans. Let the dough
rise until doubled.

Bake in a preheated oven at
375°F for 10 minutes. Reduce
the heat to 350°F and bake for
35 minutes. Cool on racks.

All Saint's Lutheran Church
Darwin, MN

RYE BREAD

3/4 cup dark molasses
1/2 cup sugar
1 tablespoon salt
1/2 cup shortening
2 cups boiling water
2 cups milk, heated to lukewarm
2 packages yeast
1/2 cup warm water
5 cups rye flour
White flour

Combine the molasses, sugar,
salt and shortening. *"Lard is also
good."* Add the boiling water and
stir until the shortening is
dissolved. Add the lukewarm
milk and the yeast that has been
dissolved in 1/2 cup of warm
water. Add the rye flour and beat
hard. *"The beating is important."*

Knead in the white flour to make
a stiff dough. Continue kneading
until a fingerprint rises. Place in
a greased bowl to rise until it is
doubled in bulk. Then shape the
dough into 5 large loaves or
more smaller loaves. Place in
greased pans and let it rise
again until doubled in size. Bake
at 350°F for 45 to 50 minutes.

Augustana Lutheran Church
Andover, IL

SWEDISH RYE LOAVES

Mix together in a large bowl:
2 1/2 cups medium rye flour
2 packages active dry yeast
1/4 cup firmly packed brown
    sugar
1 tablespoon salt

**In a saucepan heat the
following to 120°F to 130°F:**
2 cups water
1/4 cup molasses
1/4 cup butter or margarine

Add this to the flour mixture.
Blend at a low speed with an
electric beater until moistened.
Beat for 2 minutes at a medium
speed. Add 3 1/2 to 4 cups of
all-purpose white flour to form a
sticky dough. Knead the dough,
adding flour until the dough is
smooth and pliable and no
longer sticky. Place the dough in
a greased bowl and let it rise in
a warm place until doubled in
size. Shape the dough into
2 round loaves and put them in
round greased pans. Let this rise
about 30 minutes.

Bake at 350°F for 30 minutes.

Evangelical Lutheran Church
Tolley, ND

RYE BREAD

This recipe is copied exactly as
written by a 90-plus year-old
nursing home resident, Mrs.
Martha Johnson. She brought
the recipe with her from Sweden
when she came over at age 18.

*"In a good size bowl dissolve
2 dry yeast in a small cup of
varm vater add a little white flour
let rase for a short time. Then
add 2 cups of varm vater and
one big cup of rye flour and a big
half cup of dark syrup and a half
cup of sugar 2 tablespoons of salt
one tsp big of shortning then add
2 more cups of varm vater and
1 cup of rye flour, then you have
to use all white flour make quite
a stif dough and then let it rase
and then emty it out on a bread
bord and kneed some more white
flour in then you can make it into
loves or let it rase once more if
you are busy you vont have to."*

Grace Lutheran Church
Marathon, IA

SWEDISH RYE BREAD

"This is a recipe of the late Hulda Johnson whose Swedish Rye Bread was much in demand at bake sales in years past. This was a recipe which was difficult to obtain as Hulda never followed a recipe —just a scoop of this and a scoop of that— as many good cooks do. One day in desperation, her youngest daughter, Phyllis Johnson Frisk, followed her around, measuring each and every scoop, cup, etc. and came up with the following recipe which many have used with excellent results. In fact, Robert Dirks entered it in the Sioux City Journal Cookbook one year and won a prize in the bread division with it."

Here is the recipe:

2 cups potato water
2 packages yeast
3 cups white flour
4 cups rye flour
3 cups lukewarm water
1 cup sugar
2 tablespoons salt
1/2 cup shortening
1/2 cup dark molasses
White flour

Cool the potato water to lukewarm. *"If desired, add some mashed potatoes to make and keep the bread moister."*

Dissolve the yeast in this water and make a soft sponge with the 3 cups of white flour. Let this rise until about doubled.

In a large bowl sift about 4 cups of rye flour. Pour the 3 cups of lukewarm water over this to make a paste or sponge. Add the yeast sponge, sugar, salt, shortening and molasses. Add anise seed or raisins, if desired.

Mix until stiff with additional flour and knead. Let it rise in a warm place until doubled. Punch down; let it rise again, and then shape into loaves and put in pans.

Let it rise again, and bake at 350°F for about an hour. Makes 6 loaves.

While the bread is still hot, dissolve 2 teaspoons of sugar in a little hot water and brush this over the top of the loaves to make a glaze.

Immanuel Lutheran Church
Akron, IA

RYE BREAD

1 package yeast
1/2 cup lukewarm water
1/4 cup quick oatmeal
1/3 cup brown sugar
1 tablespoon salt
1/4 cup shortening
1/4 cup dark molasses
1 1/2 cups boiling water
1 teaspoon anise seed
1 teaspoon caraway seed
2 cups rye flour
4 cups white flour

Dissolve the yeast in warm water. Add the boiling water to the oatmeal, sugar, salt, shortening, molasses, anise and caraway. Stir this until the shortening melts and cools. Add 3 cups of white flour, the dissolved yeast mixture, rye flour and the remaining cup of white flour. Knead on a floured board about 10 minutes.

Put the dough in a greased bowl and cover. Let it rise in a warm place about 1 hour until doubled in size. Punch down and let it rise again. Divide into 2 loaves and place in greased pans. Let these rise about 45 minutes in a warm place. Bake at 350°F for 45 to 50 minutes.

Fridhem Lutheran Church
Hordville, NE

SWEDISH RYE ROLLS

2 packages yeast
1/2 cup warm water
1 teaspoon white sugar
2 cups milk
1/2 cup margarine
1/4 cup brown sugar
2 teaspoons salt
1/4 cup molasses
2 cups rye flour
5 cups white flour,
    approximately

Dissolve the yeast in the water and white sugar. Scald the milk and add the margarine, brown sugar and salt. Cool. Add the molasses and the dissolved yeast. Add enough flour for the batter and beat it well with a mixer. Let the dough rise until it is light.

Add the rest of the flour. When the mixture is thick, mix it with a spoon. Turn the dough out on a floured board and knead it well. Put it in a greased bowl in a warm place until doubled in size. Shape the dough into rolls. When they are light, bake at 350°F for 15 to 20 minutes.

Hebron Lutheran Church
Burdick, KS

OLD SWEDISH SOURDOUGH BREAD CULTURE

"The bread relies upon a homegrown culture that, in itself, takes three days to mature. When the dough ferments, it ages best at a warm temperature. Too warm, or too cold, and the culture will not ferment properly. So, when preparing the culture, keep it between 77°F and 95°F— preferably in the low 80's."

Day One:
Mix 1/2 cup of coarse rye flour with 1/2 cup lukewarm water and one teaspoon of honey in a covered glass or porcelain dish. The cover should be slightly ajar. The honey is not necessary, but the culture rises easier with less chance of molding.

Day Two:
Add 1/2 cup of rye flour and 1/2 cup of water.

Day Three:
If the culture is not bubbling, throw it out and begin again. If the culture is live and bubbling, begin to bake.

Note: The culture may be saved in the refrigerator for ten days, or frozen for five months.

To multiply the culture, mix 1/4 cup of the hardy culture with 3/4 cup coarse rye flour and 3/4 cup lukewarm water. The culture should be ready to use in 12 hours.

*Svenska Vänner
Jamestown, ND*

COARSE, DARK RYE BREAD

1/4 cup sourdough culture
2 3/4 cups lukewarm water
2 teaspoons of salt
2 tablespoons of oil
1 tablespoon honey
5 cups coarse, stone-ground, rye flour
2 1/2 cups white flour

Mix the culture, water, salt, honey and oil. Add the flour, saving a little for later. Work together to a very hard dough which will become looser during fermentation. Place the dough in a lightly greased bowl, spray lightly with Pam, cover the bowl with plastic wrap and let it rise in a warm place until nearly doubled in size. This may take from 8 to 12 hours. *"Bill Soper learned that placing the bowl on a heating pad turned on low works well."*

Roll the dough onto a floured baking board, knead, flatten and roll up the dough into a circular form. *To have loaf bread, simply form it for the loaf pan.* Place the dough in the greased loaf pan or on a greased cookie sheet. Let the dough rise for 45 to 75 minutes under a baking cloth.

Score the bread with a sharp knife just before placing it in the oven. Preheat the oven to 450°F, reducing the setting to 400°F as the bread is placed in the oven. Bake for about 40 minutes. The bread should sound hollow when done.

Light Rye Bread can be made with this same recipe using the following flour measurements:

4 cups sifted, stone-ground flour
3 1/2 cups white flour

"This bread will do well as a doubled batch. May also be flavored with bread spices, chopped figs, raisins, or nut meats. Enjoy!"

*Svenska Vänner
Jamestown, ND*

BLOOD BREAD

Place 1/2 bag graham flour in a big bowl. Stir in blood from a beef or a pig. Add the white flour. Use 1/2 graham flour and 1/2 of white flour. Dissolve the yeast (4 ounce cake) in warm water. Dissolve 1 tablespoon of soda in hot water and let it cool. Add this to the bowl of flour. Add 2 handfuls of salt and 1/2 cup sugar. Add more flour of both kinds until the dough is hard enough to knead. Let it rise until doubled. Then form in balls about the size of a large egg. Put it in a floured pan. NO GREASE. Let it rise again. Bake at 400°F until hard or done. Either eat it fresh, or dry it in an oven at 100°F to 150°F. Leave the oven cracked open to dry. Store after it is baked.

To serve dry: Add 1 quart of beef broth in a pan. Put a biscuit in the pan. Keep breaking. Boil until soft enough to eat, about 20 minutes. Serve with butter and cream. One biscuit serves 2 people.

*Bethany Lutheran Church
Wisconsin Rapids, WI*

SWEDISH LIMPA BREAD

2 packages active dry yeast
1/2 cup warm water
1/2 cup sugar
1/4 cup light molasses
2 tablespoons shortening
2 teaspoons salt
2 teaspoons orange peel, grated
1 cup hot water
2 1/2 cups medium rye flour,
    stirred
3 1/2 to 4 cups flour, sifted

Soften the yeast in warm water.
In a large bowl combine the
sugar, molasses, shortening, salt
and orange peel. Add the hot
water and stir until the sugar
dissolves. Cool to lukewarm.

Stir in the rye flour and beat
well. Add the softened yeast and
mix well. Stir into the flour to
make a soft dough. Continue
kneading until smooth and
satiny, about 10 minutes. Place
the dough in a lightly greased
bowl, turning once to grease the
surface.

Cover and let the dough rise in a
warm place until doubled in size
or about 45 minutes. Punch
down. Turn the dough out on a
lightly floured surface.

Divide the dough into 2 portions.
Let it rest for 10 minutes. Shape
into 2 round loaves and place
them on a greased baking sheet.
Cover and let it rise until
doubled, about 30 minutes.
Bake 20 to 25 minutes. For a
soft crust, brush with melted
butter or margarine. Cool on a
rack.

Esther Lutheran Church
Parkers Prairie, MN

HAVREGRYNSBRÖD
Oatmeal Bread

Mix together:
 2 1/2 cups lukewarm potato
    water
1/4 cup brown sugar
1 tablespoon salt
2 tablespoons soft shortening
1 package yeast

Stir in:
2 cups oatmeal
5 to 5 1/2 cups flour

Knead until smooth. Let the
dough rise until doubled. Punch
down and divide and shape into
2 loaves. Let it rise again until
doubled. Bake at 400°F for
30 to 40 minutes.

Concordia Lutheran Church
Kingsburg, CA

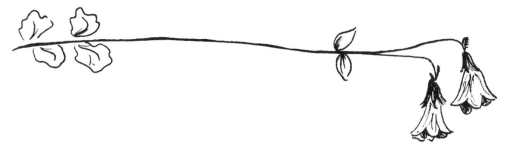

The Gulf of Bothnia is the name of the long body of water that lies between Sweden and Finland. It is also the most northern part of the Baltic Sea. Near the top of the gulf is Oulu, a coastal city in Finland. Across the gulf from Oulu is the Swedish area known as Norrbotten.

OULU PUMPERNICKEL

(Map: Appendix D)

1/4 cup warm water
1/2 cup dark corn syrup or light
  molasses
1 tablespoon grated orange peel
1 1/2 teaspoons salt
2 teaspoons caraway or fennel
  seeds
2 cups buttermilk
3 cups rye flour
3 to 3 1/2 cups all-purpose flour

Glaze:
1 tablespoon syrup or molasses
4 tablespoons water

Dissolve the yeast in 1/4 cup warm water. Set aside. Mix the syrup or molasses, orange peel, salt and seeds in a saucepan and bring to a boil. Pour into a large mixing bowl and add the buttermilk. Cool to lukewarm.

Add the yeast and blend well.

Add the white flour, beating well after each addition. When the mixture is stiff, let it rest for 15 minutes before kneading.

Turn the dough onto a floured board and knead until smooth. Then place it in a lightly greased bowl, cover tightly and let it rise until doubled in bulk, or about 1 hour.

Turn the dough out again onto a floured board and divide it into 2 parts. Shape each part into a ball or loaf. Place on a greased baking sheet and let it rise until almost doubled, about 30 minutes.

Before baking, brush with the glaze. Repeat twice during baking and again upon removal from the oven. Bake 350°F for 45 to 50 minutes. Makes 2 loaves.

Cambridge Lutheran Church
Cambridge, MN

VÖRTBRÖD

"Bread made with wort. Wort is made from malt and water. This bread is popular at Christmas.

"The Swedish tablespoon is a 'scant' American tablespoon. The Swedish tablespoon is used in this recipe."

(Metric Chart: Appendix C)

3/4 liter strong wort boiled down from 3 liter wort, or 3/4 liter port or Christmas beer and 2 tablespoons granulated sugar

2 1/2 deciliters milk

100 to 110 grams yeast

2 teaspoons salt, about 1 American teaspoon

A little bit of sugar

3 liters light rye

750 grams (1 1/2 liters) white flour

3 deciliters dark syrup

50 to 110 grams shortening or butter

5 pomegranates

2 tablespoons anise or fennel seeds

100 to 200 grams Sun Maid raisins

Boil down the wort the day before the bread is going to be made. On the same day, make a firm dough with the cold milk and the yeast, mixed with a little sugar plus the salt and some of the rye. Sprinkle the dough with flour and cover. Let it stand at room temperature until the following day.

Boil the pomegranates until soft, about 1 1/2 hours. Remove the white part and cut it into small cubes. Warm up the wort. Pour a small amount at a time into the dough and then add enough rye flour to make a firm dough. Sprinkle this with a little flour and let it stand in a warm place to rise until doubled.

Warm the syrup, shortening or butter and the cubed pomegranate. Add the crushed anise or fennel seeds and let it cool. Pour this mixture into the doubled dough and add more rye. Place the dough on a floured board and work it until it becomes elastic and shiny. Then add the raisins or the slivered almonds.

The dough should be firm enough so that it will keep its shape when formed into loaves. Make round or oblong loaves and place on a floured cloth. (Also, put the cloth between each loaf so that they don't touch each other and stick together.)

Let the loaves rise for 20 to 30 minutes or until they are puffed up. When the loaves have risen, transfer them carefully to a greased cookie sheet. (The side that was down on the cloth will be down on the cookie sheet.)

Prick them from one end to the other with a long pick and bake them in a medium oven. Brush the loaves with warm syrup-water when they are half done and once more when they are done, or brush them immediately before taking them out of the oven with the following glaze.

Potato flour glaze:
Place potato flour in a warm frying pan and let it brown. Add a little hot water and let the mixture boil for awhile. Strain and cool.

First Lutheran Church
Genesco, IL

SCANDINAVIAN CREAM BREAD

2 cups sweet cream
2 cups lard
4 cups water
10 to 12 cups of flour
Salt
1 teaspoon nutmeg or anise

Combine the first 3 ingredients and bring to a boil. Then, in a bowl sift together about 10 to 12 cups of flour, salt and 1 teaspoon of nutmeg or anise. Pour the first mixture over the flour mixture and stir well. Let this stand until it is cold.

Then roll the dough very thin and sprinkle it with sugar. Bake on a large cookie sheet in the oven. Do not turn.

"This may also be baked on top of the stove on a cookie sheet with a slow fire."

Providence Valley Lutheran Church
Dawson, MN

WHOLE WHEAT BREAD

Mix in a large bowl:
2 cups whole wheat flour
1/4 cup sugar
1 tablespoon salt
2 packages yeast

Add and beat for 3 minutes:
2 1/4 cups milk (120°F)
1/4 cup oil
1 egg, beaten

After beating, add:
1 cup whole wheat flour
3 to 4 cups white flour

Turn the dough out on a board and knead it for 1 minute. Return it to the bowl and let it rise about 45 minutes in a warm place.

Knead and let it rise again until doubled in size. Knead down and form into 2 loaves, putting them in greased pans. Let them rise for about 45 minutes. Bake for 45 minutes at 350°F.

Dalesburg Lutheran Church
Beresford, SD

HONUNGSRUSSINBRÖD
Honey Raisin Bread

Measure 1/2 cup water and add 2 tablespoons of dry yeast. Sprinkle 2 tablespoons of sugar on top. Do not stir.

Put 1 cup of small-curd cottage cheese in a bowl. Add 1/2 cup of honey and 1/4 cup of butter. Pour 1 1/2 cups of water over these ingredients. Add 1 beaten egg and mix the cottage cheese mixture with an electric handbeater or by hand. Add this to the yeast mixture. Add 2 cups of unbleached flour and stir. Beat with an electric handbeater for 2 minutes. Add 1/2 cup of ground raisins and beat again. Next add 1 cup of whole wheat flour, 4 cups unbleached flour and 3 teaspoons of salt. Mix well. Pour on a well-floured board and knead until smooth and elastic. Place in a greased bowl. Cover with foil and let it rise in a warm place about 2 hours. Punch down, shape into loaves and place in greased pans. Makes 3 loaves. Let the dough rise. Bake at 350°F for 40 minutes. Turn out on a rack to cool. Brush tops with butter.

Concordia Lutheran Church
Kingsburg, CA

KNÄCKEBRÖD

"When making rye, whole wheat, white or coffee bread, remove about 2 cups of the dough to make 'knäckebröd'."

Roll the knäckebröd dough lightly in the palm of the hand into 1 or 2 balls, depending on the amount of dough. Prepare a breadboard, well-rubbed with flour, "but no loose flour." Roll the dough with a rolling pin turning the dough over and over while rolling. Continue until the dough is round and very thin.

Have a greased and floured cookie sheet ready. Place the dough on the cookie sheet carefully. Smooth out the dough, cut off the rugged edges and let it rise. Then use a fork to pierce the dough, and a knife to mark it off into serving-sized pieces. Bake it in a hot oven, watching closely.

Remove the pieces as they are baked, returning the others to the oven if necessary.

"This takes a little practice, but practice makes perfect. The thinner the dough, the better the results."

Christ the King Lutheran Church
New Brighton, MN

POTATO "KNÄCKEBRÖD"

1 cup mashed potatoes
1/2 teaspoon salt
1 tablespoon butter
1 tablespoon thick cream
1 teaspoon sugar
Flour

Work in enough flour to make the dough stiff enough to roll. Roll thinly and place the rolled dough on cookie sheets. Prick with a fork. Bake at 350°F until delicately browned.

Prince of Peace Evangelical Lutheran Church
Grandview, MO

SWEDISH HARDTACK

1 cup milk
1/2 cup butter or margarine
1/2 cup sugar, plus a pinch
2 packages yeast
1 cup warm water
2 eggs, beaten
1/2 teaspoon salt
6 to 6 1/2 cups flour

Scald the milk. Add the butter or margarine and 1/2 cup of sugar. Set aside to cool.

Dissolve the yeast in warm water with a pinch of sugar. Let it stand for 10 minutes.

Add the beaten eggs and salt to the milk mixture; then add the yeast mixture, the flour, and stir. Next turn this out on a board and knead to a soft dough. Place it in a warm spot and let it rise until doubled in bulk.

Punch the dough down, and allow it to rest for 10 minutes. Divide the dough into 12 to 14 parts, quickly shaping into round biscuits. Preheat the oven to 400°F.

Roll out each piece of dough on a floured board to the thickness of a pie crust. Prick each piece with the tines of a fork.

Place them on a cookie sheet and bake for 5 to 6 minutes until bubbly. Turn and bake 5 to 6 minutes on the other side until they are flecked with brown spots. Turn off the oven.

Stack the pieces of bread on top of each other on the cookie sheet and let them stand in the oven until the oven is cold. This makes the hardtack dry and crisp.

Repeat the warm oven process the next morning if the crispness doesn't seem satisfactory.

"Hardtack keeps very well because it is dry. Also, it freezes well if you can keep it around that long."

*Immanuel Lutheran Church
Mediapolis, IA*

HARDTACK

2 1/2 cups white flour
2 cups oatmeal (or 1/2 cup
    wheat germ plus 1/4 cup
    yellow corn meal and
    1 1/4 cups oatmeal)
3/4 cup butter, softened
1/4 cup sugar
Dash of salt
1 1/2 cups buttermilk, mixed
    with 1 teaspoon soda
Whole wheat flour

Mix the dry ingredients together.
Work in the butter. Add the
buttermilk and mix well. Let this
stand covered for a few hours.
Using whole wheat flour, roll out
the dough very thinly. Cut the
dough into triangles or squares.

Bake at 350°F for 5 to
10 minutes until they are lightly
browned. After all of them are
baked, put them on cookie
sheets in a warm oven to dry
out.

*"Store them in a jar or can; never
in plastic containers. Do not
freeze."*

*Bethel Lutheran Church
Spicer, MN*

THIN HARDTACK

2 cups quick-cooking oatmeal
3 cups flour
1/2 cup sugar
3/4 cup shortening or butter
1 teaspoon baking soda,
    dissolved in buttermilk
1 1/2 teaspoons salt
1 1/2 cups buttermilk

Mix the dry ingredients and add
the shortening. Mix with a
pastry blender. Dissolve the soda
in the buttermilk and add it to
the dry ingredients.

Divide the dough into 7 parts.
Roll out each very thinly. Each
should fit on a cookie sheet. (The
cookie sheet should not be
buttered.) Score each into
serving pieces and prick them all
over with a fork.

Bake about 8 minutes in a
400°F oven. Turn the sheet in
the oven during baking. Cool
and break into serving pieces.

*"Delicious served with cheese or
as a replacement for rolls or
bread."*

*St Peter Lutheran Church
Canyon, MN*

FLATBRÖD
Swedish Hardtack

1 1/2 cups white flour
1 1/2 cups whole wheat (or
  graham) flour
1/2 cup sugar
1/2 cup melted butter
1/2 teaspoon soda
1/2 teaspoon salt
3/4 cup buttermilk

Mix all the ingredients, except
3/4 cup of the white flour. (The
remaining 3/4 cup will be used
in rolling out the dough.)

Take a small amount of dough
and roll it thinly on a floured
board with a pegged rolling pin.

Bake in a 375°F oven until
lightly browned. Break into
pieces to serve.

For easier handling, cut the
dough into pieces with a pizza
cutter or knife before baking.

Gethsemane Lutheran Church
Upsala, MN

FLATBREAD

1 1/2 cups graham flour
1 1/2 cups white flour
1/4 cup sugar
1 teaspoon salt
1/2 teaspoon soda
1 1/2 cups buttermilk
1/2 cup butter, melted

Combine the two flours in a
bowl. In another bowl, mix the
melted butter and the sugar.
Add the buttermilk. Pour this
mixture over the flour and stir.
Cool the dough before rolling it
very thinly. When rolling the
dough out you may add more
flour if needed. Bake in an oven.

Atwater Immanuel Lutheran
Atwater, MN

56

TUNNBRÖD
Hardtack

3 cups flour
4 1/2 teaspoons baking powder
1/2 cup sugar
1/2 teaspoon salt

Add:
Shortening
Milk

Cut 3 heaping tablespoons of shortening into the above mixture. Add 1 1/4 to 1 1/2 cups of milk, enough to handle properly in rolling.

Roll out very thinly on a floured board. Use a fluted rolling pin, if possible. Bake on a greased cookie sheet at 400°F.

"It is best to mark off the desired serving shape and size before placing the dough on a cookie sheet for the oven."

Salem Lutheran Church
Dalbo, MN

B-M-B HARDTACK

3 cups white flour
1 cup whole wheat flour
1 cup brown sugar, well-packed
1/2 teaspoon salt
1/2 cup rolled oats
1 cup butter
1 1/2 cups buttermilk
1 teaspoon soda

Sift the first 4 ingredients into a large bowl. Add the rolled oats. Cut in the butter or margarine as in making a pie crust. Dissolve the soda in the buttermilk. Add this to the mixture and chill.

Divide the dough into 12 portions. Roll out very thinly with a knobby rolling pin on a floured board. Knead each portion 3 to 4 turns before rolling. Transfer them carefully to a large ungreased cookie sheet and bake for 12 to 15 minutes at 350°F until light golden brown.

Turn them out at once on a rack and cool thoroughly. Break them into pieces and store them loosely covered to maintain crispness.

"This hardtack may be tough if it isn't rolled thin enough. It is a combination of 3 recipes perfected through trial and error, by Blenda, Maude and Barb."

Cambridge Lutheran Church
Cambridge, MN

SWEDISH "FLATBRÖD"

4 cups flour
1 cup graham flour
1 cup oatmeal
1/2 cup sugar
2 teaspoons salt
1 teaspoon soda
1/2 cup shortening *("Bacon fat is best").*
About 2 cups buttermilk

Combine and mix the dry ingredients. Cut in the shortening. Add the buttermilk using just enough to hold the dough together. Mix some white and some dark flour together on a board. Using a small amount of dough at a time, roll out as thinly as possible to a size that fits on a cookie sheet. Trim around the dough with an edger. Put the dough on the cookie sheet and cut into desired shapes with the edger.

Bake at 350°F until brown and crisp. This can be reheated in the oven.

Zion Lutheran Church
Ortonville, MN

SWEDISH TOAST

2 cups sugar
1 cup margarine or butter, softened
2 eggs
1 teaspoon almond extract
3 1/2 cups flour
1/2 teaspoon crushed cardamom seed or
    1 1/2 teaspoons ground cardamom
2 teaspoons baking powder
1 cup half and half, (1/2 milk and 1/2 cream)

Beat the sugar and butter. Add the eggs and almond extract. Combine the flour, baking powder and cardamom. Add the flour mixture alternately with the half and half to the butter, egg and sugar mixture. The batter will be thick.

Bake for 50 minutes in a 13-inch by 9-inch greased pan at 350°. Cool. Cut the cake crosswise into four 3-inch strips. Cut these strips into 1/4-inch to 1/2-inch pieces. Bake at 250°F for 45 minutes (or less) on an ungreased cookie sheet. Makes about 11 dozen.

Bethesda Lutheran Church
Chicago, IL

SWEDISH RUSKS

2 cups milk, scalded
1 cup sugar
1 teaspoon cardamom, crushed

When somewhat cool, add
2 tablespoons of yeast. Stir well
to dissolve.

Add:
2 teaspoons lemon flavor
2 small eggs, beaten
4 tablespoons soft margarine

Then, mix together:
7 cups flour
1 teaspoon salt
Grated rind of 1 orange

Add this to the other mixture.

Knead well and let it rise twice;
2 hours and then 1 hour. Shape
into 4 long rolls and place them
on 2 greased sheets 10-inch by
15-inch. Cover and let it rise
again, about 60 minutes.

Bake for 30 to 35 minutes at
350°F. Slice 3/4 inch thick.
Brown and dry them out in a
325°F oven.

Immanuel Lutheran Church
Greeley, CO

SWEDISH DUNKING TOAST

2 cups sugar
1 cup margarine
2 eggs
1 teaspoon soda
4 1/2 cups flour
1 cup cream
2 tablespoons lemon juice
2 teaspoons almond extract
1/4 teaspoon salt

Cream the sugar and margarine
together. Add the rest of the
ingredients. Divide the dough
into 3 loaf pans. Bake for
45 minutes at 350°F. Cool and
slice.

Lay the slices on a cookie sheet
and toast in a 250°F oven for
about 45 minutes or until golden
brown.

Augustana Lutheran Church
Manson, IA

RUSKS

1 cup whole wheat flour
1 cup white flour
1/2 cup sugar
2 teaspoons baking powder
1/2 teaspoon soda
1/2 teaspoon cream of tartar
1/2 teaspoon salt
1/2 cup margarine
3/4 cup buttermilk

Cut the dry ingredients and margarine together to the consistency of fine meal. Add the buttermilk. Roll out 1/4-inch thick on a floured surface. Cut the dough with a round cookie cutter.

Bake at 400°F for 10 to 12 minutes. While warm, cut in half. Toast with the cut-side up in a slow oven until the rusks are dry and browned.

Stratford Lutheran Church
Stratford, IA

MANDELSKORPOR

1/2 cup butter
1 cup sugar
2 eggs, well-beaten
3 tablespoons cream
1 teaspoon baking powder
2 cups flour
1 cup almonds, finely chopped
1 teaspoon almond extract
Egg white
Chopped nuts

Cream the butter and sugar and then add the eggs and cream. Then sift the flour with the baking powder and add these ingredients to the mixture. Lastly, add the almonds.

Sprinkle flour on a pastry board. Roll the dough into six 1 1/2-inch logs. Smear the "logs" with the egg white and sprinkle chopped nuts on top. Bake for 20 minutes at 350°F.

While warm, cut crosswise to make rusks (not too thin). When cool, place the rusks in a slow oven until they are dry and golden brown.

"These freeze well."

First Lutheran Church
Gardner, MA

DOUGHNUTS

2 eggs, beaten
1 1/4 cups sugar
1 teaspoon salt
1 teaspoon soda
1 cup buttermilk
1 teaspoon nutmeg
1 teaspoon vanilla
3 1/2 cups flour
1 teaspoon baking powder
3 tablespoons shortening,
   melted

Beat the eggs. Add the sugar and salt and beat again. Add the soda to the buttermilk first, and then add this to the mixture. Add the nutmeg, vanilla and then the flour. Lastly, add the baking powder and shortening. Add more flour if necessary.

Do not roll. Pat out and cut. Let the cut dough stand for 10 minutes and then fry.

*North Crow River Lutheran Church
Cokato, MN*

LEFSE

5 cups riced potatoes
1 teaspoon salt
1 tablespoon sugar
1/2 cup condensed milk
4 tablespoons butter
1 1/2 cups flour

Rice the potatoes. Add the rest of the ingredients, except the flour. Cream well. Let it stand until cooled, adding the flour when ready to bake. Roll thinly using as little flour as possible.

Bake on a *lefse* grill, setting the temperature at 380°F to 400°F. Brush off any extra flour from the grill with a brush.

Let each piece of *lefse* cool before stacking.

Makes 17 or 18 *lefse.*

*Highland Grove Lutheran Church
Hitterdal, MN*

LEFSE

3 cups mashed russet potatoes
1/4 cup butter
2 tablespoons half and half
1 cup flour
1 tablespoon sugar
1 teaspoon salt

Cook the russet potatoes until just done. (Don't overcook as they tend to absorb water). Drain and mash them well. Measure out 3 cups and add the butter and cream. Mix in the sugar, flour and salt.

Work on a covered board or a floured table. Have about 2 cups of extra flour to work into the *lefse* as it is rolled out. Put a small handful of flour on the board. Place a tablespoon of *lefse* dough (which has been worked into a flattened ball) on the flour. Work the flour in by patting and turning the dough until it can be easily rolled. Roll out quite thinly.

Bake on a *lefse* grill until browned on one side. Flip and bake the other side. Place the baked *lefse* rounds between 2 towels. (This prevents the *lefse* from drying out).

"It is best to store the 'lefse' in plastic bags in the refrigerator or to freeze it."

Hint: Too much flour added during rolling will make the *lefse* tough. Wipe the extra flour off the grill after each piece is baked. With a paper towel or soft pastry brush, brush off the excess flour from each piece before turning it.

*Augustana Lutheran Church
St James, MN*

LEFSE

7 cups mashed potatoes
1/4 cup melted butter
1/4 cup whipping cream
1 tablespoon sugar
2 1/2 cups flour
1/4 teaspoon salt

Chill the mashed potatoes. Add the butter, whipping cream, sugar, salt, flour and mix well. Take a big teaspoonful of the dough and make a patty. Roll out very thinly. Bake on a *lefse* grill at 500°F until lightly browned.

*First Lutheran Church
Hector, MN*

SWEDISH PANCAKES

6 eggs
1/2 teaspoon salt
1 1/2 teaspoons sugar
1 1/2 cups flour
2 3/4 cups milk

Beat the eggs until light and fluffy. Add the salt and sugar.

Stir well. Add the flour and beat well. Then add the milk gradually.

Bake on a hot griddle. These will be very thin and flat.

Pilgrim Lutheran Church
Frederic, WI

SWEDISH PANCAKES

4 eggs
1/4 cup sugar
1/2 cup flour
1/3 cup melted butter or
    margarine
1 cup milk

In a blender mix these ingredients in the order listed. Bake on a hot griddle. Spoon on small amounts of dough. Tip and turn the griddle so the batter runs all over.

"Add margarine on the griddle or electric skillet as needed."

Valley Evangelical Covenant Church
Stillman Valley, IL

PLÄTTAR
Swedish Pancakes

3 eggs, separated
2 tablespoons sugar
1/8 teaspoon salt
3 tablespoons melted butter
1/2 cup sifted flour
1 1/2 cups (plus) of rich milk

Beat the egg yolks with the sugar, salt and melted butter. Stir in alternately the flour and the milk. Let the batter stand a few hours or overnight if possible. When ready to cook the pancakes, beat the egg whites and add a drop of vanilla. Fold this into the batter.

Pour a small amount of dough onto a hot griddle or skillet. Spread the dough into a thin layer by tipping and turning the griddle. Cook until done, turning once.

Top with berries or syrup and roll up.

Ölandsklubben
New York, NY

BUTTERMILK PANCAKES

2 cups buttermilk
1 cup sweet milk
5 tablespoons sugar, heaping
1/4 teaspoon salt
2 eggs, beaten
2 tablespoons melted butter
2 cups flour, approximately

Blend the dry ingredients. Add the melted butter and eggs. Lastly, add the milks. (Use enough flour so the batter has the consistency to pour easily). Pour a small amount onto a hot griddle which has been greased with butter or shortening. Cook until done, turning once.

"Serve piping hot with syrup, or roll into 'crêpe suzettes' with jelly spread inside each pancake roll."

Stockholm Lutheran Church
Shickley, NE

BAKED PANCAKES

1/4 cup butter
1 cup all-purpose flour
2 cups milk
3 eggs
1/2 teaspoon salt
1/3 cup diced side pork

Heat the oven to 400°F. In an 8-inch by 12-inch pan, melt the butter in the oven. In a small mixing bowl, combine the remaining ingredients. Beat at a low speed, scraping the bowl often until well-mixed or 1 to 2 minutes. Pour the melted butter into the batter. Continue beating until well-mixed. Pour the mixture back into the pan.

Bake at 400°F for 30 to 40 minutes until it is puffed around the edges, set in the center and golden brown.

Serve immediately with maple syrup or preserves.

Serves 6.

First Lutheran Church
El Campo, TX

SVENSKA UGNSPANNKAKA
Swedish Oven Pancakes

1 quart milk
3 eggs
1 cup flour
2 tablespoons sugar
3 or 4 slices bacon
1/2 teaspoon salt

Cut up the bacon and fry. Beat the eggs. Add the milk and then all of the other ingredients to the beaten eggs. Pour into a large cake pan.

Bake for 1 hour at 350°F.

Serve with syrup, fruit sauce or preserves.

Serves 4.

Walnut Hills Lutheran Church
Dallas, TX

POTATISPLÄTTAR
Potato Pancakes

6 medium-sized potatoes
2 eggs
1 small onion, grated
1 1/2 teaspoons salt
1/4 teaspoon pepper
1/4 teaspoon ground nutmeg
1 tablespoon flour
Shortening

Pare the potatoes and shred about 3 cups. (If shredded ahead of time, place them in a bowl and cover them with cold water until you are ready to use them. Then drain and dry them well with paper toweling.)

Beat the eggs in a large bowl and stir in the potatoes, onion, salt, pepper and nutmeg. Sprinkle flour over the top and stir. Melt enough shortening in a large, heavy frying pan to make a depth of 1/4-inch. Drop the potato mixture (a scant 1/4 cup for each cake) into the hot shortening, flattening slightly with the back of a spoon to make thin cakes.

Fry slowly for 3 to 5 minutes or until crisp and golden, turning once. If needed, add more shortening and reheat the frying pan between batches. Serve hot.

"Potatoes stay tender on the inside, crisp on the outside, and lacy around the edges."

Makes 8 servings.

St Paul's Lutheran Church
Galeston, PA

BLOOD PUDDING

1 cup pigs blood
1/3 cup beer
2 tablespoons syrup
3 to 4 cups rye flour
3 tablespoons finely diced suet
1/2 teaspoon white pepper
1 teaspoon ginger
1 to 1 1/2 tablespoons salt
1/2 teaspoon ground marjoram
1 large red onion, chopped
1 tablespoon shortening

The blood should be put through a fine strainer and then beaten well. Add the syrup and beer. Add the flour, suet and spices. Then fry the chopped onion in the shortening and add it to the mixture. Put it into a greased tin container. Cover the bottom with dried bread crumbs and fill with the dough to 2/3 full. Bake in a water bath for 2 to 3 hours.

New Gottland Evangelical Covenant Church
McPherson, KS

BLODPLÄTTAR
Blood Pancakes

(Metric Chart: Appendix C)

1 deciliter (40 grams) rusks,
 finely crushed
2 deciliters milk
2 1/2 deciliters pig's blood
1 tablespoon syrup, light or dark
 *"Sockerbolagets ljusa eller
 morka."*
1 tablespoon butter, melted
1 teaspoon salt
1/8 teaspoon white pepper
1/8 teaspoon ginger
1/4 teaspoon marjoram, finely
 chopped
1 red onion, finely chopped
1/2 tablespoon butter (for the
onion)

Place the finely crushed rusks in
the milk for 1 hour. Strain the
blood and whip it well. Add the
blood to the crumb mixture. Add
the rest of the ingredients in
with the sautéed onion. Mix all
the ingredients together very
well. Heat and grease a *plätt*
pan. Make thin pancakes. Place
them on a warm serving platter
and serve them while warm with
lingonberry sauce, cranberry
sauce or melted butter.

First Lutheran Church
Genesco, IL

WAFFLES

1 1/2 cups cream
Pinch of salt
1 tablespoon sugar
1 1/3 cups flour (not sifted)
1/2 cup water
1 teaspoon baking powder

Beat the cream until stiff. Add
the salt and sugar and beat
again. Add half of the flour with
the baking powder mixed in. Add
the water. Fold in the remaining
flour. Makes 5 small waffles.

Faith Lutheran Church
Odebolt, IA

SWEDISH WAFFLES

1 1/3 cups plus 1 teaspoon
 whipped cream
1 cup plus 1 tablespoon flour
1/3 cup ice cold water or snow
2 tablespoons melted butter

Fold the whipped cream into the
flour. Add the other ingredients.
Let it sit for 1 hour. Bake in a
waffle iron until brown. This is a
crisp waffle.

Cool and serve with powdered
sugar or lingonberries

Swedish Club of Metropolitan Detroit
Swedish Women's Organization
Farmington Hills, MI

KAFFE PÅ SÄNGEN
A FAMILY TRADITION

"'Kaffe på s ängen', coffee in bed, on birthday mornings is a greatly anticipated event inthe family of Lucy De Remee. Coffee, on a tray with a candle and a favorite birthday coffee bread, is carried to the birthday celebrant who is still in bed. The family follows singing **Happy Birthday** *and often carries gifts and flowers. 'Kaffe på s ängen' is a very special way to begin a day of celebration. The recipe that follows is a favorite birthday coffee bread."*

MANDELKAFFEBRÖD
Almond Coffee Bread

1 package yeast
1/4 cup warm water
1/2 cup butter
1/2 cup sugar
1/2 cup boiling water
2 eggs
3 1/4 cups flour
1/2 teaspoon salt

Filling:
1/2 cup sugar
1 teaspoon almond extract
1/4 cup butter
Cinnamon

Dissolve the yeast in warm water. In a mixing bowl, pour the boiling water over the butter and sugar, and stir until dissolved. Cool to lukewarm.

Add the beaten eggs, flour and salt. Beat well. Cover and let it rise until doubled. Punch the dough down and refrigerate until cold.

Roll the dough into a rectangle. Spread it with butter. Stir the almond extract into the sugar and sprinkle it on the dough. Sprinkle generously with cinnamon. Roll and shape the dough into a tea ring. Let this rise until doubled in size, and bake at 350°F for about 30 minutes.

Drizzle with an almond-flavored glaze, or sprinkle with pearl sugar before baking.

Mt. Olive Lutheran Church
Rochester, MN

68

During the period of Lent, a wonderful Swedish speciality is served on one of the three days prior to Ash Wednesday. In Sweden, it is served on Shrove Tuesday, or "Fettisdag." Other Swedish names for this Lenten bun are "Fastlagsbullar" or "Semlor". This tradition found its way to Sweden from Germany in the 18th century.

FETTISDAGSBULLAR
Lenten Cream Buns

1/8 pound butter or margarine
1 cup milk
1 ounce yeast
1/2 teaspoon salt
1/4 cup sugar
2 eggs
1 teaspoon ground cardamom
3 cups flour

Filling:
The scooped-out portion of bread
    from the buns
2 1/2 ounces almond paste
1/4 cup cream or milk

Garnish:
1 cup whipping cream
Powdered sugar

Crumble the yeast in a bowl. Melt the butter in a saucepan. Add the milk and heat until it is lukewarm (not over 100°F). Remove it from the heat and stir in the yeast until it is completely absorbed. Gradually stir in the salt, sugar, one egg, cardamom and most of the flour. Work the dough until it is smooth and shiny. Then cover and let it rise 30 to 40 minutes. On a floured surface, knead the remaining flour into the dough. Divide into 12 parts and hand-roll into smooth round balls. Let them rise 20 to 30 minutes on a greased cookie sheet. Brush the buns with a lightly beaten egg, and bake for 8 to 10 minutes at 475°F until golden. Let cool.

To make the filling:
Cut off the top of each bun and scoop out a hollow in the bottom half with a spoon. Mix the scooped-out bits with the almond paste. Add cream to thin the mixture to a soft, smooth consistency. Fill the buns with the almond paste mixture and put the tops back on. Using stiff whipped cream in a pastry bag, squeeze out a wreath of whipped cream around the top of each bun. Sprinkle with powdered sugar and serve.

"Sweden & America"
Swedish Council of America
Eja Nilsson, Contributing Editor

SWEDISH TEA LOGS

Dough:

1 package active dry or
   compressed yeast
1/4 cup water
2 1/4 cups sifted flour
2 tablespoons sugar
1 teaspoon salt
3/4 cup butter or margarine
1/4 cup evaporated milk
1 unbeaten egg
1/4 cup raisins

Filling:

1/4 cup butter
1/2 cup brown sugar
1/2 cup chopped pecans

Cream the butter and brown
sugar and then add the nuts.

Vanilla Glaze:

Melt and brown 2 tablespoons of
butter; add 1 cup of sifted
confectioners sugar and
1/2 teaspoon vanilla. Stir in 1 to
2 tablespoons of evaporated milk
until it is the consistency of a
glaze.

Soften the dry yeast in water.
Sift the flour, sugar and salt into
a mixing bowl. Cut in 1/2 cup
butter or margarine until the
mixture has a fine consistency.

Add 1/4 cup evaporated milk,
the egg, raisins and softened
yeast. Mix well, cover and chill
at least 2 hours or overnight.

Divide the dough into thirds.
Roll 1 out on a floured board to
a 12-inch by 6-inch rectangle.
Spread with 1/3 of the filling
and then roll it up starting with
the 12-inch side.

Seal and place it on a baking
sheet lined with foil. Shape it
like a crescent. Make small cuts
along the edge, about 1 inch
apart. Turn it on the side
slightly. Repeat with the
remaining 2 parts of the dough.

Let these rise in a warm place,
80°F to 90°F, until light for
30 to 40 minutes. Bake in a
moderate oven at 350°F for
20 to 30 minutes until golden
brown. Glaze while warm.

Bethesda Lutheran Church
Morrison, IL

SWEDISH "KRINGLOR"

1/2 stick margarine
1 1/3 cups sugar
1 teaspoon salt
1 cup sour cream
1 1/2 teaspoons soda
1 teaspoon vanilla
3/4 cup buttermilk
3 cups sifted flour
2 1/2 teaspoons baking powder

Mix the first 6 ingredients until well-blended. Add the baking powder to the flour and add this to the first mixture alternately with the buttermilk. Cover the bowl and refrigerate overnight.

To bake, pinch off pieces of the dough and roll on a lightly-floured surface until the pieces are 6 inches long and as thick as a pencil. Shape into a figure 8 or a circle on a cookie sheet.

Bake at 400°F for 8 to 10 minutes.

Stratford Lutheran Church
Stratford, IA

KRINGLOR

1 cup butter
1 cup sugar
2 teaspoons baking powder
1/2 teaspoon soda
2 eggs, beaten
1/2 cup sour cream
3 cups flour

Cream the butter and sugar. Add the eggs and sour cream. Mix in the flour, baking powder and soda. Knead until it is no longer sticky, adding a little more flour, if necessary.

Let it sit for 1 hour to stiffen up. Roll the dough into pencil-like strips in sugar. Twist the strips into a knot shape.

Bake in a 350°F oven about 20 minutes.

First Lutheran Church
Hector, MN

CINNAMON OR CARDAMOM BREAD AND ROLLS

1 cup plus 2 teaspoons sugar
2 cakes (or packages) yeast
3 cups lukewarm milk
1 1/3 sticks margarine
1 teaspoon salt
10 to 12 cups flour
4 eggs, at room temperature
10 cardamom seeds crushed, or
      1 teaspoon ground cardamom

Cover the bottom of a bowl with sugar. Then add the crumbled yeast. If using package yeast, add a small amount of lukewarm milk. Add the remaining sugar on top of this. Let it stand for 10 minutes.

Gradually add the lukewarm milk containing the salt to the above mixture. Add the beaten eggs, cardamom and melted margarine. Add the flour to the mixture first by mixing it in and then by kneading the rest into it. Let the mixture rise in a warm place until doubled in bulk. Form into loaves or rolls and let it rise again.

Top with melted margarine, sugar and cinnamon after forming into bread or rolls.

Then, bake in a 350°F oven for 30 minutes for coffee bread. Bake in a 375°F oven for 15 minutes for rolls.

For caramel rolls: Place a mixture of brown sugar and cream in the bottom of the pan before putting in the rolls. Pecans may also be added.

Svea Lutheran Church
Hager City, WI

MOM'S CARDAMOM ROLLS

1 pint scalded milk
2 eggs
1/2 cup butter or lard
1 cup sugar
2 or 3 envelopes dry yeast
1 level teaspoon cinnamon
1 level teaspoon cardamom,
      mace or crushed cardamom
Flour to make a medium dough

Combine and mix the above ingredients. Roll the dough into long strips and dip into melted butter and then into a cinnamon and sugar mixture. Tie in the shape of a knot and put it in a 9-inch by 13-inch pan and bake at 350°F until light brown. *"Not real sweet, but very good."*

First Lutheran Church
Bismarck, ND

COFFEE ROLL

1 pint milk
1 package yeast
1 egg
1/2 cup sugar
1 teaspoon cardamom
3/4 cup butter or shortening
4 cups flour
1 teaspoon salt
1/2 teaspoon lemon extract

Scald the milk. When cooled, add the yeast and 3 1/2 cups of flour. Beat until smooth. Let it rise until doubled in bulk in a warm place. Then add the sugar, egg, salt, shortening, cardamom, lemon extract and the rest of the flour. Let it rise again. It will be a soft dough.

Divide the dough into 2 parts. On a floured board, pat out 1 part until it is 8-inches by 4-inches. Butter and fold it to make three thicknesses. Cut it into strips and dip in butter. Twist the dough and place it on greased pans. Let it rise 1 more hour and bake at 375°F for 25 to 30 minutes. Do the same with the second part of the dough.

Bethel Lutheran Church
Atkinson, MN

SWEDISH ALMOND BUNS

1 package dry yeast
3/4 cup very warm water
1/4 cup sugar
1 teaspoon salt
2 1/4 cups flour
1 egg
1/4 cup soft shortening
2/3 cup chopped, blanched almonds

Dissolve the yeast in water. Add the sugar, salt and half of the flour. Beat well. Add the egg and shortening and gradually beat in the rest of the flour until the mixture is smooth. Add 1/3 cup almonds.

Spoon the mixture into greased muffin tins and fill 1/2 full. Sprinkle the tops with the rest of the almonds and 3 tablespoons of sugar. Cover. Let it rise until doubled.

Bake at 375°F for about 15 minutes.

"Makes 16 to 20 rich, nutty buns."

Augustana Lutheran Church
Grand Forks, ND

LUSSEKATTER
Swedish Christmas Buns

Saffron Dough:
1 cup milk
1/4 to 1/2 teaspoon crumbled
   saffron threads or
     1/2 teaspoon powdered
     saffron
3/4 cup sugar
1 teaspoon salt
1/2 cup soft butter or margarine
3/4 cup warm water
   (110°F to 115°F)
2 packages active dry yeast
6 1/2 cups all-purpose flour,
   sifted
2 eggs
1/2 cup dark raisins
1/2 cup blanched almonds,
   ground

In a small saucepan, heat the milk just until bubbles form around the edge of the pan. Remove from the heat. Add the saffron, sugar, salt and butter stirring until the butter is melted. Let it cool to lukewarm.

Sprinkle the yeast over warm water in a large bowl, stirring until dissolved. Stir in the milk mixture and add 3 1/2 cups of flour. Beat with a wooden spoon until smooth, about 2 minutes. Beat in the eggs, dark raisins,

and the almonds. Then gradually add the remaining flour, mixing in the last of it by hand, until the dough leaves the sides of the bowl. (This is soft dough).

Turn out the dough onto a lightly floured pastry cloth. Cover it with a bowl and let it rest for 10 minutes. Turn over the dough to coat it with flour and knead it until it is smooth. This will take about 5 minutes. Place it in a lightly greased large bowl. Turn it to bring up the greased side. Cover it with a towel and let it rise in a warm place (85°F), free from drafts until doubled in bulk or about 1 to 1 1/2 hours. Punch down. Turn the dough out onto a lightly floured pastry cloth. Divide the dough and shape.

Christmas buns are often shaped into religious motifs.

(See diagram on next page).

Cardamom Dough:
Substitute 1/2 to 1 teaspoon ground cardamom and 1 teaspoon grated orange rind for the saffron.

*Mac Arthur Park Lutheran Church
San Antonio, TX*

74

SAFFRON BREAD RELIGIOUS MOTIFS

Priest's Locks

Lucia Crown

Star of Bethlehem

Lucia Twists

Christmas Goat

Lucia Cats

Christmas Cross

Easter Lilies

Sketch by Barb Pinc

SWEDISH BUNS

1 quart milk
1 1/2 cups sugar
1/4 pound butter
1 1/2 teaspoons salt
16 cardamom seeds or
   1 1/2 teaspoons ground
   cardamom
2 yeast cakes
2 eggs, beaten
11 cups all-purpose, unsifted
   flour "*King Arthur flour is
   great.*"

Scald the milk. Add the sugar, butter, salt and cardamom while the milk is still hot. Cool to lukewarm. Dissolve the yeast in 1/2 cup warm water, adding 1 teaspoon of sugar. Let it stand until foamy. Add the yeast and beaten eggs to the cooled milk mixture. Add 4 cups of the flour and beat it with an electric mixer for 4 minutes. Stir in the remaining flour or enough to make a thick batter. Let it rise until doubled in bulk. Divide the dough into thirds.

Cut the pieces of dough the size of a large egg. Roll each piece into a rope, approximately 6 inches long and tie into a knot.

Dip each piece of dough into the sugar. Place on a greased cookie sheet and let it rise until doubled in bulk.

Bake at 375°F for about 15 minutes or until medium brown.

Ebeneezer Lutheran Church
Willimantic, CT

76

SWEDISH PASTRY

1 cup flour
1/2 cup butter or margarine
1 tablespoon water
1 cup water
1/2 cup butter or margarine
1/2 cup flour
3 eggs
1/2 teaspoon almond flavoring

Frosting:
1 cup powdered sugar
1 tablespoon butter
2 tablespoons milk
1/2 teaspoon almond flavoring

Mix the first three ingredients and spread on a cookie sheet. In a saucepan, place 1 cup water and 1/2 cup butter or margarine. Heat to boiling. Take the pan from the burner and add 1/2 cup of flour at once. Stir until smooth. Cool.

When cooled, stir in 3 eggs, one at a time. Beat well after each egg is added. Add the almond flavoring. Spread this on the first pie crust mixture on the cookie sheet.

Bake at 350°F for 50 to 60 minutes. When slightly cooled, spread the frosting over the top with a pastry brush.

Frosting:
Heat the butter and milk. Add the sugar and flavoring.

*Salem Lutheran Church
Creston, IA*

SWEDISH PASTRY

Doughs:
Butter Dough:
1 1/2 cups butter
1/3 cup flour

Yeast Dough:
3 1/2 cups flour
1 1/2 cakes yeast
1 egg
1 1/4 cups cold milk
1/4 cup plus 1 tablespoon sugar

Sift 1/3 cup of flour onto a baking board. Cut the butter into the flour with two knives or a pastry mixer. Let it stand in a cold place.

Mix the yeast with 1 tablespoon sugar. Add the cold milk, egg and sugar. Add the flour gradually and beat with a wooden spoon until smooth and glossy. Roll out on a well-floured board to a 14-inch by 14-inch square. Roll out the butter dough to a 6-inch by 12-inch rectangle. Place on top of the yeast dough and fold the yeast dough over the top of the butter dough. Roll out again and fold the dough into three parts from left to right, as though folding a napkin 3 times. Leave in a cold place for 1/2 hour.

To shape "Envelopes":
Roll out the dough thinly in 4-inch by 4-inch squares. Spread with 1 tablespoon of filling. Fold the corners in toward the center and press down the edges.

To shape "Cockcombs":
Roll out the dough into thin strips 5 inches wide. Place the filling in the middle and fold both sides over. Roll this in pearl sugar and chopped almonds. Cut into pieces 4 inches long and gash one side 5 times.

To shape "Crescents":
Roll out the dough thinly and cut into strips 5 inches wide. Cut into triangles 3 inches wide at the base. Place filling in the base and roll up.

Baking:
Place the pastry on a buttered baking sheet and leave it in a cool place to rise. Brush the envelopes and crescents with slightly beaten eggs. Bake in a hot oven at 450°F until golden yellow.

When cold, spread the envelopes and crescents with icing made of confectioners sugar and water.

Fillings:
Almond Paste:
1/4 pound blanched almonds
1 egg
1/2 cup sugar

Grind the blanched almonds and mix this with the sugar. Add the egg gradually and work until the paste is smooth.

Vanilla Cream:
1/2 cup milk
1 egg yolk
1/2 teaspoon vanilla
1 tablespoon flour
1 tablespoon sugar

Mix all the ingredients, except the vanilla, in a double boiler. Cook over boiling water stirring constantly until thick. Cool, stirring occasionally. Add the vanilla.

"This is a Swedish pastry which the old Swedes made when they had extra-special guests."

Bethel Lutheran Church
Omaha, NE

JULEKAKE

2 yeast cakes
1/4 cup lukewarm water
1 cup shortening
1 cup sugar
2 eggs
1 teaspoon salt
1/2 teaspoon crushed
   cardamom seeds
1 cup raisins
4 ounces sliced citron
1 pint milk
7 cups sifted flour

Soften the yeast in water. Cream the shortening, sugar and eggs. Add the salt, cardamom, raisins and citron. Add the milk and flour. Mix well. Place in a greased bowl. Cover and let it rise until doubled. Knead down and let it rise again.

Shape into 3 round loaves. Brush the tops with egg yolk and milk that has been beaten together. Let it rise again. When it feels light, bake 50 to 60 minutes in a moderate oven at 350°F.

Immanuel Lutheran Church
Dunnell, MN

SWEDISH COFFEE RING

1 package yeast
1/4 cup sugar
1 cup warm milk
2 tablespoons butter
3/4 teaspoon salt
1 egg
2 1/2 cups flour (approximately)
Butter, brown sugar, cinnamon,
   nuts and raisins

Heat the milk to lukewarm. Add the butter, sugar and salt. Add the beaten egg. Dissolve the yeast in 1/4 cup of warm water. Mix all the ingredients well.

Add the flour and knead until it is smooth and elastic so the dough doesn't stick to the board. Place the dough in a greased bowl. Cover and let it rise until doubled in bulk.

Punch it down, cover and let it rise again for 10 minutes. Roll it into a rectangular sheet 1/2 inch thick. Brush with soft butter and sprinkle with cinnamon and brown sugar. Scatter a few chopped nuts or raisins over the dough and roll it up like a jelly roll.

Shape the dough into a ring on a greased baking sheet. Cut at one-inch intervals almost through the ring with a scissors. Turn each slice lightly on its side. Brush with melted butter and cover. Let the dough ring rise again until doubled. Bake at 350°F for 25 to 30 minutes.

Frost with confectioners icing and sprinkle with chopped nuts.

"At Christmas, use red and green maraschino cherries and pecan halves to garnish."

Amana Lutheran Church
Scandia, KS

KÖTT & VARMRÄTTER

Meats & Main Dishes

Because fish was so bountiful in Sweden, good servants could, at one time, request that their contracts include a clause guaranteeing that they would not have to eat fish more than three times a week.

GRAVAD LAX
Marinated Salmon

3 to 4 pounds salmon
Dill sprigs
2/3 cup salt
1/2 cup sugar
20 white peppercorns, crushed
Pinch of saltpeter

Dressing:
3 tablespoons olive or salad oil
1 to 1 1/2 teaspoons vinegar
1/2 teaspoon French mustard
1/4 teaspoon salt
Dash of white pepper

Mix the dressing ingredients and stir until well-blended.

Select a middle cut from a 6 to 7 pound salmon. Clean and remove the bones. Divide into two and wipe it thoroughly with a cloth. Place dill on the bottom of the pan.

Mix the salt, sugar and pepper. Rub this into the fish. To retain the red color of salmon, add a pinch of saltpeter to the spices. Place one piece (skin-side down) in the pan and sprinkle it with spices and dill sprigs.

Put the other piece on top, skin-side up. Cover with a weighted board and place in the refrigerator for 16 to 24 hours.

Remove the spices and cut the fish into thick slices.

Arrange the fish on a platter garnishing it with dill. Serve it with dressing, poached eggs, buttered spinach and boiled potatoes.

Yield: 8 servings.

*First Lutheran Church
Genesco, IL*

SALMON LOAF

Clean and rinse a fresh salmon well. Cut the fish into strips and plunge it into hot water which has been seasoned with dill, pepper, salt, bay leaf and onion.

When cooked, place the salmon carefully in a long fish mold. Boil down the stock. Strain and pour it over the fish. When hardened, turn it out and serve it with a tart sauce.

*Our Saviour's Lutheran Church
Hastings, MN*

SOAKING "LUTFISK"

Stockfish
Water
Lime

Saw dried stockfish into 4-inch pieces. Put the pieces into a stone jar and cover the fish with water. Let it stand for 4 days, changing the water every day. On the 5th day, put lime on the skin-side of the fish. Layer the fish until you have it all in a jar. Cover the fish with water. Leave it for 4 days and then wash the lime off. Put the fish in clear water changing the water every day. Keep it in a cool place. After 3 or 4 days, it is ready to use.

Lutfisk:
Soaked fish
Water
Salt
White sauce

Boil the fish in slightly salted water for a few minutes. Drain the water. Pick off the skins and bones and flake the fish. Make a cream sauce and put the fish into it. Season the *lutfisk* with salt, pepper and butter. Serve it with cooked potatoes. *"Some like to put a little mustard on top."*

Adullam Lutheran Church
Overton, NE

82

"LUTFISK", THE OLD WAY

Soak *lutfisk* in cold water for 1 day, changing the water several times. Bring a large kettle of water to a brisk boil and add 1 tablespoon of salt.

Lay a cotton dish towel or cheesecloth on the counter. Place the *lutfisk* in the center of the towel and tie the four corners together. Place the wrapped *lutfisk* in boiling water. When the water comes to a boil, let it boil for 3 to 4 minutes. Remove the fish and serve it with melted butter and/or white sauce.

Maria Lutheran Church
Kennedy, MN

WHITE SAUCE FOR "LUTFISK"

1 cup milk
2 tablespoons flour
1 1/2 tablespoons margarine
Salt, to taste

Melt the margarine and add the flour slowly. Next, slowly add the milk and cook until the mixture has thickened. Add salt to taste.

Trinity Lutheran Church
Boxholm, IA

SWEDISH "LUTFISK" PUDDING

3 pounds *lutfisk*
3/4 cup cooked rice
1/4 pound melted butter
5 eggs, separated
1 1/4 cups cream
Salt and pepper, to taste
1 cup salted almonds

Cook the fish and flake it when it has cooled. Add the cooked rice, melted butter, cream and beaten egg yolks. Fold in the beaten egg whites. Add the almonds. Place the mixture in a buttered casserole and bake at 325°F to 350°F for 1 1/2 hours.

"Do not have the casserole too full as this puffs up."

Serves 12.

Moriah Lutheran Church
Ludlow, PA

"LUTFISK" WITH HOT MUSTARD SAUCE

Bake the *lutfisk* on a layer of aluminum foil in a flat pan. Dot the fish with butter and season it with salt. Bake at 350°F for 20 to 30 minutes until it flakes or feels done. Serve the sauce over the *lutfisk*.

Sauce:
1/4 cup butter
1/4 cup flour
2 cups milk
1/2 teaspoon salt
1/8 teaspoon pepper
Colman's dry mustard

Melt the butter and stir in the flour. Add the milk and stir constantly until it thickens. Add the seasonings. Make a paste with several spoons of mustard and an equal amount of water. Stir the mustard paste into the cream sauce and heat it thoroughly. Add more mustard, if desired.

Mount Calvary Lutheran Church
Excelsior, MN

"LUTFISK" SANDWICHES
The Iverson Method

1 full sheet *lefse*
3/4 cup baked *lutfisk*
1/8 cup melted butter
3/4 cup mashed potatoes

Place the *lefse* on a large plate. Place the *lutfisk* and potatoes on the *lefse*. Pour the melted butter on top. Fold the *lefse* around the mixture and *"eat it like a burrito."*

"This is the traditional Iverson Method of eating lutfisk, passed down from generation to generation."

Highland Grove Lutheran Church
Hitterdal, MN

LUTFISK KOKT I UGN
Oven-baked "Lutfisk"

3 pounds *lutfisk*
Margarine or butter
1 tablespoon salt

Soak the fish in cold water for 1 to 3 hours. Drain. Place the fish (skin-side down) in a buttered, deep baking dish.

Sprinkle the fish with salt and cover with aluminum foil. Bake at 350°F for 30 to 40 minutes.

Trinity Lutheran Church
Benson, MN

FISKFILÉER MED SÅS
Fillet Of Flounder With Sauce

2 to 3 flounder (2 to
   2 1/2 pounds)

Stock:
3 cups water
1 cup white wine
2 to 3 slices onion
1 carrot
1/2 bay leaf
1 sprig parsley
2 whole allspice
6 white peppercorns
2 teaspoons salt

Fillet the fish and prepare the stock. Break the fish bones into pieces. Place them in a kettle and add cold water and wine. Cover, bring to the boiling point and skim. Add the onion, carrot and seasonings. Boil covered for 10 minutes and then strain. Roll the fillets and place them in the kettle. Pour in the prepared stock and simmer (covered) for 12 to 15 minutes. Place the fillets on a hot platter. Pour the sauce over the top and garnish it with any of the following: lemon slices, lettuce, tomatoes, shrimp or dill.

First Lutheran Church
Genesco, IL

84

FISKGRATÄNG
Fish Au Gratin

1 1/2 pounds fillet of cod,
   haddock, flounder or pike
3 tablespoons lemon juice
1 tablespoon butter
Salt
White pepper

Sauce:
3 tablespoons butter
3 tablespoons flour
1 1/2 to 2 cups fish stock and
   cream
2 egg yolks
2 to 3 tablespoons cold butter
Salt
White pepper
2 tablespoons grated cheese

Clean the fish and sprinkle it
with salt and pepper. Place the
seasoned fish in a buttered
baking dish and pour the lemon
juice over it. Dot it with butter
and cover it with waxed paper.
Bake it in a hot oven (425°F) for
7 to 10 minutes.

Melt the butter in a saucepan.
Add the flour and stir with a
wooden spoon until it is well-
blended. Add the cream and fish
stock gradually, while stirring.
Simmer for 10 minutes.

Remove the mixture from the
heat and add the egg yolks and
cold butter, stirring until it is
smooth. Garnish the fish with
cooked shrimp. Season the
sauce (to taste) and pour it over
the fish. Sprinkle it with grated
cheese.

Circle with mashed or riced
potatoes, and brown it under the
broiler or in a very hot oven for
10 to 15 minutes.

First Lutheran Church
Genesco, IL

CODFISH CASSEROLE

1 package frozen codfish,
   thawed
Salt
Pepper
Catsup
1 bunch green onion, sliced
1 pint whipping cream (not half
   and half)

Put the codfish on the bottom of
a 6-inch by 10-inch baking dish
and top with sliced green onions.
Mix the cream, salt, pepper and
a small amount of catsup until
well-flavored. Pour this mixture
over the fish and onions. Bake at
200°F for 45 minutes.

Augustana Lutheran Church
Tustin, MI

FISH BAKED IN MILK

2 pounds fresh or frozen fish
  (filleted or whole)
1 well-beaten egg or egg
  substitute
1/3 cup dry bread, crumbed or
  cubed
2 cups milk
1 1/2 teaspoons salt
2 tablespoons butter or
  margarine

Be sure the fish is cleaned well
and all scales are removed. If the
fish is whole, open it lengthwise
so it can be placed flat in a
baking dish. Spread the cut
sides with the beaten egg and
sprinkle the fish with part of the
salt. Place the fish (cut-side
down) in a well-greased, 2-quart,
shallow baking pan or dish.
Sprinkle 1/3 cup bread crumbs
and the rest of the salt over the
fish. Pour the milk over all and
dot it with butter or margarine.

Cover and bake for 40 minutes
at 400°F.

(Lower the heat to 325°F if a
glass pan is used.)

All Saint's Lutheran Church
Darwin, MN

"SVENSKA FISK" CASSEROLE FROM CAPE COD

1 pound white fish (Cut it in
  chunks and put it in the
  bottom of a casserole dish.)
1 cup cheese (Any kind you
  prefer.)
2 eggs (Beat and pour over the
  fish.)
14 Ritz crackers (Mix with some
  corn flakes and crush.)

Cover the top with cracker
crumbs and pats of butter. Bake
for 1/2 to 3/4 of an hour at
350°F.

First Lutheran Church
Gardner, MA

OYSTER SAUSAGE

1 pint oysters, drained and cut
1/2 pound veal, chopped
4 soda crackers, finely crumbed
  for rolling oysters
1 egg
Pepper and salt, to taste

Make into balls and fry.

Zion Lutheran Church
Rockford, IL

BAKED FRESH SARDINES OR SMELTS

2 pounds fresh sardines or
  smelts
Salt
12 Swedish anchovy fillets
3 tablespoons butter
2 tablespoons bread crumbs

Remove the heads, tails, intestines and bones of the fish. Clean well under cold running water. Drain. Cut the anchovy fillets into pieces. Sprinkle the sardines with salt and put one piece of anchovy on each sardine. Roll and place in a well-buttered and bread-crumbed baking dish. Pour a little anchovy juice over the sardines; dot with the remaining butter; sprinkle with bread crumbs, and bake in a moderately hot oven (400°F) until golden brown or for 10 to 15 minutes.

Serve from the baking dish for a *smörgåsbord* or as a main dish with boiled or fried potatoes and a green salad.

Caviar paste may be substituted for the anchovies. Blend 3 tablespoons of canned Swedish caviar and 2 tablespoons of butter until creamy. Spread this on the fillets and follow the procedure above.

Grace Lutheran Church
Sheyenne, ND

BOILED CRAYFISH

5 quarts cold water
5 tablespoons salt
1 to 3 bunches fresh dill or
  2 tablespoons dill seed
32 to 36 crayfish

Rinse the live crayfish in cold water. In a large kettle, boil the water, salt and dill. After the water has boiled for at least 5 minutes, remove the fresh dill and add the live crayfish—10 at a time.

Boil the crayfish for 6 to 7 minutes. Remove the crayfish from the boiling water and drain.

Our Saviour's Lutheran Church
Hastings, MN

JANSSON'S FRESTELSE
Jansson's Temptation

4 large baking potatoes
2 cans (3 1/2-ounce) anchovy
    fillets
1 large onion, finely chopped
1/4 cup butter
1/2 teaspoon sugar
1/4 cup juice from anchovies
1/2 cup thin cream

Pare the raw potatoes. Slice 2 of the potatoes into 2-inch thin slices and place them in a buttered, shallow 2-quart baking dish. Place the anchovy fillets on top of the potatoes. Sauté the finely chopped onion in 2 tablespoons of butter. Sprinkle the sautéed onion over the anchovies. Sprinkle the sugar over all. Cover with the 2 remaining potatoes which have been cut into long thin strips or thin slices. Dot with the remaining butter. Add the anchovy juice and half of the cream.

Cover the baking pan and bake in a moderate oven (350°F) for 30 minutes. Add the remaining cream and sprinkle with buttered bread crumbs. Bake uncovered for 10 to 15 minutes.

Zion Swedish Lutheran Church
Golden Valley, MN

JANSSONS FRESTELSE
Jansson's Temptation

"The identity of Jansson who was so sorely tempted by this dish is forever lost, but the uniquely Swedish dish retains his name."

6 raw potatoes
8 to 12 anchovies
1 onion
Pepper
2 cups milk or cream
Butter and crumbs for the
    casserole

Wash and pare the potatoes. Cut them into thin slices or thin, narrow strips. Scrape any bones from the anchovies and cut the fillets into small pieces. Spread butter and crumbs in a baking dish. Place a layer of potatoes in the casserole, then the anchovies. Sprinkle each layer with finely chopped onion and a little pepper. Alternate the layers until all has been used. The top layer should be potatoes.

Pour the milk or cream over the top. Bake at 375°F until the top is delicately browned and the potatoes are tender.

Yield: 12 small servings.

Messiah Evangelical Lutheran Church
Bay City, MI

RÄKSÅS
Shrimp Sauce

1/4 cup butter
1/4 cup flour
1/4 cup light cream
2 cups milk
1 teaspoon salt
1/4 teaspoon white pepper
2 pounds cooked, tiny shrimp
1 tablespoon chopped, fresh dill

Melt the butter in a saucepan
and gradually stir in the flour.
Remove it from the heat. Add the
cream and milk and return it to
a medium heat. Stir constantly,
until thickened and smooth. Add
the salt, pepper and shrimp.
Cook for 10 minutes. Then add
the dill, and cook for another
5 minutes to thoroughly heat the
shrimp.

Serve hot.

Swedish Council of St Louis
St Louis, MO

OXRULADER
Braised Beef Rolls

2 pounds round steak
1/4 pound pork fat or bacon,
    sliced and cut into strips
Salt
White pepper
1 to 2 cups bouillon
2 tablespoons butter
1 tablespoon flour
1/4 cup cream

Wipe the meat with a cloth. Cut
the meat into thin slices and
pound it lightly. Sprinkle it with
salt and pepper.

Place 1 strip of fat on each slice
of beef and roll it up, tying it
with a string or fastening it with
a toothpick. Sauté each slice of
beef in butter in a skillet until
browned. Sprinkle it with flour.
Add hot bouillon and more
seasonings, if desired. Simmer,
covered, 1 to 1 1/2 hours or
until tender. Remove the strings
and place the rolls in a hot, deep
serving dish.

Add the cream to the gravy.
Bring this to the boiling point
and pour it over the rolls.

Trinity Lutheran Church
Gresham, OR

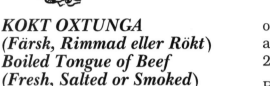

KOKT OXTUNGA
(Färsk, Rimmad eller Rökt)
Boiled Tongue of Beef
(Fresh, Salted or Smoked)

(Metric Chart: Appendix C)

1 Tongue (short and thick, about
   1 to 1 1/2 kilograms)

To Boil: For each liter of water,
add:

1 *matsked* salt
2 whole allspice
6 whole white peppercorns
1 whole clove
1/2 to 1 bay leaf
1 bit of carrot
A few slices of yellow onion or
   leek
A few sprigs of parsley

Clean the tongue and rinse it
well in cold water. If the tongue
is fresh or lightly salted, let it
soak in cold water for a few
hours. If the tongue is heavily
salted or smoked, it should soak
in lots of water for 24 hours.

If the tongue is fresh, place it in
boiling water. If it is smoked or
heavily salted, place it in cold
water. Let the water come to a
boil. Skim off the foam well.

Scrape the carrot and chop it.
Peel the onion. Add the carrot,
onion and spices to the water
and let the tongue simmer for
2 1/2 to 3 hours.

Remove the tongue. Make a slit
where the tongue is the thickest
and pull off the skin. Place the
tongue back in the broth and
simmer it until a "*stick*" will
easily penetrate the meat.

Cut off the "root" of the tongue
and slice it in thin even slices
from the root toward the tip of
the tongue at about a 30-degree
angle, ("*sneda skivor*"). Place the
meat on a warm serving platter
and garnish it with parsley,
tomatoes, and lettuce. Serve the
tongue and its broth with boiled
or mashed potatoes and boiled
or creamed vegetables.

*"Serve tomato, mushroom or
currant sauce with the tongue.*

*"The tongue can be cooked a day
in advance and cooled in its
broth. Then warm it up in its
broth, or serve it cold. The cold
tongue can be used as sandwich
meat, in an Italian salad or for
tongue in aspic. The slices can
also be put in an egg mixture and
then in crumbs and fried."*

First Lutheran Church
Genesco, IL

90

SLOTTSLEK
Royal Pot Roast

4 pounds beef roast, round or
    rump
1/2 pound pork fat, sliced and
    cut into strips or lardoons*
2 tablespoons butter
1 tablespoon salt
1/2 teaspoon white pepper
2 cups bouillon
2 onions
4 anchovies
2 bay leaves
12 whole allspice
5 white peppercorns
2 tablespoons vinegar
2 tablespoons brandy
2 tablespoons molasses

Gravy:
5 tablespoons flour
2 cups pan juice and bouillon
1 cup cream
Salt
White pepper
1 tablespoon anchovy juice

Trim and wipe the roast with a
cloth. Put white pepper and salt
on the lardoons (pork strips).
Insert the lardoons into the
roast placing them in parallel
rows. Rub the meat with salt
and pepper and brown it on all
sides in a Dutch oven.

Remove it from the heat and add
hot bouillon or water. Then add
the remaining ingredients and
cook slowly on top of the stove
for about 3 hours. Make the
gravy by straining the pan juice.
Remove it from the pan and heat
the fat. Add the flour, stirring
until it is browned. Then
gradually add the bouillon, the
pan juice and the cream.
Simmer for 10 minutes. Add the
salt, pepper and anchovy juice.

Serve the gravy with the meat.

*First Lutheran Church
Genesco, IL*

*Lardoon: A strip of pork fat
inserted into the meat, through
the muscle with a larding
needle.

Larding: Adding fat to meat.

BIF Á LA LINDSTRÖM

Wash and scrub 3 medium potatoes, (approximately 1 pound) with a vegetable brush.

Cook for 20 to 25 minutes or until the potatoes are tender when pierced with a fork. Meanwhile, dice finely, enough beets to yield 1/2 cup pickled beets.

Mix together in a bowl:
1 1/2 pounds beef, ground twice
2 egg yolks, beaten
1/4 cup cream
2 tablespoons onion, chopped
1 tablespoon capers
1 teaspoon salt
1/4 teaspoon pepper

Drain, peel and set the potatoes aside to cool.

When the potatoes are cooled, dice finely and mix them with the meat mixture and beets. Chill and refrigerate for 1 to 2 hours to allow the flavors to blend.

Shape the mixture into patties about 3/4 inch thick. Heat 3 tablespoons of butter in a skillet. Add the patties and cook over medium heat until browned.

Turn and brown the patties on the other side. Allow to cook for 10 to 15 minutes. Serve immediately.

Makes 6 to 8 servings.

First Lutheran Church
Genesco, IL

ENKEL KÖTTFÄRSRÄTT
Simple Ground Beef Dish

1 pound ground beef
1 onion, chopped
1/2 teaspoon salt
Black pepper
1 cup whipping cream
1/4 cup chili sauce
2 teaspoons curry

Brown the ground beef and the chopped onion. Add the salt and pepper. Put this mixture in a casserole dish.

Whip the cream. Fold the chili sauce and curry into the whipped cream. Spread the cream mixture on top of the beef mixture. Bake at 450°F for about 15 minutes.

Serve with baked potatoes, pasta or rice.

Swedish Council of St Louis
St Louis, MO

"Dopp i Grytan" "Dip in the Kettle" is a traditional Swedish meal served at noon on Christmas Eve– not at the table, but around the kitchen stove.

There are many theories about the origin of "Dopp i Grytan." One theory is that it was a traditional Viking meal served to fortify hungry Viking warriors who were returning from a long journey. Another theory is that "dipping of bread in the broth" was the only Christmas meal that poor house servants were able to enjoy. Yet another theory is that "Dip in the Kettle" is a meal that is served to remind people of famines which had gripped the country of Sweden at various times throughout history. However, the prevailing theory is that "Dip in the Kettle" is just an easy meal to serve for lunch on "Julafton" when the family is so busy with other preparations that no one has time to sit down and eat.

This tradition, "Dopp i Grytan," is carried on in the United States in many homes and churches of Swedish-American heritage. This wonderful tradition of serving a humble, communal meal of broth and bread is a reminder to all who partake of it of the true meaning of Christmas.

DOPP I GRYTAN
Dip In The Kettle

1 1/2 pounds short ribs, lean
1 1/2 pounds spare ribs
Salt

Cover the ribs with water and simmer for 3 hours or until the liquid has boiled down to half of its volume.

If the short ribs are fat, start them the day before and boil for 1 hour. Cool and skim off the fat before cooking them again on Christmas Eve Day. Add more water, if necessary.

Serve with flatbread, rye bread, root beer, cookies and rosettes at noon on Christmas Eve Day.

Serves about 6.

*First Lutheran Church
Hector, MN*

93

SWEDISH MEATBALLS

1 pound round steak
1/2 pound pork
1/2 pound veal *("Have the meats ground up at the market.")*
1/2 cup chopped onion (sautéed in butter until clear)
1/2 cup Ritz cracker crumbs
1 teaspoon salt
2 cups cooked potatoes (riced or mashed)
1/4 teaspoon pepper
1/4 teaspoon nutmeg
3/4 teaspoon allspice
1/4 teaspoon paprika
1 egg beaten with 1/3 cup cream

Knead until soft and fluffy and roll into meatballs.

"Lisa Lethepstrom tries to deep fat fry if possible and steam in an oven with a small amount of Spice Island beef broth until tender."

Magnolia Lutheran Church
Seattle, WA

KÖTTBULLAR
Meatballs

2 medium onions, finely chopped
1/2 cup butter
3 slices white bread (crust removed)
1 cup heavy cream
1/2 pound beef, finely ground
1/2 pound veal, finely ground
1/2 pound pork, finely ground
2 teaspoons salt
1/2 teaspoon pepper
1/2 teaspoon allspice
2 eggs
1/4 cup water

Sauté the onions in butter until golden brown. Soak the bread in a little cream. Mix the beef, veal and pork together. Add the fried onions, bread, salt, pepper, allspice and eggs. Next, add the cream and water and mix until the batter is smooth. Roll into 1-inch balls and fry in oil until they are evenly browned. *"Shake the pan frequently to keep the balls round."*

Immanuel Lutheran Church
Swea City, IA

SWEDISH MEATBALLS

3 pounds ground beef
1 cup onions, finely chopped
1 1/2 cups bread and cracker
   crumbs, mixed
3 teaspoons salt
1/4 teaspoon pepper
2 teaspoons Worcestershire
   sauce
1 cup milk
2 eggs
1/2 to 1 teaspoon nutmeg

Mix all the ingredients until
well-blended. Form into balls.
"The size is your preference."

Brown in a frying pan or on a
cookie sheet in a 350°F oven.
Chill and freeze. *"Freezing brings
out more of the flavors."*

When ready to use them, cook
them in water mixed with
instant beef bouillon. Simmer for
about 1 hour. Thicken the
bouillon mixture to make gravy.

*Pioneer Lutheran Church
Conover, WI*

KÖTTBULLAR
Swedish Meatballs

1 pound ground beef
1 egg
1 medium-sized raw potato,
   grated
1 teaspoon salt
1 teaspoon sugar
2 tablespoons dry bread, grated
2 tablespoons sweet cream or
   rich milk
1/2 teaspoon pepper
Pinch of ginger

Mix all the ingredients well and
form the meat mixture into
small balls. Fry the meatballs in
butter, browning them well on
all sides.

If an onion flavor is desired,
chop a small onion and brown it
in the butter before cooking the
meat.

*Immanuel Lutheran Church
Greeley, CO*

SWEDISH MEATBALLS

1 pound ground beef
1/2 pound ground pork
1/2 pound ground veal
1 1/2 teaspoons salt
2 eggs
2 medium onions, chopped
1 teaspoon Worcestershire sauce
4 slices bread
1 cup milk

Sauce:
1 bottle chili sauce
3/4 cup sugar
3/4 teaspoon Worcestershire
   sauce
1 1/2 tablespoons vinegar
3/4 cup water

Soak the bread in milk and break it into very fine pieces. Mix the bread pieces thoroughly with the meat. Add the remaining ingredients and mix well. Shape into small balls and place them in a roasting pan or other large, flat container. Mix the sauce ingredients and pour the over meatballs.

Bake uncovered at 350°F for 1 1/4 hours. Makes 30 meatballs.

Bethel Lutheran Church
Danville, IL

ROYAL SWEDISH MEATBALLS

2 pounds ground round steak
1 pound ground lean pork
2 beaten eggs
1 cup mashed potatoes
1 cup dry bread crumbs
1 tablespoon brown sugar
1 cup milk
2 1/2 teaspoons salt
1/2 teaspoon pepper
1/2 teaspoon nutmeg
1/2 teaspoon ginger
1/2 teaspoon cloves
1/2 teaspoon ground allspice
1 pint cream
Flour

Combine all the ingredients, except the cream and flour. Mix well. Form the mixture into small balls. Dip the meatballs in flour and brown them. Put them into a baking dish. Pour the cream over them and bake at 325°F for 35 minutes.

"This recipe was received from a relative of Esther Dawe whose friend was a cook at the Royal Palace in Sweden."

Mission Covenant Church
Foster City, MI

SWEDISH MEATBALLS

1 pound ground beef
1 cup flaked bread crumbs
1/2 cup milk
1 egg
1 teaspoon salt
1/8 teaspoon allspice
1/8 teaspoon ground cloves
1/8 teaspoon ginger
1 medium onion, minced

Soften the bread crumbs in milk. Add the well-beaten eggs, the meat and the seasonings. Mix this lightly. Make small balls with as little pressure as possible. Brown them lightly in 2 tablespoons of butter or shortening. Put the browned meatballs in a casserole.

Gravy:
Add 1 1/2 tablespoons flour, 1/2 teaspoon salt and a dash of pepper to the pan drippings. Blend and add about 1 1/2 cups of water or 1 can of beef bouillon soup. Cook until the mixture thickens. Bake at 325°F for 1 hour.

Grace Lutheran Church
Henning, MN

SWEDISH MEATBALLS

2 pounds ground round steak
1 pound ground lean pork
1 cup dry bread crumbs
1 egg
1 1/4 cups rich milk
2 teaspoons salt
1 teaspoon pepper
1 tablespoon sugar
Minced onion

Mix all the ingredients. Form into balls and fry them until they are browned. Add a little water and simmer for about 35 minutes.

First Lutheran Church
Kensington, MN

GRANDMA HERRLIE'S SWEDISH MEATBALLS

2 pounds ground beef
1 pound ground pork
2 eggs, beaten
1 cup bread crumbs
1 cup mashed potatoes
1 1/2 teaspoons salt
1 cup milk
1/2 teaspoon pepper
1 teaspoon allspice
3 tablespoons grated onion

Brown on all sides. Bake at 325°F for 1 hour.

Augustana Lutheran Church
St James, MN

SWEDISH MEAT LOAF

1 1/2 pounds ground beef
1 egg, slightly beaten
1/2 cup herb-seasoned stuffing,
    finely crushed
1/4 teaspoon ground nutmeg
1 can cream of mushroom soup
1/2 cup sour cream

Mix thoroughly the beef, egg, stuffing, nutmeg and 1/3 cup of the soup. Shape firmly into a loaf. Place the loaf in a shallow baking pan and bake at 350°F for 1 hour. Blend the remaining soup with the sour cream. Heat, stirring occasionally. Pour over the loaf for serving. Sprinkle with nutmeg. Yield: 4 to 6 servings.

First Covenant Church
Oakland, CA

SWEDISH MEAT BALLS

2 pounds ground beef
1/2 pound ground sausage
1 medium onion, chopped
1 cup bread crumbs, finely
    crushed
1 egg
1 tablespoon vinegar
2 teaspoons salt
1 teaspoon sugar
1/4 teaspoon ground allspice

Mix the onion, egg, vinegar, salt, sugar and allspice very well. Add the bread crumbs and pour the combined mixture over the meat. Mix well and form into small balls the size of a walnut. Brown the meatballs on all sides and add 1/4 cup water. Steam for about 15 minutes or until thoroughly cooked.

Northwest Iowa Associates of the
American-Scandinavian Foundation
Iowa

SWEDISH MEATBALLS

1/3 pound pork
2/3 pound hamburger
3/4 cup rusks or dry bread,
    cubed
1 tablespoon onion
3 eggs
1/2 cup water
1/2 teaspoon allspice
Salt and pepper, to taste

Form the mixture into 1 1/2-inch balls and brown in hot deep fat. Put a little fat in the bottom of an oven roaster pan and place the meatballs on top of the fat. Bake covered for 1 hour in a slow oven at 325°F.

Highlanda Lutheran Church
Langford, SD

GRANDMA'S FANCY MEAT LOAF

1 pound ground beef or a
    mixture of pork and beef
1/3 cup bread crumbs
3/4 cup milk
1/4 pound smoked ham
2 egg yolks
1 tablespoon potato flour
3/4 cup whipping cream
1 teaspoon salt
1/2 teaspoon white pepper
2 egg whites

Heat the oven to 375°F. Mix the milk and bread crumbs and let the mixture stand for 10 minutes to swell.

Chop the smoked ham into very fine pieces. Mix the meat mixture, softened bread crumbs, ham, egg yolks, potato flour, cream, salt and pepper. Work the mixture until smooth. Beat the egg whites well and fold them into the meat mixture. Press the meat into a well-greased bundt pan. Cover tightly with foil. Put the bundt pan into another pan. Put 1 or 2 cups of water into the larger pan and bake in the oven for about 1 hour.

When the meat loaf is done, turn it onto a serving platter. Cover the top with mushroom sauce. Serve the meat loaf with boiled and/or pressed potatoes and cucumbers. The sauce can also be served "on the side."

Mushroom Sauce:
1 large can of mushrooms
2 tablespoons butter
1 to 2 tablespoons flour
1 1/2 cups milk or half and half
Salt, pepper and soy sauce, to
    taste

Drain the mushrooms, but save the liquid. Brown the mushrooms in butter on a low heat. Sprinkle the flour in while stirring and add the liquid slowly. Let the sauce cook for about 5 to 10 minutes, stirring often. Add salt and pepper and/or soy sauce to taste.

Pour the sauce over the "fancy" meat loaf just before serving.

Serves 6.

Bethesda Lutheran Church
New Haven, CT

SWEDISH HAM BALLS

1 pound ground ham
1 1/2 pounds ground lean pork
2 cups bread crumbs
2 well-beaten eggs
1 cup milk

Brown Sauce:
1 cup brown sugar
1 teaspoon dry mustard
1/2 cup vinegar
1/2 cup water

Combine the meats, eggs, crumbs and milk. Form the mixture into small balls and place in a baking pan. Combine the sauce ingredients. Stir until the sugar dissolves and pour the sauce over the meatballs. Bake at 325°F for 1 hour. Baste frequently.

Augustana Lutheran Church
Sioux Falls, SD

HAM BALLS

1/2 pound ground pork, unseasoned
1 pound ground ham
2 cups crackers, crushed
2 eggs
1 cup milk
1/2 teaspoon salt
1/2 cup vinegar
3/4 cup brown sugar
1 teaspoon dry mustard
1/2 cup water
1/4 cup raisins

Combine the sausage, ham, crackers, eggs, milk and salt. Mix thoroughly and shape into round balls. Place in a casserole dish.

Combine the vinegar, brown sugar, dry mustard, water and raisins. Mix thoroughly and then pour it over the meatballs in the casserole dish. Bake for 15 minutes at 400°F and then reduce the oven temperature to 350°F and continue to bake covered for 1 hour .

Walsburg Lutheran Church
Leonardville, KS

SWEDISH POTATO SAUSAGE

9 pounds ground pork (weight after grinding)
3 pounds ground beef (weight after grinding)
15 pounds potatoes (weight after peeled)
3 tablespoons pepper
1 cup salt, approximate
1 hank of casings

Peel and grind the potatoes. Mix all the ingredients together. Stuff the mixture into casings and freeze them until ready to use.

To cook:
Cover the sausage with water. Add 1 onion (cut into quarters) to the water. Bring the water to a boil and simmer on low heat for 1/2 hour.

"Do not boil or the sausage will burst open. If it bursts, it won't hurt the sausage, but it is not attractive to serve."

St Ansgar Lutheran Church
Cannon Falls, MN

SWEDISH POTATO SAUSAGE

2 1/2 pounds pork butt, ground
6 potatoes, raw
1 medium-sized onion
3 to 4 tablespoons salt
1 teaspoon ginger
1/2 cup beef, ground
1 cup milk, scalded
1 teaspoon pepper
3/4 teaspoon allspice
1 pound casings

Grind the potatoes and onions and mix with the ground meats. Add the spices, salt and milk. Mix thoroughly and stuff the mixture into the casings.

Allow space for expansion so the casings do not break during cooking. Pierce the sausage once or twice during cooking.

Augustana Lutheran Church
Sioux Falls, SD

POTATO SAUSAGE

2 1/2 pounds pork, ground
1 1/2 pounds chuck, ground
6 raw potatoes, ground
1 cup milk
1 medium onion, ground
1 teaspoon pepper
2 teaspoons salt
3/4 teaspoon allspice

Mix all the ingredients together and stuff the mixture into the casings. Makes 6 24-inch sausages.

Evangelical Covenant Church
Milwaukee, WI

POTATO BOLOGNA

2 pounds lean pork, ground
2 pounds lean beef, ground
4 pounds potatoes, ground
2 medium onions, ground
Salt and pepper (to taste)
Sausage casings

Mix all the ingredients except the casings. *It is best to mix the ingredients with your hands.* Soak the casings in warm water and rinse them well. *If you do not have a sausage stuffer, you may use the tube of an angel food pan.* Make the bologna the length you desire and tie the ends with string. Cook the

102

bologna in gently boiling water for at least 1 hour. Pierce the bologna during cooking with a long needle so the bologna will not burst.

Cambridge Lutheran Church
Cambridge, IL

SAUSAGE SCAPPLE

1 pound pork sausage
1 cup onion, diced
5 cups water
1 3/4 cup yellow cornmeal
2 teaspoons salt
1 teaspoon poultry seasoning
1 teaspoon celery seeds

Place in a pan the sausage that has been broken into small pieces with the onion and the water. Simmer for 10 minutes. Combine the cornmeal and seasonings and add it to the sausage mixture. Simmer for 10 minutes more or until the mixture becomes thick. Place the mixture in a loaf pan and chill until it is firm. Cut slices 1/2 to 5/8-inch thick and fry them until they are warmed through.

Serve with eggs, plain or with Karo syrup.

Trinity Lutheran Church
Axtell, NE

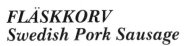

FLÄSKKORV
Swedish Pork Sausage

3 1/2 pounds lean, boneless
   pork
1 pound fat, boneless pork
1 pound veal
5/8 cup potato flour
3 to 4 cups meat stock or water
2 1/8 tablespoons salt
1 tablespoon sugar
1 1/8 teaspoons white pepper
4 yards sausage casing
1 1/8 teaspoons allspice
1 1/8 teaspoons cloves
1 1/8 teaspoons ginger

Grind the meat and place it in a large bowl. Add the potato flour and knead it about 1 hour, adding liquid a little at a time. Add the seasonings. The consistency should be like firm mush.

Cut the casings in 15-inch lengths. Run water through each casing. Fill the casings with the mixture leaving space to tie each end. Do not fill the casings too full, or they may burst when cooking.

Curing:
2 tablespoons salt
2 tablespoons sugar
3/8 tablespoon saltpeter.

Rub the filled casings with "curing" and place them in the refrigerator. To boil the sausage, place it in a pan and cover it with cold water.

Heat slowly just to the boiling point. Reduce the heat and simmer for 30 minutes. Place the sausage on a warm platter. Cut it into pieces and serve it with mashed potatoes, or with mashed turnips and mustard.

To keep the sausage for several weeks, place it in cold cooked brine.

Brine:
1 quart water
1/2 cup salt (not iodized)
1 tablespoon sugar
1/4 tablespoon saltpeter

Bring the brine ingredients to a boil and chill it again before pouring it over the sausages.

Faith Lutheran Church
Taylors Falls, MN

KORV
Sausage

1 pound barley grits
9 pounds pork shoulder, ground
    finely with the beef
6 pounds ground beef, ground
    finely with the pork
1 1/2 cups minced onion
7 tablespoons salt
3 tablespoons pepper
3 teaspoons allspice
1 1/2 pounds casings

Soak the barley grits overnight. Then cook them for 2 hours. Mix all the other ingredients into the pork and beef mixture. Rinse the casings thoroughly, inside and out. Stuff the sausage into 18 or 24-inch casings. Then tie each sausage with a strong string. Simmer for 45 minutes, or bake in 1-inch of water at 350°F for 1 hour.

"'Korv' may be frozen for a few weeks. We prefer the barley grits instead of the potatoes. The sausage is not as compact, and is lighter in color.

"The day after Thanksgiving the Julie Gustafson family has a 'korv' stuffing party. My husband says as a child, they would stuff 'korv' through a cow horn."

Gustafson Redeemer Covenant Church Beloit, WI

KORV
Grandma Irene's Swedish Sausage

40 pounds hamburger
20 pounds ground pork
3 boxes pearl barley
Casings
Canning salt, to taste
Pepper, to taste

Cook, drain, rinse and cool the barley. Mix the barley well with the meat, salt and pepper. Fill the casings and freeze the sausages.

To serve, fry the sausage until it is browned on both sides. Save the drippings for gravy.

"Korv was made in the late fall at butchering time. Beef and pork were cut up in pieces and put through the meat grinder and then made into sausages, using 2/3 beef to 1/3 pork and 1 box of pearl barley to 20 pounds of mixed meat. It was then frozen, usually in gunny sacks and hung from the clothesline.

"Traditionally, 'korv' was served as the Christmas meat. It makes a good brown gravy and with mashed potatoes, it was a real treat."

First Evangelical Lutheran Church Taylors Falls, MN

KÖTTGRYTA MED KORNGRYN
Beef and Barley Dish

1 pound barley
1 pound pork, cubed
6 cups water
2 teaspoons salt
6 whole allspice
6 peppercorns
1/2 bay leaf
1 pound ground beef
1 pound beef liver

Soak the barley overnight in 2 quarts of water. Put the pork, salt and spices in a covered pan with 6 cups of water and simmer for 1 hour.

Remove the pork for grinding and strain the stock. Add the drained barley and ground beef to the pork stock. Bring it to a boil and simmer for 1/2 hour, stirring occasionally to prevent sticking. Add water if necessary.

Simmer the liver for 5 to 10 minutes in a separate pan. Remove any membranes. Grind the liver together with the pork. Add this to the barley and beef.

To make it spicier, add onions, garlic, thyme, rosemary or marjoram to the pork stock.

This dish can be served as is, sliced and fried in butter, or browned in an oven. It may also be frozen.

"The custom is to serve this, topped with 'lingonberries' or cranberries. This is usually served on Christmas Eve."

Bethel Lutheran Church
Omaha, NE

ROTMOS

2 pounds spareribs or fresh pork
2 teaspoons salt
5 whole allspice
6 medium potatoes
1 yellow turnip (rutabaga), about
    1 1/2 pounds

Boil the meat and the spices in the water. Pour off most of the stock. Mash the vegetables, adding stock if necessary, to make a smooth "mash." Serve on a platter with meat around it.

"It is very good."

American Swedish Institute
Bemidji Affiliate
Bemidji, MN

LIVER AND BARLEY PATTIES

2 pounds beef or pork liver
1 pound barley
1/2 pound side pork
1 tablespoon salt
1 teaspoon allspice
Cinnamon
Sugar

Soak the barley in cold water. Boil the liver and the pork. When the meat is done, remove it from the kettle. Cook the barley in this same meat liquid. Season it with the salt and allspice.

When the meat is cool, grind it to a medium texture. Combine the meat with the drained barley and mix well. Form into patties, fry and serve with cinnamon and sugar.

"The mixture may also be packed into a loaf pan and sliced for frying if desired."

Faith Lutheran Church
Odebolt, IA

STEWED BREAD

1/2 pound side pork
1/2 loaf dry bread, cubed
1/2 cup water

Sauté the pork and then remove it from the pan. Add the cubed bread to the fat. Stir often, over medium heat, until the bread is softened. Add water to the softened bread.

Serve with homemade sorghum or maple syrup, along with fried pork. *"This makes a delicious breakfast meal."*

North Crow River Lutheran Church
Cokato, MN

CELERY AND ALMOND STUFFING

6 cups bread crumbs
3 cups celery, diced
1/2 cup celery leaves, shredded
1 1/2 cups almonds, chopped
1/4 cup butter, melted
1 teaspoon salt
2 eggs, beaten

Combine all ingredients, except eggs. Mix the eggs with milk or water to fill about 3 1/2 cups. This will stuff a 12-pound bird.

Faith Lutheran Church
Forest Lake, MN

FLÄSKKARRÉ
Roast Pork with Prunes

4 or 5 pounds loin of pork
20 prunes, pitted
2 teaspoons salt
1/2 teaspoon pepper

"Have the butcher separate the chops partway."

Trim the excess fat off the meat and wipe it dry. Soak the prunes for about 20 to 30 minutes, reserving the water. Then cut slits into the meat and insert the prunes deep into the meat by poking them in. Tie the meat together with a string. Brown the meat on all sides in a Dutch oven.

Cover and simmer the meat over low heat for 1 1/2 hours or until it is tender. Baste occasionally, using the water in which the prunes were soaked.

When the meat is done, place it on a hot platter. Remove the string and back bone. Slice.

Strain and skim the juice. Use it either plain, or thicken it for gravy.

First Covenant Church
Oakland, CA

FLÄSKKOTLETTER
Swedish Pork Chops

1 teaspoon salt
1/2 teaspoon black pepper
1/2 teaspoon ground ginger
2 tablespoons flour
4 pork loin chops, each 1/2-inch thick
2 tablespoons oil

Mix the salt, pepper, ginger and flour. Dust the chops with the dry mixture. In a heavy skillet with hot oil, brown the chops lightly on both sides. Lower the heat and cook until done, or about 20 minutes.
Makes 4 servings.

Swedish Council of St Louis
St. Louis, MO

JULSKINKA
Swedish Christmas Ham

1 12-pound ham, fresh
2 bay leaves
1 tablespoon peppercorns,
   crushed
2 onions, chopped
1 teaspoon allspice
1 carrot, chopped
1 egg white
1 tablespoon mustard powder
1 tablespoon brown sugar

Cover the ham with boiling water. Boil it fat-side up for 15 minutes. Skim the stock and add the bay leaves, peppercorns, onions, allspice and carrot. Turn the ham and simmer for 2 hours. Skim the stock again and slice off most of the fat. Let the ham cool for 12 hours in the stock.

Mix the egg, mustard and sugar and brush over the fat side of the ham. Sprinkle it with fine crumbs and bake it on a rack at 325°F until it browns, approximately 1 hour.

Serve cold or hot with boiled, red cabbage.

First Lutheran Church
Ault, CO

PRESSYLTA
Head Cheese

Cook the pork and veal separately until it is well done. Use half as much veal as pork. After the meat is well done, pick the meat off the bones and chop it finely or grind it.

Line a bowl with cheesecloth. (If you want the jelly on the outside, do not line the bowl.) Layer the meat into the bowl. Between each layer, season with salt, pepper, allspice and ground cloves. *"Use as much or as little as you like."*

Put the layers above the top edge of the bowl so that when it compresses there will still be a full bowl.

Put a weight or something flat on top of the meat. Then place a heavy weight on the flat top to compress the meat. Chill thoroughly.

"This dish is served sliced with pickled beets and boiled potatoes."

First Evangelical Lutheran Church
Rockford, IL

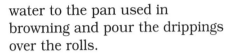

KÅLDOLMAR
Stuffed Cabbage Rolls

1 large head cabbage
1/2 cup rice
1/2 cup milk
1/2 pound ground beef
1/2 pound ground pork
1 egg
1 teaspoon chopped onion
1 1/2 teaspoons salt
3/4 teaspoon pepper
2 tablespoons butter
1 tablespoon dark corn syrup
Brown sugar

Core the cabbage and separate the leaves. Drop a few leaves at a time into boiling salted water and cook about 5 minutes. Drain on a paper towel.

Cook the rice in salted water about 20 minutes. Drain, and mix with the milk.

Combine the meats, egg, onion and seasonings and add this to the rice mixture. Put 1 or 2 tablespoons of meat stuffing on each leaf. Fold the leaf over and fasten it with a toothpick.

Brown the stuffed cabbage rolls in a mixture of butter and corn syrup. Place the rolls in a heavy baking dish and sprinkle them with brown sugar. Add a little water to the pan used in browning and pour the drippings over the rolls.

Cover and bake for 1 hour at 350°F, basting occasionally. Add more water if needed.

Remove the toothpicks before serving. Makes 25 to 30 rolls.

"Serve with boiled potatoes and lingonberries."

Wiley Heights Covenant Church
Yakima, WA

KÅLDOLMAR
Cabbage Rolls

1 pound pork
1 pound beef
1 cup rice, boiled until soft
Cabbage leaves

Grind the pork and the beef. Add the rice. Season it with salt, pepper and onion to taste.

Roll the mixture into balls and enclose each in a large cabbage leaf which has been boiled in water until tender. Tie with thread.

Fry until brown, and let them simmer in the oven until done.

Zion Lutheran Church
Minneapolis, MN

KÅLDOLMAR

1 head cabbage, solid
1 1/2 pounds beef or veal
1 1/2 tablespoons butter
1/4 cup cream
Pinch of sugar
Salt and pepper, to taste

Take one solid head of cabbage and boil it until it is half done. Drain it until it is cold.

Take the beef or veal and grind it finely. Season it with salt, pepper, butter, cream and a pinch of sugar. Work this all together until it is well-mixed.

Take the cabbage and cut off the large leaves. On each leaf, put a spoonful of the mixture. Shape it into oblong rolls, folding the cabbage leaf. Fasten the leaf with a toothpick and lay the roll carefully in a kettle or frying pan. Brown them first in hot butter. Then, add just enough hot water to cover and boil them slowly, about 2 hours.

Serve with or without brown gravy.

Stockholm Lutheran Church
Stockholm, WI

KÅLDOLMAR
Swedish Pigs in a Blanket

Remove all the fiber and waste from a portion of beef or veal. Run the meat through a grinder and pound it into a paste. Add a "lump" of butter, bread crumbs, an egg and enough milk or cream to make a smooth, creamy loaf. Season it with salt and pepper.

Form the mixture into small balls and roll a cabbage leaf around each, tying with a string. Fry them slowly in butter, basting them with milk until the cabbage is tender and browned.

"Thicken the gravy with grated Primost."

Our Saviour's Lutheran Church
Hastings, MN

PYTT I PANNA
Hash

4 tablespoons butter or bacon
    fat
2 to 3 onions, chopped
2 cups leftover meat, diced
7 or 8 cold cooked potatoes,
    diced
Salt and pepper to taste

Cook the onions in fat but do
not brown them. Add the meat,
potatoes and seasonings. Turn
the mixture over with a spatula
while browning.

*"You can serve the hash with a
fried egg on top and garnish it
with beets."*

*Grace Lutheran Church
Rankin, IL*

"PAULT"

12 medium potatoes, ground
1 large onion, ground
1 pound liver, ground
2 tablespoons salt
Dash of pepper
2 cups white flour
1 teaspoon baking powder
1 cup oatmeal
2 cups Bran Flakes, Wheaties or
    1 cup graham flour
1/2 pound salt pork, cubed

Put a large kettle of water on to
boil. Add a small handful of salt
to the kettle. While the water is
heating, grind and mix all of the
ingredients, except the salt pork.
Form into balls. Insert the salt
pork cubes into the center. Drop
them into boiling water and boil
them for 1 hour. If the mixture
becomes hard to handle while
making the balls, add more
flour. Do not let the water boil
too hard as this will cause the
balls to break. When done, the
"pault" will float. Serve with
butter.

*"Several in the Carlton Plyler
family like to dip each piece in
the butter and then the sugar. We
serve 'pault' with sauerkraut
salad and applesauce."*

*Augustana Lutheran Church
Tustin, MI*

111

KROPPKAKOR
Potato Dumplings

Dough:
10 or 12 large potatoes, boiled
   and mashed
3 eggs
Flour

Add a little milk and butter to the potatoes while mashing. Cool thoroughly. Make the dough by adding the eggs and flour to the potatoes until it will roll out without getting sticky. Roll out a square about 9-inches by 6-inches and cut this into 6 squares. Fill each square with the filling. Pinch together to make dumplings.

Filling:
1 1/2 pounds salt pork, cubed
2 or 3 onions, chopped finely
2 pounds lean ground beef
1/4 to 1 teaspoon ground
   allspice, to taste
Black pepper, optional

Fry the salt pork until golden brown and drain it on paper towels. Fry the onions in 1 tablespoon of pork fat until they are golden and tender. Drain. Fry the ground beef in a small amount of fat until thoroughly cooked. Drain, if the mixture is greasy. Combine the pork, onion and beef. Cool.

Broth:
Water
Salt Pork
6 peppercorns or whole allspice

In a large kettle put water, a small chunk of salt pork and 6 peppercorns or whole allspice. Bring to a boil.

Add the potato dumplings, 6 or 8 at a time, to the boiling broth. Let them rise to the top and remove. Continue this until all the dumplings are cooked.

Start with the coolest ones and place them in the boiling broth until all of them have been cooked twice. Serve with butter or margarine.

"Good with cranberry sauce. Warm the leftovers in a skillet with a little butter or margarine."

*St Paul's Lutheran Church
Galeton, PA*

KROPPKAKOR
Swedish Potato Dumplings

4 cups raw potatoes, grated
3 to 4 cups flour
2 teaspoons salt
1/8 teaspoon pepper
1 1/2 pounds sausage or fresh
    side pork
Large kettle of boiling water
3 cups milk

Brown about half of the meat until it is 3/4 done. Drain. If using sausage, leave it in chunks the size of a small "plum." If using side pork, cut it into small pieces and use about a rounded tablespoon for each dumpling.

In a large bowl, mix the potatoes, flour, salt and pepper. Use only enough flour to make the dough "barely manageable" when forming into 3-inch or 4-inch balls with heavily-floured hands. Place one chunk of sausage or one tablespoon of side pork onto the center of each dumpling. Be sure that the meat is completely hidden.

Using a slotted spoon that was just dipped in boiling water, lower the dumplings into the water as each one is made and boil gently. After about 5 minutes, loosen them from the bottom of the kettle and continue boiling for about 40 more minutes.

Brown the remaining crumbled meat thoroughly. Drain the grease. Add the milk and heat, but do not boil. Remove the dumplings from the water. Use the meat and milk mixture as gravy on cut up dumplings which have been dotted with butter. Salt and pepper to taste.

This makes 8 to 10 large dumplings.

"Leftovers are good when sliced thin, browned in butter and simmered for 10 minutes in enough milk to cover."

*Adullam Lutheran Church
Overton, NE*

FILLED POTATO DUMPLINGS

Bulk breakfast sausage
Onion, chopped
Potatoes
Salt, about 1/2 teaspoon per
     5 potatoes, mashed
Eggs, about 2 to 3 per
     5 potatoes, mashed
Flour, equal amounts of flour to
     prepared mashed potatoes

Skillet-fry the sausage and onion slowly until the onions are tender and the pork is done. Do not brown. Cook the potatoes in salt water until they are done. Mash and put them in a bowl to cool. Then, add the salt and eggs and mix them together.

Add the flour, 1/2 cup at a time until the dough is firm. At the end, mix more using your hands. (It usually takes equal amounts of flour to potatoes.)

Cut the dough "in the size of a jumbo egg." Work the dough around the precooked sausage and onion mix so that the meat is in the center of the dumpling. Drop the dumpling in boiling, salted water.

Use a 4-quart kettle (or larger) and fill it 3/4 full with water. Watch the water so it does not boil over. It takes about 20 minutes for the dumplings to rise to the top and get done.

"This is an Erickson five-generation recipe."

Cambridge Lutheran Church
Cambridge, MN

KROPPKAKOR
Potato Dumplings

Grate 6 medium potatoes. Add 1 tablespoon salt and enough flour to handle the mixture.

Grate or grind 2 medium onions and add them to 1 pound of ground beef. Add 1/4 teaspoon salt and pepper, to taste.

Put enough water in a large kettle to cover *the kroppkakor* or dumplings. Add salt. Bring it to a boil and keep it boiling.

To make kroppkakor:
Put about 1/2 cup of potato-mix in your hand. Take a piece of the meat-mix the size of a walnut and put it in the middle of the potato-mix in your hand. Bring the potato-mix around the entire meatball and form a ball so only the potato-mix is on the outside. Gently drop it in boiling water and simmer for 45 minutes.

Karen Olson
Lindsborg Community Library
Lindsborg, KS

LAMB ROLL

1 good-sized lamb flank, boned
   and skinned
Onion
Mustard seed

Sprinkle the boned and skinned
lamb flank with salt and pepper,
some finely chopped onion and
mustard seed. Roll it up tightly
and tie it with a string to hold its
shape. Boil the lamb flank in
slightly salted water about
1 1/2 to 2 hours.

Place the lamb flank on a platter
and cover it with waxed paper.
Weight it down with a small
board and leave like this until it
is cold.

Immanuel Lutheran Church
Holden, MA

SWEDISH BOILED DINNER

Cut a portion of lamb into
individual pieces. Place the
pieces into a kettle of water and
parboil the pieces of lamb. Have
the following vegetables (that
have been cooked separately)
ready: cabbage, carrots,
parsnips, (cut the cabbage,
carrots and parsnips into strips)
cauliflower, onions, fresh peas,
and fresh, young, tender peas in
the pod. Add all of the vegetables
to the meat. Season with whole
allspice, salt and parsley.
Potatoes may also be added.

Our Saviour's Lutheran Church
Hastings, MN

MUTTON STEW WITH CABBAGE

4 pounds mutton, for stew
1 large head of cabbage
1 teaspoon whole pepper
1 tablespoon salt
1/2 cup flour

Boil the mutton and pepper,
scantily covered with water, for
1 hour. Divide the cabbage into
eighths. Remove the core.
Arrange the meat and cabbage
with the pepper in alternate
layers, sprinkling each layer
with salt. Pour the water (in
which the mutton was boiled)
over the meat and cabbage. Add
a little boiled water, if necessary.
Boil about 45 minutes or until
done.

Bethany Lutheran Church
Siren, WI

SWEDISH VEAL BIRDS

2 1/4 to 2 3/4 pounds veal
   cutlets
3/4 tablespoon salt and pepper
1 large sprig parsley or onions,
   minced
5 tablespoons butter
3/4 cup cream
Water or meat stock
2 tablespoons flour
Meat juice or stock
Worcestershire sauce
Salt and pepper

Wipe the meat with a damp cloth
and pound it with a meat
hammer. Season each piece of
meat with the salt, pepper,
parsley or onions and
2 tablespoons of butter. If
necessary, cut the meat into
uniform-sized pieces suitable for
individual servings. Roll and tie
each with a string. Sear the rolls
in 3 tablespoons of butter.

Rinse the pan with a little hot
water and pour the drippings
over the rolls. Return the rolls to
the pan and baste with the
cream and water or stock. Cook
over a slow fire for about
1 1/2 to 2 hours or until the
meat is tender. Baste
occasionally. When done, remove
the meat and strain and skim
the pan juice. Thicken the pan
116

juice with flour blended with a
little water. Season to taste. Cut
away the strings and lay the
rolls in the gravy to reheat.
Serve with new boiled potatoes
and a light salad.

Zion Lutheran Church
Minneapolis, MN

FRIKADELLER
Swedish Veal Meatballs

1 pound veal, well-ground
1/2 cup crumbs
Chicken or veal broth
1/2 cup cream
1 egg separated, stiffly-beaten
   whites
1/2 pound mushrooms, sautéed
1/2 cup parsley, chopped
1/4 teaspoon mace
Salt and pepper

Mix the veal with the crumbs,
broth, egg yolk, mace, salt and
pepper. Fold in the stiffly beaten
egg whites. Form the mixture
into small, round balls and cook
slowly in enough stock to cover.
Cook for 30 minutes. Thicken
the sauce with 1 tablespoon of
flour. Add the sautéed
mushrooms, parsley and cream.
Season to taste.

Prince of Peace Evangelical Lutheran
Church
Grandview, MO

KALVSYLTA
Pressed Jellied Veal

1 veal shank
3 pounds veal neck
2 1/2 tablespoons salt
Pepper
1 tablespoon gelatin
1 tablespoon vinegar

Wipe the meat with a damp cloth. Place the meat in a kettle, add 2 quarts of water and bring it to a boil. Skim. Add the salt and pepper and a few whole cloves, allspice and a bay leaf. Simmer until the meat is tender. Remove the meat from the bones and cut it into cubes. Strain the stock, return it to the kettle, and let it boil down to 1 quart. Dissolve the gelatin in cold water and add it to the stock. Add the diced meat and vinegar. Pour it into a mold.

Faith Lutheran Church
Forest Lake, MN

VEAL SYLTA

5 pounds veal shank
1 medium size onion
Salt and pepper
Bay leaf
Few whole cloves

Select a lean and meaty shank. Put this in a pan with a small amount of water. Add sliced or diced onion, the bay leaf, a few whole cloves and the salt and pepper. Cook this slowly until it is tender.

When the mixture has cooled, take out the meat and put it through a meat grinder. Strain the stock and add enough of the stock to the meat to make a soft mixture. Season to taste. Mix well and bring it to a boil again. Pour the meat mixture into a loaf pan and refrigerate. Slice and serve the *sylta*.

This will keep for several weeks in the refrigerator.

Mount Zion Lutheran Church
Hudson, WI

STEKT GÅS
Roast Goose

1 10 to 12 pound goose
1/2 lemon
1 teaspoon salt
1/4 teaspoon black pepper
8 apples, cored and quartered
30 pitted prunes

Wash and dry the goose. Remove the fatty portion inside the cavity. Rub the cavity with the lemon, salt and pepper. Fill the cavity with the apples and prunes. Close the goose with skewers.

Bake the goose in a shallow roasting pan on a rack for 4 1/2 hours at 325°F. Pierce the goose to check the juices making sure the color is yellow and not pink.

Serve the goose with potatoes with parsley. Use the apples and prunes as decorations as well as for serving them with the goose. The apples and prunes absorb the fat from the goose. The goose is served after an earlier course of black soup and sausage.

"This is the second course in the Feast for Martin's Day."

Superbly Swedish
Penfield Press
Iowa City, IA

UGNSOMELETT
Baked Omelet

5 eggs
1 tablespoon flour
1/2 teaspoon salt
Few grains of pepper
2 cups milk
1 tablespoon butter
Creamed asparagus, mushrooms
    or lobster, optional

Beat the eggs until the yolks and whites are well-mixed. Beat in the flour, salt and pepper. Add the milk. Melt the butter in a 9-inch or 10-inch frying pan. Pour in the omelet mixture and bake in a moderate oven at 350°F for 30 minutes. Fold over and serve at once.

Serve plain or fill with creamed asparagus, mushrooms or lobster.

Yield: 5 to 6 servings when plain or 6 to 8 servings when filled.

Swedish Council of St Louis
St Louis, MO

SWEDISH HAM OMELET

3 eggs
2 1/2 cups milk
1 cup ham cubes
Salt and pepper to taste
1 tablespoon melted butter

Mix the milk, eggs and butter. Beat thoroughly. Add the salt and pepper. Place the ham cubes in the bottom of a buttered pie pan and pour the liquid mixture over the ham. Bake at 350°F until the mixture sets lightly.

Yield: 4 to 6 servings.

First Lutheran Church
Genesco, IL

EGGS Á LA GOLDENROD

1/2 cup butter
1/2 cup flour
4 cups milk
1 teaspoon salt
1/4 teaspoon white pepper
4 cups chopped, hard-boiled egg
    whites
Yolks from the hard-boiled eggs,
    grated

Melt the butter and stir in the flour. Gradually add the milk, salt and pepper. Cook the mixture until it thickens and bubbles. Add the hard-cooked egg whites. Serve on buttered toast. Grate the hard-boiled yolks over the toast and sauce.

Augustana Lutheran Church
St James, MN

ÄGG MED OSTLÅDA
Egg Cheese Casserole

1 cup Velveeta cheese, cubed
1/2 cup mushrooms
1/4 cup butter, melted
Onion, to taste
4 cups hard-boiled eggs,
    chopped
3 1/2 cups hamburger buns,
    crumbled
1 can cheddar cheese soup
1 soup can milk

Moisten the crumbs with the butter. Alternate layers of the crumbs, eggs, cheese and mushrooms. Pour the cheese soup mixture over the top. Bake for 25 minutes at 350°F.

First Lutheran Church
Genesco, IL

"Egg Gravy. It has always been the staple meal, no matter how poor or rich we've been. No matter how low the staples were in the pantry or cellar – we always had eggs, milk and a little flour."

Egg Gravy
Linda K. Hubalek

EGG GRAVY

Fry any meat and reserve the drippings. Set the meat aside. Add the milk to the drippings.

Mix together approximately 1/4 cup flour and 1 egg yolk per 2 cups of milk. Make a thin paste by adding the flour to some of the milk that has been warmed. Pour the remainder of the milk in the skillet, gradually adding in the thin paste mixture.

Use a low heat and stir constantly to prevent curdling. Add milk until you get the right consistency. Pour this over Swedish rye bread.

Grace Lutheran Church
Aurora, IL

SWEDISH "DOPPA"

Heat about 2 1/2 cups of rich milk to the boiling point. Mix in, separately, 2 beaten eggs. Add a heaping tablespoon of flour and 1/4 cup more of milk. Stir in the hot milk and heat through.

"This will look like custard. Then, add some salt so it won't taste flat."

Serve on toast with a side of bacon.

Maria Lutheran Church
Kennedy, MN

EGG GRAVY

2 cups milk
1 tablespoon flour
1/2 teaspoon salt
3 egg yolks
1 tablespoon bacon drippings

Fry the bacon and reserve 1 tablespoon of the drippings in the pan. Add flour as in making gravy. Then add the egg yolks, slightly beaten, and the milk and the salt. Stir the mixture until it is thick. Do not let the mixture curdle.

Serve this hot on toast or homemade rye bread and with bacon or side pork.

First Evangelical Lutheran Church
Oakland, NE

EFTERRÄTT & SÖTSAKER

Nancy Morgan

Desserts & Sweets

Risgrynsgröt or rice pudding as we call it in the United States is a favorite Christmas dessert that most Swedish-Americans have eaten. Usually a whole almond is mixed into the pudding. The one who gets the almond in their bowl is said to be in for good fortune; or if the person is single, they will be the next one to marry.

RISGRYNSGRÖT
Rice Pudding

1 cup long-grained white rice
2 cups water
6 cups milk
1 teaspoon salt
1/2 cup sugar
1/2 cup raisins

Cook the rice in water until all the water is absorbed. Add the milk and bring it to a boil. Cover and continue cooking over low heat until it is thickened, or about 2 hours. After the mixture has cooked for 1 hour, add the sugar and the raisins. Stir occasionally with a fork to keep the mixture from sticking to the bottom of the kettle.

Serve hot with cinnamon, sugar, a pat of butter and milk.

*Immanuel Lutheran Church
Clarissa, MN*

RISGRYNSGRÖT
Rice Porridge

Bring 3 pints of milk to a boil and add 1/4 pound rice which has been washed well in cold water. Stir for a few minutes, and then reduce the heat. Cover and let this simmer gently for 1 hour. Stir occasionally to prevent the rice from boiling over. Five minutes before the porridge is ready, add 1 teaspoon of salt.

Serve with a "knob" of butter in each helping, and with sugar and ground cinnamon sprinkled over the top.

"This may be served with cranberry sauce."

*Augustana Lutheran Church
Grand Forks, ND*

RISGRYNSGRÖT
Swedish Rice Porridge

6 cups milk
1 cup rice
3 tablespoons sugar
1/2 teaspoon salt
1 or 2 sticks cinnamon
1/4 cup chopped, blanched
   almonds
1 whole, blanched almond

Mix together the first
6 ingredients in top of a double
boiler. Cover and cook over low
heat for 2 1/2 to 3 hours, or
until the rice is soft and the
mixture is quite thick. (Remove
the cover the last 10 minutes if
the mixture is not thick enough.)

Just before serving, mix in
1 whole, blanched almond.

Serve with cream, sugar and
cinnamon or with a thickened
fruit sauce.

*"In some families, the one who
gets the whole almond receives a
gift!"*

*First Covenant Church
Oakland, CA*

RICE CUSTARD
PUDDING

1/2 cup rice
2 eggs
1 1/2 cups rich milk, heated
1/4 teaspoon salt
1/2 cup raisins (cooked 8 to
   10 minutes)
3/4 cup sugar
1/4 teaspoon cinnamon

Cook the rice in 2 quarts of
boiling, salted water for
20 minutes. Beat the eggs. Add
the warm milk and the
remaining ingredients. Mix well.

Pour into a baking dish and set
the dish in a pan of hot water in
the oven. Bake at 325°F until
brown, approximately
45 minutes. Test with a knife to
see if the custard is set.

Double this recipe for an 8-inch
by 13-inch Pyrex dish.

*St. Paul Lutheran Church
Oakland, CA*

RØMMEGRØT
Cream Porridge

"The amount of cream used to start out with will determine the quantity of the finished product. A suggestion would be 4 cups of cream and 4 cups of scalded milk."

Cook the cream over low heat until rich, yellow goose eyes, or small drops of butterfat form on the top.

While boiling, stir in enough flour so the cream has the consistency of thick gravy. The butterfat will rise to the top of the mixture. Dip the butterfat into a bowl.

While the cream is still boiling, add enough flour to make a thick batter. Next, add the scalded milk, stirring until it is back to the consistency of very thick gravy. Add a little salt and blend well.

Pour into a serving dish and top with butter, sugar and cinnamon.

"Today 'rømmegrøt' is often stirred with a wooden spoon, but we used to use a 'visp' or 'turu'."

*Highland Grove Lutheran Church
Hitterdal, MN*

RØMMEGRØT
Cream Porridge

24 ounces soured cream
3 tablespoons flour
1 teaspoon salt
1 1/2 to 2 quarts hot milk

Heat the soured cream until boiling. Add the flour and cook until the butter comes to the top. Skim off the butter and save it.

Heat 1 1/2 to 2 quarts of milk. Add 1 cup of flour to the cream. Stir in the hot milk, 1 cup at a time.

Add 1 teaspoon of salt and boil for at least 2 minutes. The mixture should have the consistency of thick gravy.

Serve with the reserved melted butter, cinnamon and sugar.

*Bethel Lutheran Church
Atkinson, MN*

RØMMEGRØT
Cream Porridge

1 pint very thick, slightly
    soured, cream
1/2 cup water
1/2 cup sifted flour
1/2 teaspoon salt
1 pint hot milk
Sugar and cinnamon to taste

Simmer the cream and the water slowly over low heat for 45 to 60 minutes, stirring occasionally. Combine the flour and the salt and sift the mixture into the hot cream. Beat until smooth. Cook slowly until it is thick and the butter comes out of the pudding. Stir in the hot milk and beat well. Pour into bowls. Serve hot with cinnamon and sugar.

Spring Garden Lutheran Church
Cannon Falls, MN

FIPOUNDUNKE
Fermented Milk

Heat 1 pint of milk just to the boiling point. Cool the milk to room temperature (72°F). Mix together 3 tablespoons of plain yogurt and 3 tablespoons of thick cream. Stir into the cooled milk.

Pour into 4 serving bowls. Cover the bowls and let them stand at room temperature until set. Refrigerate until serving time.

Sprinkle the tops with cinnamon and sugar or ginger and sugar before serving.

Vasa Lutheran Church
Vasa Village
Welch, MN

FIPOUNDUNKE
Fermented Milk

Heat 1/2 liter (1 pint) of milk until it is just on the point of boiling. (Boiling fermented milk will cause it to curdle). Cool the milk to normal room temperature (22°C/72°F). Mix in 3 tablespoons of fermented milk and 3 tablespoons of thick cream. Pour into bowls. Cover the bowls and let them stand at room temperature until they have set, or overnight. Place the bowls in the refrigerator until they are to be served.

Serve with ground ginger and crushed gingerbread biscuits. Makes 4 servings.

Bethesda Lutheran Church
New Haven, CT

"Kalvdans" is a special Swedish delicacy to be had only after a cow has given birth to a calf as the recipe calls for milk from the 1st, 2nd or 3rd milking. Such milk is referred to as "beestings" in both English and Swedish. The name of this recipe–which translates literally into "calf dance"– can also be translated from Swedish as "Beestings Pudding."

KALVDANS

3 cups *"fresh cow's milk from the 2nd milking"*
3 cups raw milk
1 cup sugar
1 tablespoon vanilla
Dash of nutmeg

Mix all the ingredients together well. Pour into a casserole and set the casserole in a pan of hot water. Bake with the casserole resting in the pan at 350°F in the oven for 1 hour.

First Lutheran Church
Hector, MN

VELLING
Gruel

4 cups milk
1 1/2 cups flour
1/4 teaspoon salt

Bring the milk to a boil and stir it into the flour-salt mixture a little at a time to make a soft dumpling. Place a spoonful of dough in your hand and press it through your fingers in fine strings into the milk. Cook for a few minutes. Serve in bowls.

"You may add a little butter and cinnamon. Some people also like a sprinkling of sugar."

Maria Lutheran Church
Kennedy, MN

SWEDISH "KALVDANS"

2 cups regular milk
1/2 cup sugar
2nd or 3rd milking from a fresh cow
1/4 tablespoon cinnamon

Mix all the ingredients well. Bake at 325°F for 1 hour in a glass casserole.

"You can add 2 beaten eggs to make it like a baked custard."

Bethel Lutheran Church
Willmar, MN

RICE PUDDING WITH MERINGUE

1/2 cup rice
Grated rind of 1 lemon
1/2 cup sugar
1 tablespoon potato flour
2 egg yolks
2 cups milk
1 tablespoon butter, melted

Meringue:
2 egg whites
1 scant cup sugar
3 tablespoons lemon juice

Wash the rice in cold water. Cook the rice in boiling water for 15 minutes. Drain. Mix the potato flour, rind and sugar. Beat and add the egg yolks. Add the milk and beat all together. Add the rice and the melted butter to the custard and put this mixture into a baking dish. Bake at 325°F.

Stir 3 or 4 times while baking. Bake until barely set. Cool for a few minutes.

Top with meringue and return the pudding to the oven to brown.

Hope Lutheran Church
Minneapolis, MN

"SMÖRGÅSBORD" RICE PUDDING

1 cup Le Gourmet Rice
2 cups cold water
1 teaspoon salt
3/4 cup sugar
4 cups rich milk
5 eggs, separated
1/2 teaspoon salt
1 teaspoon vanilla
1 tablespoon cornstarch

Cook the rice as directed on the package. Add the milk and cook slowly for 5 minutes. Beat the egg yolks and mix with the salt, sugar, vanilla and cornstarch. Mix the egg and rice mixture very slowly. Simmer about 5 minutes watching carefully.

Place the mixture in a glass Pyrex pan 7 1/2-inches by 12-inches. Bake at 350°F for 12 to 15 minutes.

Top with meringue:
Beat 5 egg whites with 1/4 teaspoon cream of tartar until stiff. Gradually beat in 3/4 cup of powdered sugar and 1/4 teaspoon vanilla.

"Enjoy hot or cold!"

First Evangelical Lutheran Church
Oakland, NE

HILDUR'S RICE PUDDING

1 quart milk (reserve 1/4 cup)
1/2 cup rice plus 1 tablespoon
1/3 cup sugar
1/2 teaspoon salt
Dash of cinnamon
2 egg yolks (save egg whites)
1 teaspoon vanilla

Cook the first 5 ingredients in a double boiler about 1 hour. Stir occasionally. During the last few minutes of cooking time, slowly add 2 slightly beaten eggs yolks mixed with the remaining 1/4 cup of milk. Stir gently until the mixture coats the spoon. Add 1 teaspoon of vanilla. Pour the mixture into a casserole.

Meringue:
2 egg whites
1/2 teaspoon vanilla
4 tablespoons sugar
1/2 teaspoon cream of tartar

Beat well and pour over the pudding.

Brown in the oven at 425°F for 5 minutes.

Bethany Lutheran Church
Negaunee, MI

LEMON CREAM RICE

1/2 cup rice
3 cups milk
1/2 cup sugar
Grated lemon rind
1 1/2 tablespoons lemon juice
3/4 teaspoon salt
2 egg yolks, slightly beaten
2 egg whites, beaten stiff
2 tablespoons powdered sugar
1/4 teaspoon lemon extract

Cook the rice and milk in a double boiler until the rice is soft. Add the sugar, lemon rind, lemon juice, salt and egg yolks. Stir and cook until the mixture is thickened. Pour into a buttered baking dish and cool.

Meringue:
Add powdered sugar and lemon extract to the beaten egg whites. Put over the top of the pudding.

Bake at 350°F just long enough to brown the meringue.

Serves 5 or 6.

Arlington Hills Lutheran Church
St. Paul, MN

SWEDISH RICE MOLD

3/4 cup rice
3/4 teaspoon salt
6 cups milk, scalded
3 envelopes gelatin
1 cup water
6 tablespoons butter
3/4 cup sugar
6 teaspoons vanilla
3 cups whipping cream
1 package currant junket
1 package frozen raspberries,
    thawed

Cook the milk and rice for
30 minutes or until the rice is
tender. Add the gelatin dissolved
in 1 cup of water, butter, sugar,
salt and vanilla to the cooked
mixture. Put it in the refrigerator
until the mixture thickens. Fold
in the whipped cream and spoon
the mixture into a 12-cup mold.
Refrigerate until set.

Cook the junket and add the
thawed raspberries. Unmold the
rice and spoon the junket and
raspberries over the top, or serve
the junket and raspberries on
the side.

Keep refrigerated.

Bethel Lutheran Church
Willmar, MN

RICE PUDDING

1/2 cup rice (not Minute)
1/2 teaspoon salt
3 cups milk

Cook in a covered, double boiler
until done, or about 1 1/2 to
2 hours. Stir occasionally.

Soak and add to the cooked rice.

1 package Knox gelatin
3 tablespoons water

Stir gently and chill. Add 1 cup
of whipping cream whipped and
1 1/2 cups sugar to the cooked,
cooled rice. Put the pudding in
an oiled ring mold.

Sauce:
Thaw 2 packages of frozen
raspberries or strawberries. Save
1 cup of the juice. Mix and add
2 1/2 tablespoons of cornstarch
and 1/2 cup of sugar to the juice
and cook until thick. Add
1 tablespoon of lemon juice after
the mixture has cooked. Pour the
mixture over the thawed fruit
and cool.

Unmold the rice and serve the
sauce in a dish placed in the
middle of the rice ring.

Our Saviour's Lutheran Church
Hastings, MN

OSTKAKA

1/2 gallon whole milk, heated to
   lukewarm
Soak 1/4 rennet tablet in
   1/8 cup water

Mix 1/2 cup flour with a little
milk. Pour it into the warm milk
and add the rennet mixture. Let
it set.

Stir with a spoon "crisscross"
and pour off the excess liquid.

2 or 3 beaten eggs
1/2 cup cream
1/2 to 3/4 cup sugar
1/2 teaspoon salt
1/2 teaspoon vanilla

Add the milk mixture to the egg
mixture. Mix and place in a
casserole. Bake at 350°F for
1 hour or until set.

*Swedlanda Evangelical Lutheran
Church
Hector, MN*

OSTAKAKA

Stir well:
1 gallon of warm milk *"The curds
   will get tough if the milk is too
   hot."*
2 well-beaten eggs

Add 1 cup of flour mixed with
some of the warm milk. Stir well
so the flour does not settle in the
milk. Stir again to keep it mixed.

Add half of a rennet tablet which
has been dissolved in a bit of
water. Stir this into the milk
mixture. Let it stand until the
mixture is thick, but stir it so
the curds and whey separate.
Let it stand until the whey is
formed, and then drain off most
of the whey.

For flavoring, add 1 teaspoon
cinnamon to 1 cup of sugar and
mix into the curds. Add
1/2 teaspoon salt and crushed
cardamom seed to taste. Add
1 cup of sweet cream. Vanilla or
almond flavor may also be used.

Bake at 350°F for 1 1/2 hours.

*Zion Evangelical Lutheran Church
Newman Grove, NE*

OSTKAKA

1/3 cup milk, lukewarm
1 rennet tablet
1 gallon whole milk, heated
1 cup flour
2 cups milk (for flour mixture)
6 eggs
1 1/3 cups cream
1 1/3 cups sugar

Heat the 1/3 cup of milk to lukewarm. Add the rennet tablet to this to dissolve. Heat the gallon of whole milk to 100°F. Mix the flour with the remaining 2 cups of milk to form a paste. Add the "paste" to the heated whole milk. Then add the milk (in which the rennet has dissolved) to the heated whole milk. Stir until the milk begins to curdle. Set this aside until it forms firm curds, and then drain off 2 quarts of whey.

Beat the eggs and add the cream and sugar. Add this mixture to the curds, and stir. Pour the entire mix into a pan and bake at 400°F for 10 minutes. Then lower the temperature and bake at 350°F for 1 hour.

Serve topped with lingonberries or with *"kram"* .

Andover Lutheran Church
Windom, KS

QUICK-MIX "OSTKAKA"

1 package dry curd cottage
    cheese
6 beaten eggs
1/2 cup sugar
1/2 teaspoon salt
1/2 teaspoon almond extract
1 pint cream

Mix the first 5 ingredients together and add the cream. Pour the mixture into a 2-quart dish and place the dish in a pan of water in the oven.

Bake at 350°F for 20 minutes. Reduce the heat to 325°F and bake again for about 30 minutes or until done. *"Insert a knife in the middle of the custard. The custard is done when the knife comes out clean."*

Zion Lutheran Church
Ortonville, MN

OSTKAKA

"1 pail of milk
1 rennet tablet
5 eggs
To each egg 1 tablespoon flour
Milk lukewarm"

Concordia Lutheran Church
Kingsburg, CA

130

OSTKAKA

1 gallon whole raw milk
1/2 cup flour
1 teaspoon salt
1/2 rennet tablet
2 tablespoons warm water
3 eggs
3/4 cup sugar
1 teaspoon vanilla

Let the raw milk stand unrefrigerated overnight in a 6 quart kettle. In the morning, take off about 1 1/2 cups of the milk and set it aside. Heat the milk on low heat to 89°F or lukewarm. (Do not overheat.)

While the milk is heating, put the flour and salt in a small bowl. Put the rennet tablet in a cup with 2 tablespoons of warm water to dissolve. (The tablet may have to be mashed with a spoon so it dissolves easier.)

When the milk is warm, mix 1 cup of it with the flour and salt. Beat this with an egg-beater until it is smooth and the lumps are gone.

Pour the flour-milk mixture and the dissolved rennet mixture into the large kettle of milk. Heat and stir gently. Continue stirring slowly and gently until the milk

thickens and curdles. Remove from the heat immediately.

Set it aside "to cheese" for 30 minutes. Then cut through the milk with a knife in both directions, about 1 1/2 inches deep. Let it stand another 15 minutes to separate the whey from the cheese.

Drain through a colander for at least 3 hours turning occasionally. Crumble the mixture into a buttered 3-quart casserole.

Beat the eggs, sugar, reserved 1 1/2 cups of milk and vanilla until slightly mixed. Pour this over the cheese and stir gently.

Bake at 300°F for 1 1/2 to 2 hours until it is firm like custard and an inserted knife comes out clean. The top should be lightly browned.

Mission Covenant Church
Foster City, MI

OSTKAKA

"1 liter milk
1/2 rennet tablet
2 tablespoons sugar
2 hands full of flour"

Concordia Lutheran Church
Kingsburg, CA

SNOW PUDDING

1 tablespoon plain gelatin
1/4 cup cold water
1 cup boiling water
1 cup sugar
1/4 cup lemon juice
3 egg whites

Soak the gelatin in cold water and then dissolve it in the boiling water. Add the sugar and the lemon juice and cool the mixture. When the mixture thickens, beat it with a rotary egg-beater adding the stiffly beaten egg whites. Place this in the refrigerator to chill and become firm.

"Serve with custard sauce."

First Lutheran Church
Gardner, MA

CHRISTMAS ALMOND PUDDING

2 cups cream
4 egg yolks
1 package unflavored gelatin
1 package slivered almonds
1/2 cup sugar
1/3 teaspoon almond extract

Beat the eggs and sugar until cream-colored. Add the cream to the eggs and cook in a double boiler until the mixture thickens. Add a little water to the gelatin and add this to the cream mixture. Add the almond extract and slivered almonds. Pour it into a 1-quart mold and refrigerate.

"Serve topped with lingonberries or raspberries."

First Lutheran Church
Hector, MN

LEMON CREAM PUDDING

1 cup sugar
3 tablespoons flour
1/2 teaspoon salt
2 eggs, separated
1 cup milk
Juice of 1 lemon (The rind may
    also be used.)

Mix the sugar and flour. Add the salt and lemon juice. Add the beaten egg yolks and milk. Fold in the stiffly beaten egg whites. Pour this into a baking dish which has been set in a pan of water and bake for 1/2 hour at 325°F until set and browned on top. When baked, the custard settles on the bottom, and cake on top. Serve with whipped cream.

Faith Lutheran Church
Forest Lake, MN

LEMON RICE PUDDING

Boil 1 cup of rice in a pint of water for a few minutes. Add 1 quart of milk and cook until tender and thick. Add 1 cup of sugar, a pinch of salt, the grated rind of 1 lemon and the yolks of 3 eggs. Bake for 1/2 hour in a casserole.

Place a meringue on top made from 3 stiffly beaten egg whites, 1/4 cup sugar and the juice of 1 lemon. (Vanilla extract may be used instead of the lemon.) Spread the meringue on the pudding and place in the oven until the meringue is browned.

North Park Covenant Church
Chicago, IL

SWEDISH KISS PUDDING

1 cup egg whites, (approximately
    8 eggs)
1/4 teaspoon salt
3/4 teaspoon cream of tartar
2 cups sugar
1 1/2 teaspoons vanilla

Beat the egg whites and salt until foamy. Add the cream of tartar and beat until stiff. Add the sugar, one tablespoon at a time, while beating. Add the vanilla.

Spread the mixture in an ungreased 9-inch by 13-inch baking dish and place this in a preheated 450°F oven. Turn the oven off and leave the dish in the oven for 4 hours, or overnight. Frost with whipping cream, and serve with strawberries.

Swedish Council of St. Louis
St. Louis, MO

WHIPPED BERRY PUDDING

3 cups cranberry (or other fruit)
   juice
1/2 cup uncooked farina
1/2 cup sugar

Heat the juice to boiling and add the sugar. Sprinkle in the farina and stir quickly to prevent lumping. Cook slowly for about 30 minutes, or until the farina is done.

Pour the mixture into a large bowl and whip with an electric mixer or a food processor at high speed. Whip until the mixture has a very light color and is fluffy. If the juice is too bland, add lemon juice to taste.

Serve with cream.

"Whipped berry pudding is sometimes called 'Air Pudding'."

Big Lake Covenant Church
Cloquet, MN

VANILLA PUDDING

"A fluted mold is needed to make this look just right."

Melt 2 to 3 tablespoons of butter in a heavy saucepan. Blend in 5 and 5/8 cups milk, 2 eggs slightly beaten, 4 tablespoons white flour, 4 tablespoons potato starch and 4 tablespoons sugar. Stir continuously and cook until mixture leaves the edge of the pan. Stir in 1 teaspoon vanilla.

Steam and sugar the mold. To steam the mold, hold it upside-down over the hot pudding in the saucepan until the mold is completely steamed. Then turn the mold over and shake in the sugar until the mold is fully coated. Spoon in the pudding.

Cover and refrigerate the pudding in the mold for several hours or overnight. Serve with *"sylt* to pass" and a fruit sauce.

A favorite fruit sauce is the Swedish cherry sauce. To make, drain a can of pitted sour pie cherries. Heat and sweeten the juice with approximately 1/2 cup sugar, and pour the juice over the cherries and chill.

Vasa Lutheran Church
Vasa Village
Welch, MN

CRANBERRY STEAM PUDDING

2 cups cranberries
1 1/2 cups flour
1/2 teaspoon salt
2 teaspoons soda
1/4 teaspoon mace
1/3 cup hot water
1/2 cup mild molasses
1/4 teaspoon cloves
1/4 teaspoon cinnamon

Sauce:
1 cup sugar
1 cup heavy cream
1/2 cup butter
2 teaspoons vanilla

Chop the cranberries coarsely. Mix the flour, salt, soda, hot water, molasses, cloves, cinnamon and mace. Add the cranberries last. Put the batter into 3 16-ounce cleaned cans and cover with foil. Place the covered cans in a Dutch oven and steam for 2 1/2 hours.

Combine the sugar, heavy cream, butter and vanilla and simmer for a few minutes.

Re-steam the pudding and serve with the warm sauce.

Bethel Lutheran Church
Willmar, MN

STEAMED SUET PUDDING

1 cup sweet milk
1 cup suet
1 cup raisins and currants
1 cup molasses or brown sugar
3 cups flour
2 tablespoons cinnamon
1 teaspoon cloves
1 teaspoon soda

Steam for 3 hours.

Tre Kronor Scandinavian Society
Holdridge, NE

MOM'S BREAD PUDDING

3 slices bread, cubed
3 eggs
1 cup sugar
2 1/2 cups milk
1 cup raisins or diced apples
1 teaspoon cinnamon
1 tablespoon butter

Place the cubed bread in a greased baking pan 9-inch by 9-inch by 2-inch. Beat the eggs. Add the sugar, milk, raisins and cinnamon. Pour this over the cubed bread. Dot with butter and sprinkle with a dash of cinnamon.

Bake slowly at 325°F for 1 hour. Serve with cream, berries or a lemon sauce.

Serves 6.

North Crow River Lutheran Church
Cokato, MN

SWEDISH BREAD PUDDING

4 cups whole milk
4 eggs
2 cups bread, in pieces
2/3 cup sugar
1/2 teaspoon almond flavoring

Mix all the ingredients together until the bread is dissolved.

Bake in a moderate oven at 350°F for 1/2 hour or until light brown on top. Place the mixture in a 9-inch by 12-inch pan or a round baking dish.

Yield: 10 servings.

"This can be served with any fruit topping or served alone with half and half."

Fremont Lutheran Church
Essex, IA

SWEDISH BREAD PUDDING

Put 1 cup of sugar in a pan over the heat to brown. Soak bread in water, squeeze the moisture out, and add this to the sugar. Mix some stale cake or cookies and 3 or 4 pared and sliced apples or some canned fruit into it.

Beat 3 eggs. Add 1/2 cup sugar and enough milk to cover the pudding. Stir it all together and pack it in a buttered baking dish. Set the dish in a pan of water and bake the pudding. Serve with a flavored, sweetened hot cream or sauce.

Our Saviour's Lutheran Church
Hastings, MN

GIFTAS

2 or 3 16-ounce cans whole
   cranberry sauce
1/4 cup sugar (optional)
2 cups graham cracker crumbs
2 tablespoons melted butter
2 cups whipping cream
1/4 cup confectioner's sugar
1 teaspoon vanilla

Mix the sugar and cranberries.
Combine the melted butter and
cracker crumbs. Whip the cream
and add the confectioner's sugar
and vanilla.

Layer the cracker crumbs,
cranberries, and whipped cream
in a *"fancy clear glass bowl."*
Repeat the layers and refrigerate
for 2 to 3 hours before serving.

*Soda crackers or rusks can be
used in place of the graham
crackers. 'Giftas' should be eaten
the same day it is prepared.*

*Augustana Lutheran Church
St. James, MN*

GIFTAS

1 quart cranberries
1 1/2 cups sugar
1 1/2 cups crumbs
1 1/2 cups heavy cream

Wash and "pick over" the
cranberries. Put them in a
saucepan with enough cold
water to cover. Bring to a boil.
Cook until all of the berries have
popped or are soft. Stir in the
sugar. Remove from the heat,
pour into a bowl and cool. Put in
the refrigerator and chill.

To make crumbs:
Crush or roll with a rolling pin
1 of the following:

1 1/2 dozen graham crackers, or
1 1/2 cups crumbs from
   homemade rusks, or
8 cinnamon toasts, or
An equal amount soda crackers

Whip the heavy cream until it is
stiff. Cover the bottom of a glass
bowl with a small layer of
cranberries, crackers and cream.
Repeat layers until all the
ingredients have been used.

Garnish with a layer of whole
berries or cream, and sprinkle
lightly with crumbs.

*Arlington Hills Lutheran Church
St. Paul, MN*

RHUBARB "KRÄM"

5 or 6 rhubarb stalks
1/2 quart water
1 cup sugar
2 tablespoons cornstarch

Cook the rhubarb in the water and sugar until it is soft, but not mushy. Add the cornstarch which has been dissolved in cold water. Stir while cooking.

Pour mixture into a bowl which has been rinsed in hot water. When the *kräm* has cooled, sprinkle with sugar. Serve with plain or whipped cream.

First Covenant Church
Minneapolis, MN

SWEDISH KRÄM

2 1/2 cups grape juice (or any
    other juice)
1/4 teaspoon salt
1 tablespoon lemon juice
1/2 cup sugar
1/4 cup tapioca (cornstarch may
    be used as a substitute)

Mix all ingredients and cook in a double boiler until the mixture thickens. Pour into a serving bowl. Sprinkle with cinnamon and serve warm with cream.

Svea Lutheran Church
Hager City, WI

TARTBERRY SAUCE

"This may be used as a substitute for cranberry or lingonberry sauce."

1 quart gooseberries
1 quart raspberries
1 quart currants
1 quart cherries

Add a small amount of water and sugar to taste.

"If the berries are not obtainable at one time, preserve them when they are available."

First Lutheran Church
Genesis, IL

KRÄM
Fruit Pudding

Cook any ripe berry or fruit with water to cover until the fruit is tender. Run it through a strainer or sieve.

To 4 cups of this thin purée, add 3 to 6 tablespoons cornstarch or potato flour mixed with a little cold water. *("How many tablespoons depends on how thick you want it")*. Cook the sauce until it is clear. Serve cold with plain cream. Serves 4 to 6.

Immanuel Lutheran Church
East Moline, IL

GOOSEBERRY SAUCE

"Use unripened—but full grown—berries."

Cook the berries with sugar and lemon rind in water until they fall apart when potato flour, mixed with water, is added.

"Some like a cinnamon stick in this sauce. Serve cold with half and half, garnish with jam, and serve with a biscuit."

(1904 Cookbook)

GOOSEBERRY SAUCE

(Metric Chart: Appendix C)

1/2 liter green gooseberries
1 liter water
1 1/2 *"kkp"* or about
   3 1/4 deciliters sugar
3/4 *"kkp"* potato flour

Clean, rinse and cook the berries in the water until they are very soft. Add the sugar. Remove the pan from the heat. Add the potato flour, which has been dissolved in a little cold water. Boil the sauce again.

"Potato flour doesn't have to boil for any length of time."

(1930 Cookbook)

KRUSBÄRSKRÄM
Gooseberry Sauce

(Metric Chart: Appendix C)

1/2 to 3/4 liters fresh
   gooseberries
6 deciliters water
Grated rind and juice of half a
   lemon
1 to 2 deciliters granulated
   sugar
2 tablespoons of flour (potato,
   tapioca, sago or corn)

Clean and rinse the berries. Place them in boiling water with the sugar and grated lemon rind. Cook the berries until they are soft but not falling apart. Dissolve the flour in a little water. Bring the sauce to another boil with the potato flour, but cook it for about 3 minutes with the other flours.

Serve the sauce with half and half or whipped cream; almond, wheat or graham rusks; pound cake etc.

(1950 Cookbook)

*First Lutheran Church
Genesis, IL*

These three recipes are from Sonja Anderson's cookbook collection Genesco, IL.

139

LINGONBERRIES

1 quart lingonberries, solidly
   packed
2 cups water
1 cup sugar
3 tablespoons cornstarch,
   dissolved in 1/4 cup water

Drain the liquid from the
lingonberries and wash them.
Bring the berries, sugar and
water to a boil. Let it cook slowly
for 10 minutes, stirring
occasionally. Then add the
cornstarch mixture. (Tapioca
may be used instead of
cornstarch.) Stir to dissolve and
continue to cook 4 to 5 minutes.
Cool. (The lingonberries will
thicken as they cool.)

Serve over *ostkaka*, custard, rice
pudding or pancakes.

Thabor Lutheran Church
Wausa, NE

RAISIN SAUCE

1/2 cup brown sugar
2 tablespoons cornstarch
1 teaspoon mustard
1 tablespoon vinegar
1 cup raisins

1/4 teaspoon grated lemon peel
2 tablespoons lemon juice
1 1/2 cups orange juice

Put all the ingredients in a pan
and stir over medium heat until
the sauce is thick and bubbly.

Makes 2 1/2 cups.

First Lutheran Church
Genesco, IL

MAPLE MOUSSE

6 egg yolks, beaten
1 glass maple syrup
Whipped cream

Cook the beaten egg yolks and
syrup in a double boiler until
thick. Cool the mixture. Add 1
quart (or more) of cream which
has been whipped. Put the
mousse in the freezer.

"When Mrs.William Lundgren got
this recipe from her mother-in-
law, they didn't have electric
refrigerators or freezers so this
was put outside in the snow
when the temperature got below
zero. This was a special treat
then."

Red River Lutheran Church
Hallock, MN

NYPONSOPPA
Rosehip Soup

(Metric Chart: Appendix C)

"Red rosehips are called the 'false fruits of the wild rosebush' because the 'real fruit is inside the red hip.'"

2 to 2 1/2 *"kkp"* dried hips
2 to 2 1/2 liters water
1 *"kkp"* sugar
2 *matsked* potato flour

Rinse the hips. Place the hips in water the day before you plan to use them. Cook them in this same water in a covered saucepan until they are very soft. Whip the hips several times during cooking. Purée them through a sieve. Pour a small amount of hot water over the remaining pulp in the sieve and press again.

Put the purée back into the saucepan. Add the sugar and test for sweetness. Add the potato flour which has dissolved in a little cold water and boil the soup for a short time.

"The soup will have a richer taste when served with whipped cream."

*First Lutheran Church
Genesco, IL*

NYPONSOPPA
Rosehip Soup

2 1/2 cups fresh rosehips
2 quarts water
6 tablespoons sugar
2 tablespoons cornstarch
3 to 4 tablespoons Madeira wine
10 to 15 blanched almonds

Clean the rosehips removing the blossom ends. Wash and cook the hips in water until tender. Force the cooked hips through a strainer or a purée sieve. Return the purée to the pan.

Add the sugar and water to this, and stir in the cornstarch which has been blended with a little cold water. Cook until thickened. Add wine and chill.

"Serve with shredded almonds, whipped cream, or rusks in vanilla sauce."

*Zion Lutheran Church
Minneapolis, MN*

FRUKTSOPPA
Fruit Soup

1 12-ounce package dried fruit
   soup mix
6 cups water
3/4 cup sugar
2 tablespoons lemon juice
2 sticks cinnamon
1/2 to 3/4 cup "Red Hots"
2 tablespoons tapioca

Cut up the fruit into small
pieces. Add the water, sugar,
lemon juice, cinnamon sticks,
"Red Hots" and tapioca. Boil
slowly for one hour. As it cools,
the juice will thicken.

*"Serve warm or cold. It will keep
for several weeks in the
refrigerator."*

*Elim Lutheran Church
Marquette, KS*

FRUKTSOPPA
Fruit Soup

1/2 pound prunes
1/4 pound dried apricots
1/4 pound dried peaches
1 cup raisins
4 tablespoons of "large-variety"
   tapioca
1 cup sugar
1 stick cinnamon
1/4 teaspoon salt

Soak the dried fruits and tapioca
overnight. In the morning,
combine all the ingredients in
2 quarts of water and cook until
the fruit is soft.

*"This soup may be served hot or
cold. It is very good served cold
with cream."*

*East Sveadahl Lutheran Church
St James, MN*

SWEDISH FRUIT SOUP

1 8-ounce package dried
  apricots
1 8-ounce package pitted prunes
1 cup golden raisins
1 cup sugar
1/2 cup "small-pearl" tapioca
2 1/2 cups water
1/4 teaspoon salt
1/2 cup sugar
1 can cherry pie filling

Cook the apricots, prunes and raisins in 2 1/2 cups water until soft. Use plenty of water. Add 1 cup of sugar after the fruit is cooked. Next, remove the cooked fruit and cook the tapioca in the same water for 20 minutes. Add the salt to the water. *"Cook it in the microwave 8 minutes at Level 8."*

Then add the 1/2 cup sugar and the cooked, sweetened fruit.

When cooled, add the pie filling.

Immanuel Lutheran Church
Mediapolis, IA

SWEDISH FRUIT SOUP

1/2 pound prunes
1 cup seeded raisins
1 orange, sliced
4 tablespoons tapioca
1/4 pound dried apricots
1 lemon, sliced
1 cup sugar
1 stick cinnamon
1 cup canned cherries
3 apples, diced

Soak overnight the dried apricots, prunes, raisins, tapioca, sugar, cinnamon, orange and lemon in enough water to cover.

In the morning, add the apples and some more water and cook until the fruit is soft. Add the canned cherries last.

"This soup can be served either hot or cold."

Sillerud Lutheran Church
Balaton, MN

SWEDISH FRUIT SOUP

12 ounces of dried apricots, cut
  into halves or fourths. (Dried
  peaches and apples may also
  be used.)
1 cup white raisins
1 cup dark, seedless raisins
1 tablespoon currants
3 tablespoons tapioca

Boil the fruits in 1 gallon of
water and simmer 45 minutes to
1 hour. Thicken with
3 tablespoons of tapioca.

Cook separately:
1 pound of small prunes.

(If adding sugar, add it to the
prunes. Often no sugar is
needed).

Add this to the fruit mixture.

Add:
1 can (14 ounces) crushed
  pineapple tidbits
1 can cherries
1 can grapefruit sections
1 can (14 ounces) fruit cocktail
1 cup orange juice

Serve hot or cold. *"Fresh berries
or bananas may be added when
serving, or the soup may be
topped with whipped cream."*

*Trinity Lutheran Church
Carthage, SD*

FRUKTSOPPA
Fruit Soup

1 cup prunes
1 cup raisins
1 cup peeled apple, chopped
1 orange, cut up and peeled
1/4 teaspoon salt
1 teaspoon orange rind, finely
  cut
4 cups water
1 tablespoon lemon juice
1/4 cup sugar
1 stick cinnamon
2 tablespoons quick-cooking
  tapioca
1 10-ounce package frozen
  raspberries (to be thawed)

Combine all the ingredients,
except the tapioca and
raspberries in a large saucepan.
Simmer slowly for 1 hour.
Sprinkle the tapioca over the
soup and stir to avoid lumping.
Cook for 15 minutes more. Add
the thawed raspberries to the
hot soup.

Serve hot or chilled with
whipped cream. This makes
about 5 cups of soup, or 8 to
10 servings.

*Svenska Vännerna
South Central Minnesota*

144

MOTHER'S SWEDISH FRUIT SOUP

2 quarts water
4 cups mixed dried fruits;
    apricots, prunes, raisins
1/4 cup pearl tapioca
1 stick cinnamon
1/2 cup sugar
1 tablespoon lemon juice
1/4 cup grape juice, or other
    leftover juice (more can be
    used, if desired).

Combine the dried fruits, water and tapioca and soak overnight. *"Be sure the tapioca is well-soaked or 'fish-eyes' may result."*

In the morning, add the cinnamon stick and simmer the soup until the fruit is tender.

Add the sugar and cook another 15 minutes. Remove the cinnamon stick and add the lemon and grape juices. Simmer until thoroughly heated.

"Fruit soup may be served hot as a first course for a luncheon or dinner, or cold as a dessert."

"Dried fruits were not easily obtained. Occasionally dried pears were available, but they were costly as were apricots. Dried apples would also be added. Harvest apples from the orchard were peeled, sliced medium-thin and spread in cake pans. These then dried slowly in the oven of the wood-burning kitchen range with the oven door kept open for warmth on cool autumn days."

First Evangelical Lutheran Church
Winthrop, MN

SWEDISH FRUIT SOUP

1 cup prunes
1/2 cup raisins, washed
1 stick cinnamon
1/2 cup sugar
1 tablespoon lemon juice
6 cups hot water

Simmer for 15 minutes.

Add:
1 peeled apple, cut up into small
    pieces
1 16-ounce jar of canned
    peaches, with juice
3 tablespoons tapioca

Simmer for 10 minutes more.

May be served hot or cold.

Evangelical Covenant Church
Warren, MN

FRUKTSOPPA
Fruit Soup

1/2 cup pearl barley
Salt
Water
1 pound prunes
1 cup raisins
1 can frozen grape juice
1 stick cinnamon
1/2 cup sugar
3 large apples, sliced

Boil the pearl barley and salt in "a quart or so" of water. (Then add water as needed.) Add the prunes, raisins, grape juice, cinnamon, sugar and apples and simmer. Add more water as needed.

Evangelical Covenant Church
Stanton, IA

SWEDISH PRUNE SOUP

1 pound prunes
1 pound raisins
2 broken cinnamon sticks
1 cup pearl tapioca for
    thickening (*"Large tapioca*
    must be soaked").

Add enough water to cover and cook until thickened.

Siloa Lutheran Church
Morris Run, PA

RUSKS IN VANILLA CREAM

8 to 10 round, tender rusks
1 cup milk
A little salt
1/2 teaspoon vanilla
3/4 cup thick cream, whipped

Add the vanilla to the milk. Place the rusks in the milk until they are saturated. Remove them with a ladle and layer them in a large glass serving bowl with whipped cream between the layers and on top.

"Chill and serve with fruit soups, either hot or cold."

Zion Lutheran Church
Minneapolis, MN

ÄNGLAMAT
Angelic Food

1 cup whipping cream
1/2 package rusks
2 tablespoons lingonberry
    preserves

Break the rusks into 1-inch cubes. Whip the cream and add the lingonberry preserves. Pour this mixture over the rusks and stir until they are well-covered.

Serve immediately. Serves 5 or 6.

First Lutheran Church
Ottumwa, IA

SWEDISH CREAM

"This smooth cream may be made 3 to 5 days ahead of time."

2 envelopes unflavored gelatin
1/4 cup cold water
2 cups heavy cream
1 cup sugar
2 cups commercial sour cream
1 teaspoon vanilla extract
1 teaspoon rose water (optional)

Sprinkle the gelatin over the water and let it stand for 5 minutes. Heat the heavy cream, but do not let it come to a boil. Add the gelatin and sugar. Stir it until it is completely dissolved. Cool the mixture to room temperature.

Fold the sour cream, vanilla extract and rose water into the gelatin mixture. Then, pour this into a dish and chill until the mixture is set.

"Serve the cream plain or topped with sugared fresh fruit, frozen fruits or jam.

"When the mixture begins to set, add fresh, grated or canned coconut and fresh or canned fruit which has been chopped."

Makes 4 to 6 servings.

North Crow River Lutheran Church
Cokato, MN

SWEDISH CREAM

Mix together:
2 cups heavy cream
1 cup sugar
1 envelope gelatin

Heat gently and stir until the gelatin is dissolved. Cool until it is slightly thickened. Fold in 1/2 pint of sour cream. Add 1 teaspoon of vanilla and 1/2 teaspoon of almond extract.

"Serve with fruits and crepes."

St, Phillips Lutheran Church
Hastings, MN

SWEDISH CREAM

1 cup milk
3/4 cup sugar
1 egg
1 envelope Knox gelatin
1 pint whipping cream, whipped

Scald the milk in a double boiler. Mix the sugar and egg and add it to the milk. Add the gelatin that has been dissolved in 1/4 cup cold water and bring it to a boiling point. Let cool. When beginning to set, add it to the whipped cream. Mold as desired.

"Top with fresh raspberries."

Interbay Covenant Church
Seattle, WA

SWEDISH CREAM

1 cup whipping cream
1 cup sugar
1 envelope unflavored gelatin
1 cup sour cream (cultured)
1/2 teaspoon vanilla
Sweetened strawberries or
    raspberries

Combine the cream, sugar and
gelatin. Heat until the sugar and
gelatin are dissolved. Add the
sour cream and vanilla. Put the
mixture in separate molds or in
a larger bowl and chill it.

*"Serve topped with sweetened
fruits, such as raspberries or
strawberries."*

Serves 4 to 6.

*Augustana Lutheran Church
Cumberland, WI*

ÄPPELMARÄNG
Meringue-Covered Apples

(Metric Chart: Appendix C)

Meringue:
3 to 4 egg whites
1 1/2 *"kkp"* sugar

Cook sugar and water until it is
clear. Let it cool. Peel the apples
and remove the stems. (Do not
core the apples. If the apples are
to be cored, fill them with sugar
and bake them in a slow oven.)
Place the apples in the cooled
sugar syrup and let them
simmer without a cover until
they feel soft. Remove the apples
and place them in an oven-proof
baking dish and let them cool
again.

Beat 3 to 4 egg whites until
frothy. Add the sugar
1 tablespoon at a time and beat
it until stiff peaks form.

Cover the apples with the
meringue. The apples are then
placed in a medium-hot oven
and baked until the meringue is
golden brown.

*"The boiled or baked apples can
be put on a greased cookie sheet
after they are cooled. Then they
should be individually covered
with meringue and baked until
they are golden brown.*

*"Place them in individual serving
dishes or on a platter."*

Serve cold.

*First Lutheran Church
Genesco, IL*

148

APPLE DUMPLINGS

Put 1 1/2 cups sugar, 2 cups water and some butter in a baking dish and place it on a stove to boil.

Mix 4 tablespoons shortening, 2 cups flour, 2 teaspoons baking powder, 1/2 teaspoon salt and 3/4 cup milk together. Roll out until they are 1/2 inch thick.

Cut the dough into squares and place a cored apple slice in the center of each square. Fill the apple centers with sugar and cinnamon or mace, and bake for 25 minutes after placing them in the sugar syrup.

"Pour some of this syrup on each dumpling when they are ready to be served."

Salem Lutheran Church
Duluth, MN

ÄPPELKAKA
Apple Cake

2 cups thick cream
1/4 cup sugar
2 cups dried apples, cooked and
    sweetened
2 cups bread crumbs

Whip the cream until thick and add the sugar. In a serving dish, put a layer of apples, a layer of bread crumbs and a layer of whipped cream. Repeat the layers, ending with the whipped cream on top. Decorate with cinnamon.

Immanuel Lutheran Church
Greeley, CO

APPLES WITH ALMOND TOPPING

Peel and halve 8 cooking apples and simmer for 6 minutes in 1 1/2 cups of water and 1 cup of sugar. Place the apples on a serving dish.

Topping:
4 tablespoons butter
2 tablespoons flour
1/2 cup sugar
4 tablespoons milk
2/3 cup sliced almonds
1/2 teaspoon vanilla

Combine all the ingredients and cook over a low heat, stirring constantly for 2 to 3 minutes. Spoon the topping over the apples. Chill for 1 hour before serving.

"Pears may be used instead of apples."

North Central Svenska Klubben
North Central Iowa

149

APPLE PUDDING

1 egg, beaten
3/4 cup sugar
1 tablespoon butter, melted
3/4 cup milk
1 cup flour
1 teaspoon baking powder

Mix the ingredients together in the order listed. Place sliced apples in a buttered baking dish. Sprinkle cinnamon or nutmeg on top of the apples and pour the batter over them.

Bake for 1/2 hour. Serve with sauce or cream.

Faith Lutheran Church
Forest Lake, MN

MOM'S DELICIOUS PIE CRUST

2 cups flour
1/4 cup water with 1 teaspoon
    vinegar
Dash salt
1 cup shortening

Mix the flour, shortening and salt until crumbly. Add the water and the vinegar. Mix well.

Makes 2 crusts.

Amana Lutheran Church
Scandia, KS

NEVER-FAIL SWEDISH PIE CRUST

Dry Ingredients:
3 cups flour
1 cup lard or shortening
1/4 teaspoon salt

Mix these ingredients together well until the mixture is moist.

Liquid Ingredients:
1 egg slightly beaten
1 teaspoon vinegar
1/4 to 1/2 cup water

When the flour and shortening are well-mixed, gradually add the liquids using just enough to hold the dry ingredients together.

Roll the dough out on a floured board.

"This recipe keeps well in the refrigerator but if a smaller batch is to be made, use 1/3 as much shortening as flour. If the dough hangs together well, it might not be necessary to use all the liquid.

"If making the crust for a meat dish, add 1 1/2 tablespoons of Parmesan cheese.

"This is a tender, flaky crust."

First Lutheran Church
Lincoln, NE

PUMPKIN PIE

2 cups cooked pumpkin or
squash
4 eggs, separated
1 cup sugar
1 tablespoon cornstarch
1/3 cup cream
1/4 cup margarine, melted
1 teaspoon whiskey
Cinnamon

Bake the pumpkin or squash in an oven. Mash it lightly and drain it overnight in a colander which has been placed in the refrigerator.

Combine the pumpkin and slightly beaten egg yolks with a mixture of sugar, cornstarch and cinnamon. Beat for 5 minutes. Mix in the cream, margarine and whiskey.

Beat the egg whites until they form rounded peaks. Fold this into the pumpkin mixture and pour the whole mixture into a pastry-lined pan.

Bake at 375°F for 45 minutes or until a knife inserted in the center comes out clean.

First Lutheran Church
Gardner, MA

GRAPE PIE

1 pint of grapes, seedless
3/4 cup sugar
4 tablespoons cornstarch

Add the sugar to the grapes and mix the cornstarch with some water to make a thin paste. Add the cornstarch paste to the grapes and sugar. Pour this into a pie crust and cover it with another crust. Coat the upper pie crust with milk.

Bake in a 450°F oven for 10 minutes. Turn the temperature down to 350°F and bake for another 30 minutes.

First Lutheran Church
Genesco, IL

SWEDISH SOUR CREAM RAISIN PUDDING OR PIE

1 cup sour cream
3/4 cup sugar
3/4 cup raisins
1/2 teaspoon cloves
1/2 teaspoon cinnamon
2 or 3 eggs, separated

Cook all the ingredients together except the egg whites until the mixture has the consistency of pudding. For a pie, place the pudding mixture in a pie pan on a baked bottom crust.

Beat the egg whites with 1 tablespoon of sugar for a meringue topping.

Faith Lutheran Church
Forest Lake, MN

SWEDISH PIE

Mix:
1 egg, beaten
1/2 teaspoon vanilla
1/2 cup flour
Pinch of salt
1/2 cup nuts, chopped
1/4 cup plus 2 tablespoons
   sugar
1/4 cup plus 2 tablespoons
   brown sugar
1 teaspoon baking powder
1 cup apples, chopped

Combine all the ingredients and bake in a pie pan at 350°F for 45 minutes.

Serve with whipped cream topped with a cherry or ice cream.

North Central Svenska Klubben
North Central Iowa

SWEDISH APPLE PIE

2 cups apple slices, slightly
  cooked
2 tablespoons flour
3/4 cup sugar
Pinch of salt
1 egg
1 teaspoon vanilla
1 cup commercial sour cream
9-inch pie shell, unbaked

Lightly mash the apples and add
the flour, sugar and salt. Beat
the egg and vanilla together and
add this to the apple mixture.
Then add the sour cream.

Pour the apple mixture into a pie
shell and bake it at 350°F for
40 minutes.

Topping:
1/3 cup sugar
1/3 cup flour
1 stick margarine, softened
1 teaspoon cinnamon

Spread this topping on the
baked apple mixture and return
the pie to the oven for 15 more
minutes.

Bethesda Lutheran Church
Morrison, IL

MERINGUE FOR CREAM PIE

Syrup:
1/2 cup sugar
1/4 cup water
Boil these together until the
mixture *"spins a thread."*

Add:
2 egg whites
1/4 teaspoon cream of tartar,
  beaten until stiff

Pour the syrup slowly into the
beaten egg whites stirring until
the mixture is fluffy.

Cool the meringue and put the
meringue on a cooled pie. (Do
not bake). Refrigerate the
meringue.

Salem Lutheran Church
Rock Island, IL

SWEDISH APPLE CAKE

1 cup flour
2 teaspoons baking powder
1/2 teaspoon salt
2/3 cup sugar
1 egg
1/2 cup milk
1 teaspoon vanilla
2 cups sliced apples

Sift the flour, baking powder, salt and sugar together in a bowl. Add the egg, milk and vanilla. Beat for 1 minute. Put into an 8-inch by 8-inch buttered pan. Arrange the sliced apples evenly over the top.

Mix the following ingredients:
1/3 cup brown sugar
3 tablespoons softened butter
2 teaspoons cinnamon
1/2 teaspoon black walnut
　flavoring, optional

Sprinkle this mixture over the apples. Bake at 350°F for 30 to 40 minutes. Serve warm with milk or cream.

Immanuel Lutheran Church
Omaha, NE

AMAZING RAISIN CAKE

3 cups flour
2 cups sugar
1 cup real mayonnaise
1/3 cup milk
2 eggs
2 teaspoons soda
1 1/2 teaspoons cinnamon
1/2 teaspoon nutmeg
1/2 teaspoon salt
1/4 teaspoon cloves
3 cups chopped apples
1 cup raisins
1/2 cup chopped nuts

Mix the first 10 ingredients at low speed for 2 minutes. Stir in the apples, raisins and nuts. Pour the mixture into 2 pans. Bake at 350°F for 35 to 45 minutes. Cool for 10 minutes. Remove the cake from the pans and cool. Fill and frost the cake with whipped topping or serve plain.

Brantford Evangelical Covenant Church
Brantford Township
Washington County, KS

SWEDISH APPLE CAKE WITH VANILLA SAUCE

1 1/3 cups applesauce
2 cups zwieback crumbs or stale
Swedish *limpa*, grated
4 tablespoons butter

Melt the butter in a skillet. Add the bread crumbs and stir until nicely browned. Butter a baking dish well and arrange the crumbs and applesauce in alternating layers, finishing with the crumbs on the top.

Bake at 375°F for 25 to 35 minutes. Cool the cake before removing it from the pan. Serve with vanilla sauce.

Vanilla Sauce:
1 cup cream
3 egg yolks
2 tablespoons sugar
2 teaspoons vanilla extract
3/4 to 1 cup whipped cream

Beat the egg yolks and sugar in the top of a double boiler. Add the heated cream and cook until thick, stirring constantly. Remove the pan from the heat and add the vanilla. Cool the sauce, beating occasionally.

When the mixture is cold, carefully fold in the whipped cream.

Trinity Lutheran Church
Gresham, OR

DELICATE SPICE CAKE

1/2 cup butter
1 1/2 cups brown sugar
2 eggs, separated
2 teaspoons ground cardamom
2 teaspoons cinnamon
1/2 cup rich cream
1 1/2 cups flour
1 teaspoon baking powder

Cream the butter and sugar thoroughly. Add the beaten egg yolks. Then add the dry ingredients alternately with the cream. Fold in the egg whites which have been beaten stiff, but not dry.

Grease a pan with butter and dust it with bread crumbs. Bake the cake in a slow oven.

North Park Covenant Church
Chicago, IL

155

LINGONBERRY CAKE

1 1/4 cups sifted flour
1 cup sugar
1 teaspoon cinnamon
1 teaspoon baking soda
1/2 teaspoon ground cloves
1 stick butter, melted
1 cup milk
1/2 cup lingonberries

Sift all the dry ingredients together. Add the melted butter, milk and lingonberries. Mix well. Bake at 350°F in a small greased bundt pan for 40 to 45 minutes or until a toothpick comes out dry.

Ladies Auxiliary of the Suncoast Swedish Veterans Chorus Florida

LINGONBERRY CRUMB CAKE

Mix together:
1 3/4 cups flour
3/4 cup sugar
3 teaspoons baking powder

Add:
1 egg
5 ounces butter or margarine

Beat the mixture and put it in a pan.

Spread:
2 tablespoons lingonberry jam over the crust. *"Cranberry jam can be used in place of lingonberry jam."*

Topping:
1 1/5 cups old-fashioned oatmeal
1 cup sugar
2 teaspoons vanilla sugar
4 ounces butter or margarine

Mix these 4 ingredients together and spread the topping over the lingonberries. Bake in a 400°F oven for 20 minutes.

Catherine Tenebeck Rock Hill, SC

SWEDISH COFFEE CAKE

3 cups all-purpose flour
2 cups sugar
2 teaspoons baking powder
1/2 teaspoon salt
1 cup butter or margarine
1 cup milk
2 eggs, slightly beaten
1 teaspoon vanilla
1 teaspoon cinnamon
1/2 teaspoon nutmeg
1/2 teaspoon ginger

Preheat the oven to 350°F. In a large bowl combine the flour, sugar, baking powder and salt. Cut in the butter until crumbly. Reserve 1 cup of the crumb mixture. To the remaining crumb mixture add the milk, eggs and vanilla. Beat until well-mixed. Pour this into a greased 9-inch by 13-inch baking pan.

Stir the spices into the 1 cup of reserved crumbs and sprinkle spiced crumbs evenly over the batter.

Bake for 30 to 40 minutes or until a wooden pick comes out clean.

Yield: 15 to 18 servings.

First Lutheran Church
Lincoln, NE

CRANBERRY CHRISTMAS CAKE

3 tablespoons butter, softened
1 cup sugar
2 cups flour
3 teaspoons baking powder
1/4 teaspoon salt
1 cup milk
3 cups cranberries

Put all the ingredients in a bowl, except the cranberries and beat the mixture by hand. Fold in the cranberries. Spread the batter evenly in a greased 8-inch or 9-inch square pan. Bake for 40 to 45 minutes at 350°F. Serve warm with hot butter sauce.

Butter Sauce:
1 cup sugar
1 tablespoon flour
1/2 cup cream or half and half
1/2 cup butter
1 tablespoon vinegar
1 teaspoon vanilla

Mix the flour and sugar. Place all the ingredients, except the vanilla, in a saucepan. Cook on high heat stirring constantly until the sauce is hot and bubbly. Add the vanilla. Serve warm over the cake.

Immanuel Lutheran Church
Dunnell, MN

SWEDISH PINEAPPLE

2 cups flour
2 cups sugar
1/2 teaspoon salt
2 teaspoons soda
2 eggs
1 large can pineapple plus the
    juice
1 teaspoon vanilla
1/2 cup chopped nuts

Sift the dry ingredients together.
Beat the eggs well. Mix together
the pineapple, its juice and the
vanilla. Stir. Add the sifted dry
ingredients and mix thoroughly.
Add the chopped nuts. Pour into
a well-greased 9-inch by
13-inch pan. Bake 40 to
45 minutes at 350°F.

Topping:
8 ounces cream cheese at room
    temperature
1 3/4 cups powdered sugar
1 stick of butter at room
    temperature (not margarine)
1/2 cup nuts

Beat the cream cheese, butter
and powdered sugar until fluffy.
Spread this on the cooled cake
and sprinkle the topping with
nuts.

First Lutheran Church
Genesco, IL

ORANGE CAKE

Squeeze the juice from 1 orange
and then grind up 2 whole
oranges, including the rinds.
Grind 1 cup of raisins with the
oranges.

Mix together:
1 cup sugar
1/2 cup margarine
2 eggs
1 cup sour milk (add
    1 tablespoon of vinegar to the
    milk so it will sour)
1 teaspoon soda mixed in with
    the milk
2 cups flour
1 teaspoon baking powder

Mix the ground-up raisins and
orange mixture into the batter.
(Mix well with a wooden spoon.)
Bake in a 9-inch by 12-inch
greased and floured pan at
350°F for 25 to 30 minutes or
until a toothpick comes out
clean.

While still warm, spread the cake
with a glaze made by mixing the
orange juice with the powdered
sugar until it has a spreading
consistency.

Bethlehem Lutheran Church
Florence, WI

SOLSKENSKAKA
Sunshine Cake

2 eggs
1 extra egg white
3/4 cup sugar
1/2 teaspoon baking powder
1/2 cup regular flour
1/4 pound margarine, melted
1/2 teaspoon almond extract

Beat the eggs lightly. Add the sugar and beat well. Add 1/2 teaspoon baking powder, 1/2 cup flour, 1/4 pound melted margarine and 1/2 teaspoon almond. Grease a pan with shortening and flour. Mix together nuts and some sugar and sprinkle this on top of the batter. Bake in a 350°F oven for 25 minutes. Decorate the cake with candied orange peel. Chop up the peels and put an inch around the cake that has been frosted with a thin coat of confectioners sugar, water and vanilla extract.

Candied Orange Peel:
3 oranges
2 cups sugar
3 tablespoons light corn syrup
3/4 cup water

Peel the fruit in large strips, using only the "zest" (the outer colored peel) and the white peel.

If the white is very thick, trim it down. Put the peel in a pan, cover it with cold water and simmer for 30 minutes. Drain, cover with cold water and simmer until tender. Drain and cut the peel into small strips about 1/4-inch wide by 2-inches long. Mix 1 cup of sugar with the corn syrup and the water in a heavy saucepan. Stir over low heat until dissolved. Dip a pastry brush in cold water and wash down the sides of the pan. Then add the peel and cook very gently over low heat until most of the syrup has been absorbed. Cover and let it stand overnight. Reheat and bring the syrup to a simmer again. Cool it for a little while and drain it. Spread out several thicknesses of paper towels. Empty the remaining cup of sugar onto the towels and roll the peel in it, turning it frequently so all pieces are well-coated. Let them stand until dry enough to handle.

"The orange peels will stay fresh for several months if they are stored in an airtight container. If they become too dry, put a lemon in the container for a day or two and the peel will soften."

Elsa Larson, friend
Shrewsbury, MA

SUNSHINE CREAM CAKE

7 eggs, separated
Pinch of salt
1/3 teaspoon cream of tartar
2 1/4 cups sugar
1 1/2 cups flour
1 teaspoon "flavoring"
2 1/4 cups milk
1 "cube" butter, chilled
1 cup coconut

Combine the whites of the 7 eggs with the salt and cream of tartar. Beat this until stiff. Next, slowly add 1 1/4 cups of the sugar to the egg white mixture. Beat the 7 egg yolks and fold this into the mixture. Finally, fold in 1 cup of the flour and the flavoring. Bake this at 325°F for 45 minutes to 1 hour.

When the cake has cooled, split it into 3 layers and prepare the filling. Combine 2 1/4 cups milk, 1/2 cup flour and 1 cup of sugar. Cook this until thick, or about 10 minutes. Let this cool completely and beat in 1 cube of cold butter. (Add flavor if you like.) Brown 1 cup of coconut and sprinkle it over the top and on the sides.

Concordia Lutheran Church
Kingsburg, CA

OLD-FASHIONED MARZIPAN CAKE

Use any brand of mix for a yellow poundcake. For the filling, combine a vanilla pudding mix with half a cup of whipped cream. (The batter should be 1/4-inch thick.)

Marzipan mixture:
1/2 cup cream, or half and half
2/3 cup flour
1 pound powdered sugar
4 ounces of scalded almonds

"Since all marzipans are usually colored in light pastels, carefully add green or red food coloring, one drop at a time, to obtain a light green or pink color." Microwave the cream and flour until it becomes thickened, usually about 2 minutes on high. Let it cool. Grind the almonds into a fine powder. Pour the powdered sugar on a baking board and cover the sugar with almond powder. Pour the wet marzipan mixture on top of the powder and knead the mixture together until it feels like pie dough. Using a rolling pin, shape the dough large enough to cover cake. Place the marzipan on top of the cake and trim.

Lisa Dahlfjord-Nelson
Clackamas, OR

KRONANSKAKA
Crown Cake

2 eggs
1/2 cup granulated sugar
1/4 cup butter or margarine
2/3 cup ground almonds
2 boiled medium potatoes,
    chilled and grated
2 tablespoons bread crumbs

In a bowl, beat the eggs and sugar until thick and foamy. In another bowl, cream the butter. Add the ground almonds to the butter. Gradually add the egg mixture to the butter and almonds and blend well. Add the grated potatoes.

Grease an 8-inch cake pan and sprinkle it with bread crumbs, shaking off excess crumbs. Pour the batter into the pan. Bake in a moderate oven at 350°F for 25 minutes. Cool the cake.

"If desired, serve the cake with lemon sauce."

*Swedish Council of St. Louis
St. Louis, MO*

KARDEMUMMAKAKA
Cardamom Cake

2 cups flour
2 teaspoons baking powder
3/4 cup sugar
2 teaspoons ground cardamom
1/2 cup butter, softened
1 cup milk

Sift the first 4 ingredients together in a large bowl. Cut the butter into this with a pastry blender until crumbly. Add the milk all at once and mix it together quickly. (The batter will be slightly lumpy and rather thick.)

Pour the batter into a well-greased, 9-inch square pan.

Prepare a topping of:
1 teaspoon cinnamon
2 tablespoons sugar
1/4 cup chopped almonds

Sprinkle the topping on the cake and bake it at 350°F for 35 to 40 minutes.

"Delicious served warm."

*Bensonvale Covenant Church
Omaha, NE*

MERINGUE CAKE

Cake:
1/2 cup butter or margarine
1/2 cup sugar
4 egg yolks
1/4 cup half and half
1/2 teaspoon vanilla
1 cup cake flour, sifted
1 1/4 teaspoons baking powder
1/8 teaspoon salt

Cream the butter with the sugar.
Add the egg yolks one at a time,
beating after each addition. Add
the half and half and vanilla. Sift
the flour, baking powder and
salt together in a separate bowl.
Add the wet ingredients to the
flour mixture and stir. Beat the
combined mixture for 2 minutes.
Spread the batter into 2 greased
and floured 9-inch layer-cake
pans.

Meringue:
4 egg whites
Pinch of salt
1 cup sugar
1 teaspoon vanilla
1/4 cup walnuts or pecans,
   chopped

Beat the egg whites and salt
until stiff. Gradually add the
sugar; then add the vanilla. Beat
for 1 minute.

Spread the meringue on top of
the cake batter in the pans.
(Make sure the meringue has
uneven peaks and is about
1/2 inch from the edge.) On top
of one of the layers, sprinkle the
chopped nuts.

Bake at 350°F for 35 minutes.
Allow the cakes to cool in their
own pans on wire racks.

Assembling the cake:
Place one layer meringue-side
down. Spread the plain top with
fruit and whipped cream. Then,
place the other layer that has
nuts on it meringue-side up on
top of the whipped cream filling.

Makes 12 servings.

Dala Heritage Society
Mora, MN

162

STINA'S AMBROSIA TORTE

2 eggs
2/3 cup sugar
2/3 cup soft butter
2/3 cup all-purpose flour
1/2 teaspoon baking powder
Butter for greasing the pan
Soft bread crumbs

Icing:
1 tablespoon orange juice
1/2 cup powdered sugar
3 tablespoons candied orange
   peel or sliced almonds

Beat the eggs and sugar together until light and fluffy. Beat in the butter. Next, add the flour and baking powder. "Butter" an 8-inch round cake or tart pan. Sprinkle the bread crumbs to cover the bottom and sides of the pan. Pour the cake into the pan and bake in a slow oven (300°F for 30 to 45 minutes) or until a toothpick inserted into the center of the cake comes out clean. Cool slightly and turn the cake out on a rack.

Combine the icing ingredients and frost the top of the cake.

Svenska Vänner
Jamestown, ND

TOSCATÅRTA

2 eggs
2/3 cup sugar
3/4 cup flour
1 teaspoon baking powder
2 tablespoons table cream
1 stick butter
Frosting:
1/2 stick butter
1/3 cup almonds
3 tablespoons sugar
1 tablespoon flour
1 tablespoon table cream

Preheat the oven to 325°F. Beat the eggs and sugar until light and foamy. Sift the flour with baking powder and add it to the egg mixture. Melt the butter over a low heat and let it cool. Add the cream and melted butter to the batter.
Butter and flour (or "bread") a round cake form. Pour the batter into the pan and bake until it is half done, about 15 to 20 minutes. Chop the almonds.

Combine the ingredients for the frosting in a pan, stirring constantly. Heat until the butter is melted and surface begins to bubble. Pour this over the half-done cake and bake another 15 to 20 minutes.

Tre Kronor Scandinavian Society
Holdredge, NE

163

KRISTINA'S TORTE

3 egg yolks
1 1/2 cups sugar
5 tablespoons milk
1/2 cup melted butter
2 1/2 cups wheat flour
5 teaspoons baking powder
1 teaspoon vanilla

Meringue:
2 egg whites
2 1/2 cups powdered sugar

Garnish:
1/2 pound almonds, peeled and
   chopped

Filling:
3 cups whipped cream

Grease a "long pan" with butter.
Begin with the meringue. Beat
the egg whites until stiff and sift
in the powdered sugar, a little at
a time, while beating. In another
bowl, beat the egg yolks and
sugar. Then add the milk and
melted butter. Combine the flour
and baking powder and stir this
into the yolk mixture. Add the
vanilla.

Put the cake batter into a pan.
Top it with the meringue and
sprinkle it with almonds. Bake
at 350°F for 25 minutes.

Let it cool.

Cut the cake into 2 layers and
put half of the whipped cream
on top of the bottom layer. Then,
put the top layer on and frost it
with the remaining whipped
cream.

Top with sliced bananas, if
desired.

Braham Evangelical Lutheran Church
Braham, MN

SOCKERKAKA
Sponge Cake

4 eggs, beaten until foamy
1 cup sugar
1/2 cup oil
1 cup cake flour
1/2 teaspoon salt
1 teaspoon vanilla
1 teaspoon baking powder

Grease and flour a large bundt
pan. Fill it with the cake mixture
and bake it for 1 hour at 350°F.

When cool, sprinkle the cake
with confectioners sugar.

Linneas of Texas
Houston, TX

DELICIOUS CHRISTMAS "TÅRTA"

2 cubes butter (1-inch by 1-inch)
7/8 cup sugar
2 eggs
2 teaspoons baking powder
1 1/2 cups unsifted flour
1 tablespoon grated orange rind
1/2 cup milk
1 cup raisins
Orange juice
Powdered sugar
Sliced almonds

Melt 1 2/3 cubes butter. Add the sugar and blend. Add the eggs. In another bowl, stir the baking powder into the flour. Combine these with the egg mixture. Now add the orange rind, raisins and milk. Pour the batter into a small, fluted tube-pan which has been greased with the reserved 1/3 cube of butter and floured. Bake at 390°F for 30 to 40 minutes or until done.

Make a glaze from the orange juice and powdered sugar. Pour this over the cooled cake and sprinkle the cake with sliced almonds.

First Covenant Church
Oakland, CA

BRUN SOCKERKAKA
Brown Sponge Cake

2 eggs
1 cup brown sugar
1 cup granulated sugar
1/2 cup butter
1 cup sour cream
1 teaspoon soda
1 teaspoon cinnamon
1 teaspoon cloves
2 cups flour

Mix the ingredients together in the order given. Bake at 350°F in a greased tube-pan.

Linneas of Texas
Houston, TX

SOUR CREAM FILLING FOR CAKE

1 cup sour cream
1 cup sugar
4 egg yolks, beaten well
1 cup pecans, chopped

Mix the first 3 ingredients together and cook until thick, stirring constantly.

Remove from the heat and add 1 cup of chopped pecans. Let it cool and spread it between 2 layers of cake.

Salem Lutheran Church
Rock Island, IL

CREAM BAKE

2 eggs
Sour cream (about 1 cup)
1 1/2 cups flour
1 cup sugar
1/4 teaspoon soda
1 teaspoon baking powder
1 teaspoon vanilla
Whipping cream

Break 2 eggs into a 1-cup measuring cup. Fill the remaining cup with sour cream. Beat well. Sift the dry ingredients together. Add this to the egg and cream mixture. Add the vanilla. Pour it into an 8-inch square pan which has been greased and floured lightly. Bake for 30 minutes in a 325°F oven. Let it cool. Frost with whipped cream.

Balsam Lutheran Church
Amery, WI

FRUIT CAKE

1 pound butter
3 cups sugar
3 cups flour
12 eggs, separated
5 pounds white raisins, seeded
1 pound citron, shredded
1 pound candied cherries
1 pound candied pineapple
1 pound blanched almonds, cut
    and browned
1 pound pecans
1 glass grape jelly
1 tablespoon cinnamon
1 scant tablespoon nutmeg
1/2 teaspoon allspice
1 teaspoon cloves
1 glass grape juice
2 tablespoons rose water
1/4 pound candied orange peel
1/4 pound candied lemon peel

Soak the almonds in rose water overnight and soak the fruit in grape juice overnight.

Cream the butter and sugar thoroughly and add the beaten egg yolks. Add the spices in the order named and the grape jelly. Next add the flour and the soaked fruit, reserving a little of the flour to mix with the fruit before it is added to the mixture. Then add the beaten egg whites. Add the nuts last.

Line baking pans with several layers of greased wrapping paper. Bake for 2 1/2 hours in a low-temperature oven. Makes 6 fruit cakes.

Moriah Lutheran Church
Ludlow, PA

WHITE FRUIT CAKE

2 3/4 cups cake flour, sifted
1/3 cup almonds, blanched and
  shredded
7/8 cup butter or shortening
2/3 cup sugar
4 eggs, unbeaten
1 cup seedless raisins
1 1/3 cups seeded raisins, finely
  cut
1/4 cup preserved orange peel,
  finely cut
1/4 cup preserved lemon peel,
  finely cut
2 tablespoons orange juice
1 teaspoon orange extract
12 almonds, blanched and split
  in half
12 candied cherries, halved
12 pecan meats

Sift the flour once. Measure and
sift it three more times. Add the
almonds. Cream the butter and
the cream until light and fluffy.
Add the eggs separately, beating
well after each addition. Add the
flour mixture.

Combine the fruits and peel with
the orange juice and orange
extract. Add this to the batter,
mixing well. Spoon a layer of the
dough, with pieces of preserved
cherries, into three greased and
paper-lined pans 4 1/2-inches
by 2 3/4-inches by 2-inches.
Dot this layer with green candied
pineapple and whole pecan nuts.
Spoon another layer of dough
over this fruit. Decorate the top
of each cake with whole nuts
and candied fruit. Bake in a slow
oven at 275°F for 50 minutes to
1 hour.

Moriah Lutheran Church
Ludlow, PA

167

CHOKLADRULLTÅRTA
Chocolate Roll

3 eggs
1/3 cup potato flour
3/4 cup sugar
2 tablespoons cocoa
2 teaspoons baking powder

Beat the eggs and sugar until white and fluffy. Sift together the flour, cocoa and baking powder. Add and stir until well-blended. Pour the batter into an oblong pan lined with buttered waxed paper. Bake at 425°F for 5 minutes. Turn onto waxed paper sprinkled with sugar and let it set until it is cold.

Filling:
1/2 cup butter
2 egg yolks
1/2 cup powdered sugar
1 teaspoon vanilla

Work the butter and sugar until the mixture is light and fluffy. Stir in the egg yolks and vanilla. Spread the cake with the filling. Roll it up lengthwise. Wrap the cake in waxed paper and leave for several hours before serving.

Faith Lutheran Church
Balsam Lake, WI

SWEDISH SHORTBREAD

1 cup butter
2 1/2 cups flour
Raspberry or strawberry jam

Frosting:
1 cup powdered sugar
2 to 3 teaspoons water
1 teaspoon almond extract

Mix the butter and flour working in the flour with your hands. Chill the dough. Heat the oven to 350°F. Roll the dough and flatten it with your fingers into 2-inch strips. Place it on a lightly greased baking sheet. Make a furrow or depression in the center of each length. Put jam in each depression.

Bake for 10 to 12 minutes at 350°F. Frost and cut diagonally in 1-inch slices.

Cambridge Lutheran Church
Cambridge, MN

TUSENBLADSTÅRTA
Thousand Leaves Torte

Dough:
1 cup cold butter
4 tablespoons ice water
1 2/3 cups flour

Filling:
Applesauce
Vanilla cream

Icing:
1 cup powdered sugar
1/2 tablespoon lemon juice
1 1/2 tablespoons water

Garnish:
1 cup whipped cream
Sliced almonds
Candied orange peel

Sift the flour on a baking board. Cut in the butter with 2 knives or pastry blender. Place the mixture in a bowl. Gradually, add the ice water and work the dough with a wooden spoon until smooth. Cover and chill for 1/2 hour.

Divide the dough into 6 or 7 portions. Roll each portion out thinly on waxed paper. Cut out circles and prick them with a fork. Place the circles with waxed paper on baking sheets. Brush with ice water, sprinkle with sugar and bake at 450°F for 6 to 8 minutes or until golden brown.

Keep on waxed paper until cold. Spread the layers alternately with the applesauce and vanilla cream filling. Cover the top with icing.

Garnish with candied orange peel strips, thinly sliced almonds and sweetened whipped cream which is forced through a pastry tube.

Vanilla cream filling:
2 egg yolks
1 1/2 tablespoons butter
3/4 tablespoon potato flour
1 cup cream
1 teaspoon vanilla
2 tablespoons sugar

Mix all the ingredients, except the vanilla, in a double boiler and cook until smooth and thick. Stir constantly. Remove from the heat. Add the vanilla and beat occasionally until cold.

Faith Lutheran Church
Balsam Lake, WI

169

SWEDISH JELLY ROLL

4 eggs, separated
3/4 cup sugar
1/3 cup potato flour
1/3 cup flour
1 teaspoon baking powder

Filling:
5 tablespoons butter
1/2 cup powdered sugar
2 tablespoons orange
   marmalade
2 teaspoons vanilla sugar or
   extract

Beat the egg whites until stiff.
Add the yolks and sugar. Blend
well. Add both flours and the
baking powder. Blend well.

Pour into an oblong pan lined
with buttered waxed paper. Bake
about 8 minutes or until golden
brown. Turn onto waxed paper
sprinkled with sugar. Let it cool.

Spread the filling on and roll
lengthwise. When cold, cut it
crosswise in slices.

*"Good with whipped cream and
fruit!"*

*Inger Karlsson, cousin to
Janet Martin's Husband, Neil
Lima, Sweden*

RULLTÅRTA
Jelly Roll

5 eggs
1 cup sugar
3 tablespoons water
1 cup flour
2 teaspoons baking powder

Beat the eggs until very light
and fluffy. (*"The longer they are
beaten, the better the jelly roll."*)
Lightly mix in the rest of the
ingredients. Line an 11-inch by
15-inch pan with waxed paper.
Bake at 350°F for 20 to
25 minutes.

Take the jelly roll from the oven
and tip it out on a cloth that has
been dusted lightly with
powdered sugar. Peel off the
waxed paper and roll the cake
up in the cloth for a few
minutes.

Unroll, and spread it with jelly
or lemon pie filling. Roll the cake
up again.

*Augustana Lutheran Church
Manson, IA*

LISA BARS

(Metric Chart: Appendix C)

2 cups sugar
2 eggs
2 teaspoons vanilla
1 cup milk
3 cups flour
2 teaspoons baking powder
120 grams butter or margarine,
    melted

Beat the eggs with the sugar.
Add the rest of the ingredients
and mix.

Bake the bars in a 9-inch by
13-inch cake pan (or larger) at
350°F until done.

Frost with:
2 hectograms powdered sugar
2 tablespoons cocoa
3 tablespoons strong coffee
7 tablespoons butter, melted
1 teaspoon vanilla

Mix and spread the frosting on
the bars as soon as they come
out of the oven. Then return the
frosted bars to the oven so that
the frosting can melt into the
bars. Take the bars from the
oven and sprinkle them
generously with shredded
coconut.

*Balsamlund Lutheran Church
Verndale, MN*

SWEDISH BLOND BROWNIES

2 eggs
1 cup sugar
1/2 cup butter or margarine,
    very soft
Pinch of salt
1 cup flour
1 teaspoon almond flavoring or
    vanilla
Powdered sugar frosting
Sugar (preferably, medium-
    grained crystal sugar)
Chopped pecans

Beat the first 6 ingredients
together and spread in a
buttered 9-inch by 9-inch pan.
Bake at 325°F for 30 minutes.

Frost with powdered sugar
frosting. Sprinkle generously
with granulated sugar and
pecans. Cut into squares.

*Salem Lutheran Church
Minneapolis, MN*

SWEDISH BUTTER CRISPS

1 cup butter
3/4 cup sugar
1 egg yolk
2 cups all-purpose flour, sifted
1 teaspoon vanilla

Topping:
1 egg white, whipped almost stiff
1/4 cup brown sugar
1/4 cup pecans, finely chopped

Cream the butter and sugar. Mix all the other ingredients into this. Spread this mixture on a cookie sheet 15-inches by 18-inches. Flatten the mixture with the palm of your hand. Spread whipped egg white on the top and sprinkle with brown sugar and nuts. Bake for 30 minutes in a moderate oven.

Watch carefully while baking so it doesn't burn. Remove it from the oven and cut this into squares while still warm. Trim off the edges.

This makes about 4 dozen.

*First Lutheran Church
Genesco, IL*

INGS SMÅTÅRTOR
Ing's Squares

1/4 cup butter
2 cups brown sugar
2 eggs, separated
1 cup nutmeats
1 1/2 cups flour
2 teaspoons baking powder
1 teaspoon vanilla

Cream the butter together with 1 cup of the brown sugar. Add the egg yolks. Sift the flour together with the baking powder. Add these to the mixture. Stir well and add 1/2 teaspoon vanilla. Pat this mixture into a 9-inch by 9-inch cake pan. Sprinkle with nutmeats.

Beat the egg whites until they are stiff. Beat in the second cup of brown sugar and the remaining 1/2 teaspoon vanilla. Spread this over the top of the nuts. Bake for 30 minutes at 350°F.

Cut in squares to serve.

*Hebron Lutheran Church
Burdick, KS*

VATENKAKA

Crust:
1 cup flour
1/2 cup butter
2 tablespoons water

Mix together and spread into a 12-inch by 15-inch ungreased pan.

Cake filling:
1 cup water
1/2 cup butter
1 cup flour
3 eggs
1 teaspoon almond extract

Bring the water and butter to a boil. Add the flour and beat until the mixture is smooth. Add the eggs and almond extract. Spread this over the crust.

Bake at 350°F for 1 hour.

Frost with:
1 cup powdered sugar
1 tablespoon cream
1 tablespoon butter
1/2 teaspoon almond extract

Augustana Lutheran Church
Sioux Falls, SD

TUPPKAKA

2 eggs
1 1/4 cups sugar
1 1/4 cups flour

Beat the eggs and sugar. Add the flour and mix well. Pat this mixture into a greased pizza pan.

Spread 2 to 3 tablespoons of butter over the dough. Sprinkle with 3 tablespoons of almonds. Bake at 400°F for 12 to 15 minutes. *"No more!"*

St. Paul Lutheran Church
Oakland, CA

SWEDISH PUFF COFFEE CAKE

Mix as for pie dough:
1/4 pound butter
1 cup flour
1 tablespoon cold water

Form into 3-inch by 12-inch rectangles and place on 2 cookie sheets.

Spread:
1/2 pound butter
1 cup boiling water
1 cup flour
3 eggs
1 teaspoon almond extract

Bring the water to a boil and add the butter. Stir until melted. Remove from the heat and add the flour. Beat vigorously. Add the eggs one at a time, beating after each addition. Spread the prepared mixture on the rectangles on the cookie sheets and bake at 350°F for 1 hour.

Cool slightly and frost with powdered sugar frosting that has been flavored with 1 teaspoon almond extract.

First Evangelical Lutheran Church
Rockford, IL

TUPPKAMMAR
Cockscombs

1 cup butter
3 cups flour
1 teaspoon baking powder
1 egg plus 2 egg yolks
1 cup sour cream
2 teaspoons lemon extract
Sugar

Mix the first 3 ingredients together as in making a pie crust and then add the sugar. Next, beat 1 egg and 2 egg yolks. Add the sour cream and lemon extract. Blend this with the dry ingredients.

Roll half of the dough 3/4-inch thick. Sprinkle the top of the dough with sugar and cut it into 1-inch by 3-inch strips. Make three short cuts on 1 side and curve.

Repeat the entire procedure with the other half of the dough.

Bake at 375°F. *"Watch so the bottom of the cookie doesn't brown too much before the rest gets done."*

Maria Lutheran Church
Kennedy, MN

SWEDISH SOUR CREAM TWISTS

3 1/2 cups flour, sifted
1 teaspoon salt
1 cup shortening
1/4 cup warm water
1 package dry yeast
1 whole egg and 2 egg yolks,
   well-beaten
3/4 cup sour cream
1 teaspoon vanilla
1 teaspoon ground cardamom
Sugar, as needed

Sift the flour and salt into a mixing bowl. Cut in the shortening. Dissolve the yeast in warm water and add it to the flour mixture. Stir in the sour cream, eggs, and vanilla. Add the ground cardamom. Mix it well with your hands. Cover the bowl with a damp cloth and refrigerate for 2 hours or overnight.

Roll half of the dough on a sugared board to fit an 8-inch by 16-inch oblong pan. Fold the ends towards the center with the ends overlapping. Sprinkle with sugar and roll again into the same size. Repeat a third time. Roll the dough about 1/4-inch thick and cut into strips 1-inch by 4-inches. Twist the ends into the opposite direction, slightly stretching the dough.

Place on an ungreased baking sheet as is, bar-shaped or turn the ends into a horseshoe shape. Press the ends so the twists keep their shape. Repeat with the rest of the dough and bake in a preheated oven at 375°F.

Bake for 15 minutes or until delicately browned. Remove the twists from the baking sheet immediately. This recipe makes about 5 dozen.

Stockholm Lutheran Church
Shickley, NE

BUTTER TARTS

"Do not try to make these in the summer time!"

1 egg
4 teaspoons sugar
1 cup cold water
A pinch of salt
Flour
Butter, unsalted

Beat the first 4 ingredients together. Mix with enough flour to make a stiff dough. Weigh the dough and use the same weight of unsalted cold butter. Roll the dough out and place the butter in the center. Turn the sides of the dough over to cover the butter.

"Take this out to the garage or a cold room and beat it with a rolling pin (or some such firm item). Keep turning the dough over and beating it until it is thoroughly mixed. Keep plenty of flour on the pastry cloth or the dough will stick to it. Keep the dough in a cold place and it will be easy to handle."

When the butter is thoroughly beaten into the dough, roll the dough out about 1/4-inch thick. Cut into strips 1-inch wide and 4-inches or 5-inches long. Slash the strips 3 or 4 places halfway through and dip them in sugar. Then form them in half circles on the baking sheet. Bake in a hot oven until light brown.

Keep any extra dough in the refrigerator. This makes about 1 2/3 pounds of dough.

"We also called these 'reindeer horns' since they resembled them. These are very flaky and delicious!"

Immanuel Lutheran Church
Akron, IA

SAND TARTS

(Metric Chart: Appendix C)

250 grams flour
225 grams butter
150 grams sugar
2 teaspoons baking powder
1 teaspoon vanilla

Mix all the ingredients together and press the dough into small, tin fluted forms. Bake at 250°F for approximately 15 minutes.

Balsamlund Lutheran Church
Verndale, MN

LITTLE SWEDISH TEA CAKES

1 cup butter
1/2 cup sugar
1 egg
2 scant cups of flour
1/4 teaspoon salt
1 teaspoon vanilla

Cream the butter and add the sugar slowly, mixing these well. Add a well-beaten egg and blend. Sift the flour before measuring and then sift it again with the salt. Add the flour and salt and blend in the vanilla.

Place a rounded teaspoon of dough in very small muffin tins or molds 1 1/2-inches in diameter. Press the batter up the sides and over the bottom so that there is a hollow in the center. Fill this with almond filling.

Almond filling:
2 eggs
1/2 cup sugar
1/4 teaspoon salt
1 cup almonds, finely ground

Beat the eggs until very light. Add the sugar and salt. Add the ground almonds last. Place a teaspoon of the filling in the hollow of the cakes.

Bake for 30 minutes in a slow oven at 325°F.

Immanuel Lutheran Church
Akron, IA

MUSSLOR
Butter Tarts

Cream together:
2 cups butter
1 1/4 cups sugar

Add:
1 whole egg and 1 yolk
1/2 teaspoon almond extract
1 teaspoon vanilla
4 cups flour

Blend all the ingredients well. Press into small fluted tins. Bake on a cookie sheet in a moderate oven at 350°F until light brown, about 10 minutes.

Turn upside down and tap the tins to remove the cookie.

First Lutheran Church
Granville, IL

TOSCATÅRTOR
Swedish Tosca Tarts

6 tablespoons butter
1/4 cup sugar
1 cup flour, sifted
2/3 cup blanched, slivered
    almonds

Cream the butter and sugar together. Blend in the flour and add the almonds. Place a tiny bit of dough into each *sandbakkel* tin and press into place.

Bake for 10 minutes at 350°F. Remove from the oven. Add the cream mixture and bake for 10 to 15 minutes longer.

Cream mixture:
1/2 cup sugar
1/4 cup butter
3 tablespoons cream
4 teaspoons flour

Combine the above ingredients and cook over a high heat until boiling. Stir constantly, as the mixture tends to scorch easily. When the mixture is thickened and well-cooked, fill the baked tarts.

Augustana Lutheran Church
Grand Forks, ND

STRUVOR
Swedish Rosettes

1 egg
1 tablespoon sugar
1 cup milk
Fat (for frying)
3/4 cup sifted flour
Dash of salt
Powdered sugar

Beat the egg slightly and add the sugar, salt and a little of the milk. Add the flour and the remaining milk alternately, beating only enough to blend after each addition. Heat the fat to 370°F as indicated on a "frying thermometer." Heat the rosette iron in fat, then dip it into the batter. Do not let the batter cover the upper edges of the iron. Immerse the dough-covered iron in hot fat and keep it down until the edges of the rosette brown. Slide the rosette off the iron to brown the under side, using a fork to push the rosette off, if necessary. Drain the rosettes on absorbent paper. Heat the iron again and repeat until all the batter is used. Sprinkle the rosettes with powdered or granulated sugar. Makes 3 to 4 dozen.

Emanuel Lutheran Church
Blackfoot, ID

KLENÄTER

*These "cookies" are known as
"Klenäter" in Swedish and
"Fattigmann" in Norwegian.*

2 whole eggs plus 3 egg yolks
1 teaspoon ginger
2 tablespoons sugar
2 tablespoons cream
Melted butter
2 1/2 cups flour

Beat the eggs. Add the ginger,
sugar, cream and melted butter.
Add the flour until the dough is
hard enough to roll out. Roll
thinly and with a pastry wheel
cut the dough into pieces
3/4-inch wide and 3-inches
long. Cut a slit in the center and
pull one corner through the slit
stretching the dough slightly.

Fry in deep fat until golden
brown. Drain on absorbent
paper.

*First Covenant Church
Oakland, CA*

KLENÄTER

4 egg yolks
1/4 cup powdered sugar
3 tablespoons soft butter
1 1/2 cups sifted flour
1 tablespoon brandy
1 tablespoon grated lemon rind

Mix all the ingredients and stir
until well-blended. Chill the
dough. Then roll it out in thin
sheets on a floured board. With
a pastry wheel, cut the dough
into strips 1-inch wide and
3-inches long. Cut a gash in the
center of each strip and slip one
end of each strip through the
gash making a twist.

Fry in deep fat at 375°F until
light brown. Drain on absorbent
paper.

*First Lutheran Church
Ottumwa, IA*

MOM'S KRUMKAKER

1 cup melted butter
2 cups whipping cream (not
    whipped)
2 cups sugar
2 eggs
5 cups flour
Cardamom for flavoring

Beat the eggs. Add the sugar
and cream. Add the flour. Add
the melted butter and
cardamom.

Preheat a *krumkake* iron on both
sides. Test a small amount of
batter to see if it holds together
while baking in the iron. If not,
add a small amount of
additional flour so the batter
holds together. Watch carefully.
When browned as desired,
remove from the iron and roll it
on a *krumkake* cone form. Cool.

Yield: Approximately
100 *krumkake*.

Arlington Hills Lutheran Church
St. Paul, MN

"KRUMKAKE"

4 eggs
1 cup sugar
1/2 cup melted butter
2 tablespoons cornstarch
1 1/2 cups flour
1/2 teaspoon almond extract

Beat the eggs slightly and add
the sugar. (Do not overbeat.) Add
the butter, cornstarch, flour and
flavoring. Mix together well. Put
about 3/4 teaspoon dough on a
hot *krumkake* iron and bake
until slightly browned.

Mamrelund Lutheran Church
Pennock, MN

KRUMKAKER

1 pint whipping cream
1 cup powdered sugar
Whites of 3 eggs
1 1/2 cups flour
1 teaspoon cardamom

Beat the cream until thick. Add
the sugar, cardamom and the
flour. Carefully stir in the stiffly
beaten egg whites.

Drop by spoonfuls into the
krumkaka iron and bake. Roll
up.

Grace Lutheran Church
Mankato, MN

SVENSKA KRANSAR
Swedish Wreaths

1/2 cup soured cream
1 cup sugar
1 cup butter
4 cups flour
1/2 teaspoon soda
4 egg yolks
Cardamom

Blend the cream and sugar. Add the rest of the ingredients. Turn the dough out onto a board and knead it thoroughly. Shape the dough into a long roll and slice it into pieces. Roll each piece of dough into 7-inch lengths and form them into wreaths.

Bake in a hot oven.

Zion Evangelical Lutheran Church
Newman Grove, NE

KANAPÉER
"Palm Leaf Cookies"

1 cup flour
1/2 cup butter
2 tablespoons ice cold water

Mix all of the ingredients like a pie crust. Roll the dough out 1/8-inch thick into an oblong shape. Add 1/2 cup sugar while folding over 4 times and re-rolling. Do not tear. "Roll as for a cinnamon roll" from each end to the center. Chill.

Slice and place on a cookie sheet to bake at 400°F. Do not brown.

Bethlehem Lutheran Church
Cherokee, IA

THREE BITE COOKIES

1 cup commercial sour cream
1 egg
1/2 cup sugar, heaping
1 cup margarine or butter,
    softened
1 teaspoon baking powder
1/2 teaspoon soda
3 1/2 cups flour
1 teaspoon vanilla

Beat the egg and stir in the sour cream. Add the butter and sugar. Mix well. Add the vanilla and then the remaining ingredients. Mix well again and chill for several hours.

Roll out half of the dough until it is 1/2-inch thick. Cut in strips 1-inch by 2-inches long. Cut two slits on one side of the strip and sprinkle with sugar. Shape in a semi-circle and place on an ungreased cookie sheet. Repeat with the other half of the dough.

Bake at 375°F until very lightly browned on the bottom.

Zion Lutheran Church
Gowrie, IA

"KRONASMÅKAKOR"
Wreath Cookies

3/4 cup butter
1/4 cup lard
1 egg
1 cup sugar
4 tablespoons sweet cream
2 tablespoons vinegar
1/2 teaspoon almond extract
3 1/2 cups flour
1 teaspoon soda

Combine all the ingredients and "work the dough." Mold it in sticks with your hands and cross it in a circle like a wreath.

Bake on a greased cookie sheet in a moderate oven.

Christ the King Lutheran Church
New Brighton, MN

"KEFFLINGS"

3/4 pound butter
1/2 pound red-skinned
   almonds
2 dry vanilla beans
2 teaspoons vanilla extract
4 cups flour
2/3 cup sugar

Grind the vanilla beans and almonds in a food chopper. Cream the butter and sugar. Add the flavoring. Sift the flour, ground beans and nuts. Add this to the butter mixture. Mix until well-blended.

This makes a thick dough. Roll the dough until it is 1/2 inch thick. Cut the rolled dough into crescent shapes and bake in a moderate oven until "barely brown." When cooled, roll the crescents in powdered sugar.

If unable to obtain vanilla beans, use 3 teaspoons of vanilla instead of the 2 teaspoons listed.

Audubon Park Covenant Church
Orlando, FL

SWEDISH TEA COOKIES

1 cup butter
2 eggs
1 teaspoon soda
1 cup chopped nuts
2 cups brown sugar
3 1/2 cups flour, sifted
1/2 teaspoon salt

Cream the butter and sugar. Add the eggs. Sift the flour with the soda and salt three times. Add the nuts. "Mold in a narrow leaf" and chill.

Slice thinly and bake in a hot oven.

Walnut Hill Lutheran Church
Dallas, TX

GRANDMA'S SWEDISH COOKIES

1 cup powdered sugar
1 pound butter
3 1/2 cups flour
2 cups chopped nuts
1/4 teaspoon salt

Cream the sugar and butter. Add the rest of the ingredients and mix thoroughly. Chill for 2 hours. Roll into 1-inch balls and bake. Sprinkle with powdered sugar.

Augustana Lutheran Church
Sioux Falls, SD

SWEDISH HEIRLOOM COOKIES

1/2 cup Crisco
1/2 cup butter
1 cup powdered sugar
1/2 teaspoon salt
1 1/4 cups ground almonds
2 cups sifted flour
1 tablespoon water
1 tablespoon vanilla

Cream the Crisco and butter. Gradually add the powdered sugar and salt, creaming well. Add the almonds and blend in the flour, mixing thoroughly. Mix the vanilla and the water together with a fork and add this to the mixture.

Shape into balls or crescents using 1 level tablespoon of dough for each cookie. Place the shapes on an ungreased cookie sheet flattening a little.

Bake at 325°F for 12 to 15 minutes. Take the cookies out of the oven and roll them in confectioner's sugar while still warm.

Yield: About 4 1/2 dozen.

Siloa Lutheran Church
Morris Run, PA

BUTTER BALLS

1 cup butter
3 tablespoons powdered sugar
1 teaspoon vanilla
2 cups flour
1 cup chopped pecans

Cream the butter. Add the sugar and vanilla. Next add the flour and nuts. Shape the dough into small balls and bake on an ungreased cookie sheet in a moderate oven at 350°F for 20 minutes. Roll in powdered sugar while hot.

Yield: 6 dozen.

Concordia Lutheran Church
Kingsburg, CA

CREAM CHEESE SPRITZ COOKIES

1 cup margarine or butter
1 3-ounce package cream cheese
1 cup sugar
1 teaspoon vanilla
1 egg yolk
1/8 teaspoon salt
2 1/2 cups flour

Mix the butter and cream cheese well. Cream with the sugar and mix in the other ingredients. Chill the dough. When ready to bake, put the dough through a cookie press.

Bake in a 350°F oven for 12 to 15 minutes or until slightly browned.

Dalesburg Lutheran Church
Beresford, SD

SPETSKAKOR
Lace Cookies

2 cups dark brown sugar, firmly
  packed
1 cup butter, melted
1 egg
2 cups rolled oats, uncooked
1 teaspoon vanilla

Mix the sugar and melted butter. Stir in the egg. Add the rolled oats and vanilla. Mix well. Take 1/2 teaspoon of batter at a time and use another teaspoon to drop the amount on an unbuttered cookie sheet. Drop the dough about 2 inches apart as the mixture will spread while baking.

Bake in a 350°F oven for 7 minutes. Remove from the oven and allow the cookies to cool a few minutes. Remove with a spatula while holding the cookie sheet over a warm burner.

"The cookies will be paper-thin and lacy-looking."

Yield: 100 cookies

First Evangelical Lutheran Church
Rockford, IL

SWEDISH NUT WAFERS

3/4 cup sugar
1/4 cup shortening
1 egg, beaten
1 1/3 cups flour
1 teaspoon baking powder
1/2 teaspoon salt
2 tablespoons milk
1 teaspoon vanilla
1/2 cup nuts, chopped

Cream the shortening and sugar. Combine the other ingredients, except the nuts. Spread the dough on a buttered baking sheet as thinly as possible. Sprinkle with nuts.

Bake in a moderate oven. Cut into strips 2-inches by 4-inches while warm. Shape on a cone or rolling pin.

Augustana Lutheran Church
Sioux Falls, SD

SWEDISH COUNTRY LASSES

2 cups flour
1 1/2 teaspoons baking powder
3/4 cup sugar
3/4 cup coarsely chopped
   almonds
1 tablespoon molasses
2/3 cup margarine or butter

In a large mixing bowl, blend all the ingredients. Knead it to make a smooth, firm dough.

Divide the dough into 3 parts and roll it into cylinders about 1 1/2-inches in diameter. Refrigerate until firm. Cut the cylinders into 1/4-inch slices.

Bake on a greased cookie sheet in a hot oven at 400°F about 10 minutes. Makes 5 dozen cookies.

Swedish Council of St. Louis
St. Louis, MO

CIRKUSARENA
Ring Cookies

1 cup butter
2 cups flour
3 tablespoons cream

Cream the butter and flour. Add the cream and chill the dough.

Roll the dough out on a floured board and cut with a doughnut cutter. Bake at 350°F. Do not brown.

Carefully roll the cookies in sugar when they are done baking.

Bethlehem Lutheran Church
Cherokee, IA

SCANDINAVIAN SOUR CREAM COOKIES

1/2 cup butter
3/4 cup sugar
1 egg
2 1/4 cups flour
1/2 teaspoon baking soda
1/2 teaspoon baking powder
1/4 teaspoon salt
1 teaspoon ground cardamom or
    grated nutmeg
1/2 cup sour cream

Cream the butter. Then gradually add the sugar. Beat in the egg. In another bowl mix the flour, baking soda, baking powder, salt and cardamom. Then add the flour mixture into the butter mixture alternately with the sour cream, beginning and ending with flour. Chill overnight or until firm enough to roll.

Roll the dough out on a floured board until it is about 1/4-inch thick. Cut out pieces with a round cookie cutter.

Bake at 375°F on ungreased cookie sheets for 12 minutes or until golden brown. Sprinkle the tops with sugar.

Gloria Dei Lutheran Church
Huntington Station, NY

GRANDMOTHER'S SWEDISH "MOVER WAGON" COOKIES

1 cup sugar
1 cup butter
4 eggs, beaten
2 tablespoons milk
1 teaspoon vanilla
2 teaspoons baking powder
3 1/2 cups flour (approximate)

Cream the sugar and butter. Add the eggs, milk, and vanilla. Add the baking powder and enough flour to roll the dough out, about 3 1/2 cups. This makes quite a stiff dough.

Roll the dough into sheets and cut it into rectangular pieces about 2-inches by 5-inches. Arrange these pieces on half-cylinder shaped tins.

Bake at 350°F for 8 to 10 minutes.

Remove them carefully from the tin. Frost them with boiled icing and decorate them with colored sugar and candies.

Evangelical Covenant Church
Stanton, IA

SWEDISH CHRISTMAS STARS

1 cup butter
4 tablespoons sugar
1 egg, or 2 egg yolks
1 teaspoon vanilla
2 cups flour (approximate)
1/2 teaspoon cardamom seed, crushed
1/2 cup walnuts, finely chopped
1 egg white, slightly beaten

Cream the sugar and butter. Add the egg yolks, vanilla, flour and crushed cardamom seed. Roll a small amount of dough out on a floured board and cut the dough into stars. Brush the stars with egg white and dunk them in a dish of sugar and chopped nuts, or sprinkle them with sugar and nuts. Repeat until all the dough is gone.

Bake at 350°F.

Cambridge Lutheran Church
Cambridge, MN

SWEDISH SUGAR COOKIES

Cream together:
2 cups sugar
2 cups butter

Add:
1 cup coconut
1 teaspoon soda
1 teaspoon baking powder
1 teaspoon vanilla
Dash of salt
3 cups flour

Add these ingredients, in the order listed, to the creamed mixture.

Take a heaping teaspoonful of dough and drop it onto a baking sheet.

Butter the bottom of a glass and dip it in sugar. Flatten the dough with the bottom of the glass.

Bake until light brown, about 10 minutes in a 350°F oven.

Normandale Lutheran Church
Edina, MN

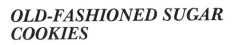

OLD-FASHIONED SUGAR COOKIES

Cream together:
1 cup sugar
3/4 cup butter
2 eggs, beaten
1/4 cup cream
1/2 teaspoon cardamom seeds, crushed

Sift:
2 3/4 cups flour
3 teaspoons baking powder
Pinch of salt

Roll the dough out into thin sheets and cut. Bake in a quick oven at 425°F. Sprinkle with sugar.

Faith Lutheran Church
Forest Lake, MN

SWEDISH CREAM WAFERS

Mix well:
1 cup butter
1/3 cup thick cream
2 cups flour

Chill. Roll the dough out and cut it with a small, round cookie cutter. Place the cookies on sugar-coated, waxed paper and flip the cookies so both sides get coated.

Bake on an ungreased sheet at 375°F for 7 to 9 minutes.

Put together with this filling:
1/4 cup butter
3/4 cup powdered sugar
1 egg yolk
1 teaspoon vanilla

Spring Garden Lutheran Church
Cannon Falls, MN

MY MOM'S "PEPPARKAKOR"

Mix well:
2 cups flour
1 1/2 cups dark brown sugar
2 teaspoons baking powder
A pinch of baking soda
1 teaspoon ground cardamom
1 teaspoon ground cinnamon
1 teaspoon ground cloves

Beat 1 egg well with 1 cup of milk and add it to the dry ingredients. Melt 2 tablespoons of butter and fold it into the batter.

Pour the batter into a greased bundt pan. Bake in a 350°F oven for 30 to 50 minutes or until a toothpick inserted in the center comes out clean.

Marion Anderson
Ft. Montgomery, NY

PEPPARKAKOR
Gingersnaps

2 1/2 cups flour
1/2 cup maple syrup
1/2 cup butter, melted
1/3 cup brown sugar
1 teaspoon ginger
1 teaspoon cloves
1 teaspoon cinnamon
1 teaspoon lemon rind, grated
1 tablespoon rum or extract
1 teaspoon baking soda

Melt the butter with the sugar and syrup. Add the spices, rum and soda. Set aside until lukewarm, and then mix in the flour. Wrap the dough in waxed paper and chill for several hours.

Roll the dough out paper-thin, 1/8 inch thick, and cut in rounds or fancy shapes.

Bake 1/2 inch apart on a greased cookie sheet. Bake at 350°F for 5 to 8 minutes.

First Lutheran Church
Ault, CO

SWEDISH "PEPPARKAKOR" COOKIES

1 cup butter (not margarine)
1 1/2 cups sugar
1 egg
1 tablespoon dark syrup
3 cups flour, sifted
1 teaspoon soda
1 teaspoon ginger
1 teaspoon cloves
1 or 2 teaspoons cinnamon

Cream the butter, sugar, egg and syrup. Sift in the flour and the spices. Cover and chill for at least 2 hours or overnight. For easier rolling, use a rolling pin "stocking." Bake at 375°F for 10 minutes.

Trinity Lutheran Church of
Minnehaha Falls
Minneapolis, MN

GAMMALDAGS PEPPARKAKOR

3 1/2 cups flour
1 teaspoon soda
1 1/2 teaspoons ginger
1 1/2 teaspoons cinnamon
1 teaspoon cloves
1/4 teaspoon ground cardamom
1/2 cup butter
3/4 cup granulated sugar
1 egg, unbeaten
3/4 cup molasses
2 teaspoons orange rind, grated
Almond halves (optional)

Sift together the flour, soda and spices. Cream the butter. Add the sugar gradually, creaming until the mixture is light and fluffy. Add the egg, molasses and orange rind. Beat well. Stir in the dry ingredients gradually, mixing until well-blended. Cover and chill overnight.

Roll the dough out on a well-floured pastry cloth or board until it is 1/8 inch thick. Cut the dough into a variety of shapes with cookie cutters and place the cookies on lightly buttered baking sheets. If desired, place half of a blanched almond in the center of each cookie before baking.

Bake in a moderate oven at 375°F for 8 to 10 minutes. This makes 7 to 10 dozen cookies. *"The dough will keep for one week."*

Stockholm Lutheran Church Shickley, NE

SWEDISH "PEPPARKAKOR"

1/2 pound butter
1 1/2 cups sugar
1 egg, beaten
2 tablespoons dark syrup
3 3/4 cups flour
2 teaspoons soda
1 teaspoon cinnamon
1 teaspoon cloves
1 teaspoon ginger
1 teaspoon cardamom, crushed

Cream the butter and sugar. Add the beaten egg and syrup. Sift the flour with the other dry ingredients. Add this to the first mixture and mix well.

Keep the dough overnight in a refrigerator. Roll the dough out thinly and bake for 5 to 10 minutes at 375°F.

"Makes over 100 thin cookies."

MacArthur Park Lutheran Church San Antonio, TX and Grace Covenant Church Stambaugh, MI

SWEDISH MELTAWAYS

1 cup butter
1 cup sugar
1/2 teaspoon vanilla
2 teaspoons baker's ammonia,
    crushed well
2 cups flour

Whip the butter. Add the sugar and beat together until the mixture is white. Add the vanilla and the baker's ammonia. (Baker's ammonia may be bought at a drugstore.)

Mix in the flour. Shape the dough into small balls. Bake in a 250°F oven until light brown.

Bethel Lutheran Church
Willmar, MN

SERINA CAKES

4 cups flour, sifted
2 cups sugar
2 cups butter, cold
2 eggs
1/2 cup blanched almonds,
    chopped
1 1/2 teaspoons baking powder
4 teaspoons vanilla sugar

Mix the flour with the baking powder. Whip in the sugar, vanilla sugar, egg yolks and one egg white. Add the cold butter.

Shape the dough into small balls. Flatten them slightly with a fork. Smear them with the white of the second egg and sprinkle the tops with chopped, blanched almonds.

Bake until golden brown in a 350°F oven for 12 minutes. Makes 60 cookies.

Augustana Lutheran Church
Grand Forks, ND

HVITE NÖTTER
"Little White Mice"

1 cup butter
1/4 cup powdered sugar
2 cups flour
1 teaspoon water
1 teaspoon vanilla
1 cup nutmeats including
    pecans, cut finely

Cream the butter and sugar. Add the water and vanilla. Add the flour and nuts. Roll the dough into the shape of dates, but a bit larger.

Bake at 300°F for about 30 minutes. Shake the cookies in powdered sugar after they have cooled slightly.

Augustana Lutheran Church
Grand Forks, ND

CURRANT COOKIES

1/2 cup sugar
2 cubes butter
1 3/4 cups flour
2 teaspoons vanilla
1 cup currants

Mix all the ingredients together making a soft dough. (Add more flour, if needed.) Divide the dough into 3 parts. Roll each part into a 1-inch diameter roll the length of the cookie sheet.

Place all three rolls on an ungreased cookie sheet and bake at 400°F until just golden brown.

Remove the pans from the oven and cut the rolls into 3/4-inch diagonal slices while still warm. Remove the slices from the cookie sheet.

First Covenant Church
Oakland CA

HOLIDAY NUT COOKIES

1/2 cup shortening
1/2 cup brown sugar
1 egg, beaten
1/4 cup sour milk
1 3/4 cups flour
1/2 teaspoon soda
3/4 cup pecans, cut
3/4 cup dates, cut
3/4 cup candied cherries
1/2 teaspoon salt

Cream the shortening. Add the sugar and beaten egg. Sift the flour, soda and salt together and add this alternately with the sour milk. Add the fruit and pecan pieces. Drop the dough from a spoon onto a cookie sheet. Bake in a moderate oven.

Faith Lutheran Church
Forest Lake, MN

SYRUP COOKIES

Combine and heat until almost boiling:
1 cup dark molasses
1 cup sugar

Remove mixture from the heat and add:
1/2 cup butter
1/2 cup lard

Let this stand until lukewarm.

Sift together:
4 1/2 cups flour
1 teaspoon ginger
1 teaspoon cinnamon
1/2 teaspoon allspice
1/2 teaspoon cloves

Add this to the molasses mixture.

Then add:
2 eggs, slightly beaten
1 teaspoon baking soda
   dissolved in warm water

Chill the dough for 1/2 hour or until it is easy to handle. "Mix with plenty of flour." Roll the dough out thinly.

Cut the dough into Christmas shapes and press half an almond into the center of each cookie or sprinkle them with colored sugar.

Bake at 350°F for 8 to 10 minutes.

Balsamlund Lutheran Church
Verndale, MN

OLD-FASHIONED MOLASSES COOKIES

1 cup molasses
1 tablespoon baking soda
1 cup sugar
1 cup shortening (lard preferred)
2 eggs
1 teaspoon cinnamon
1 teaspoon ginger
1 teaspoon cloves
1 teaspoon salt

Boil 1 cup of molasses. As soon as it is removed from the stove add 1 tablespoon of soda. Then add 1 tablespoon of vinegar and enough flour to make a stiff dough. Bake at 350°F.

"Either roll thin and cut with a cookie cutter, or make into a roll and chill in the 'ice box' and slice."

Faith Lutheran Church
Forest Lake, MN

194

SWEDISH BROWN COOKIES

Cream together:
1 cup sugar
1 cup margarine
2 teaspoons honey

Add:
2 cups flour
1 teaspoon soda

Press the dough onto a cookie sheet and sprinkle it with granulated sugar.

Bake at 300°F for 20 to 25 minutes. Cut into desired shapes while the dough is still warm.

Evangelical Covenant Church
Clay Center, KS

SWEDISH SOUR CREAM GINGERSNAPS

1/2 cup plus 2 tablespoons
    molasses
1 3/4 cups sugar
1/3 cup sour cream
2/3 cup butter or margarine,
    melted and cooled
1 tablespoon orange rind, grated
4 egg yolks

5 cups flour
2 teaspoons soda
1/4 teaspoon salt
1 teaspoon ginger
1 teaspoon cloves
1 teaspoon allspice
2 teaspoons cinnamon

Heat the molasses and add the sugar. When the sugar has dissolved, stir until the mixture cools. Add the cream, butter, orange rind, salt and spices. Next, add the egg yolks, one at a time and then add the flour and soda (mixed together) in small amounts.

Add more flour, if needed, to make a firm smooth dough. Chill the dough before rolling it out and cutting it.

Bake in a 375°F oven about 10 minutes.

"You can make the dough ahead and store in the refrigerator."

Capron Lutheran Church
Capron, IL

ALMOND GINGERSNAPS

1 cup butter
1 cup sugar
1/2 cup dark syrup (Karo)
1 teaspoon baking soda
1 cup blanched almonds
2 teaspoons ginger
1 teaspoon cinnamon
1 teaspoon cloves
3 cups flour

Work the butter until creamy. Add the sugar, syrup, spices, baking soda, almonds and flour. Turn the mixture onto a floured baking board and knead it until the dough is smooth. Shape it into 2 or 3 thick, slightly-flattened rolls. Wrap the dough in waxed paper and chill thoroughly. (The dough can be frozen).

Cut the dough with a sharp knife into thin, 1/2-inch slices. Place the slices on a greased cookie sheet. Bake at 325°F for 8 to 10 minutes. Remove the cookies from the pan when slightly cooled.

Cambridge Lutheran Church
Cambridge, MN

MOTHER'S GINGER COOKIES

1 cup shortening, lard and
    butter, mixed
1/2 cup sugar
3/4 cup "good" molasses
1 egg, beaten
2 teaspoons soda (mixed in with
    a little cold water)
1 teaspoon ginger
1/8 teaspoon salt
Flour (enough to make a stiff
    dough)

Roll thinly, sprinkle with sugar and bake.

Faith Lutheran Church
Forest Lake, MN

SWEDISH OATMEAL COOKIES

1/2 cup melted butter
1 cup sugar
2 cups rolled oats
2 beaten egg whites

Mix and shape into 1-inch balls. Place them on a greased cookie sheet and flatten them out with the bottom of a water glass. Bake at 350°F about 8 minutes. *"Put melted milk chocolate chips between two cookies."*

First Lutheran Church
Ault, CO

196

RUSSINKLIPPAR
Swedish Raisin Rock

Cook 1 1/2 cups of raisins in
1 cup of water until the raisins
have absorbed the water. Add
1 teaspoon soda.

Cream together:
1 cup shortening
1 1/2 cups sugar
3 eggs

Add:
3 cups flour
1 1/2 teaspoons baking powder
1/2 teaspoon cinnamon

Form the dough into small balls
and roll them in sugar. Bake about
10 minutes at 350°F.

ch
Sioux Falls, SD

SWEDISH RAISIN COOKIES

3 eggs
1 1/2 cups sugar
1 cup butter
1 cup raisins (chop raisins into
    some of the flour)
2 cups flour (or enough to roll the
    dough)

1/4 teaspoon cloves
1 teaspoon cinnamon
1 teaspoon soda

Bake at 375°F until the
cookies are light brown, about
10 to 12 minutes.

Bensonvale Covenant Church
Omaha, NE

SARA'S "FLARN"

2 cups sugar
1 1/2 cups melted butter
2 cups flour
2 1/4 teaspoons baking
    powder
1/2 cup cream (heavy cream
    works the best)
1/2 cup syrup
2 cups quick-cooking oats
4 teaspoons vanilla

Mix all the ingredients
together until smooth. Place a
heaping teaspoonful of dough
onto a lightly greased baking
sheet for 10 minutes at 350°F.

Carefully remove the cookies
from the cookie sheet and
*"hang them over a wooden
dowel."* Let them cool. Makes
75 cookies.

Concordia Lutheran Church
Kingsburg, CA

SPICED FRUIT COOKIES

1 cup butter or margarine
1/2 cup granulated sugar
1/2 cup brown sugar, packed
2 tablespoons egg, beaten
4 cups all-purpose flour
1 teaspoon baking powder
1/2 tablespoon cardamom,
   ground
10 tablespoons whipping cream
1 cup candied fruit, diced

In a mixing bowl combine the butter and sugars, beating until fluffy and creamy. Stir in the egg. In a separate bowl, combine the flour, baking powder and cardamom. Add this to the first mixture alternately with the cream. Stir in the candied fruit, mixing to distribute evenly.

Shape the dough into 2 long smooth rolls about 2 inches in diameter. Wrap the rolls in waxed paper or plastic wrap. Refrigerate overnight.

The next day, cut the rolls into 1/4-inch-thick slices. Place them slightly apart on greased cookie sheets.

Bake at 350°F for 10 to 15 minutes.

Hebron Lutheran Church
Burdick, KS

REAL SWEDISH COOKIES

1 cup butter
1/2 cup brown sugar, packed
2 eggs, separated
2 cups flour, sifted
Grapenuts

Cream the butter and sugar. Add the beaten egg yolks and stir well. Add the flour and mix well. Roll the dough into small balls. Dip them in 1 unbeaten egg white and roll the balls into grapenuts that have been crushed finely. Press the centers down with a rounded thimble top. Place the cookies on a greased cookie sheet and bake them for 5 minutes at 325°F.

Remove the cookies from the oven and press down the centers again. Bake for 15 minutes longer.

Cool slightly. Fill the centers with jelly or a maraschino cherry.

First Lutheran Church
Ottumwa, IA

198

SWEDISH MACAROONS

1 1/3 cups blanched almonds,
   ground
1 1/2 cups powdered sugar
1 1/2 to 2 egg whites

Put the almonds through a
grinder twice, the second time
with the sugar. Add the egg
whites gradually, working the
mixture until it is smooth and
firm. Drop by teaspoonfuls onto
a well-greased and floured
cookie sheet. *("The mixture can
also be forced through a fluted
pastry tube in various shapes.")*

Decorate tops with strips of
candied orange peel, cherries
and nuts. Bake in a slow to
moderate oven at 325°F until
light yellow or about 30 minutes.

*Trinity Lutheran Church
Gresham, OR*

SWEDISH COCONUT COOKIES

1 cup butter
1 cup shortening
1 cup toasted coconut
1 teaspoon vanilla
1 teaspoon soda
1 teaspoon baking powder
3 cups flour
2 cups sugar

Cream the sugar, butter and
shortening. Add the dry
ingredients and then add the
coconut and vanilla. Roll the
dough into balls. Bake for 8 to
10 minutes at 300°F until lightly
browned.

*"A true melt-in-your-mouth
cookie."*

*Augustana Lutheran Church
St. James, MN*

SWEDISH NUTS

1 12-ounce package mixed nuts
2 egg whites, stiffly beaten
1 cup sugar
1 teaspoon salt
1/4 pound melted butter

Toast the nuts in a 200°F oven for 20 minutes. Beat the egg whites until they are stiff, adding the sugar and the salt to the egg whites. Melt the butter. Mix the nuts in with the egg-white mixture and melted butter. Stir the mixture on a cookie sheet and bake at 200°F for 30 minutes, stirring frequently until all the butter is absorbed.

Rochester Covenant Church
Rochester, MN

CREAM FUDGE

2 cups granulated sugar
Butter (the size of an egg)
3/4 cup sweet cream
1/4 cup water

Mix the above ingredients and boil until it forms a "soft ball" when tried in cold water. Remove the pan from the heat and allow it to stand for 20 minutes. Add 1/2 teaspoon of vanilla and beat until it reaches the consistency of fudge. If desired, add 1 cup chopped walnuts or any candied fruit that is cut into small pieces. Spread the fudge in a buttered pan and cut it when hardened.

Lindsborg Kansas Mission Church
Lindsborg, KS

SWEDISH CARAMELS

4 1/2 cups white sugar
1 1/3 cups white Karo syrup
1 rounded tablespoon parafin
  wax, shaved
3 pints whipping cream
1 teaspoon vanilla

Using a heavy aluminum 4-quart kettle, and stirring frequently, bring the sugar, syrup, wax and 1 pint of the whipping cream to a boil. Add a 2nd pint of cream and cook until it reaches the soft ball stage. Add a 3rd pint of cream and continue boiling until it reaches the medium hard ball stage (240° on a candy thermometer). Add the vanilla and pour the mixture at once into a buttered 12-inch by 18-inch jelly roll pan.

Cool and cut into small squares, wrapping each piece in waxed paper. This takes 4 to 6 hours of cooking time and makes about 180 pieces.

Braham Covenant Church
Braham, MN

SMÖRGÅSBORD

Ann Nilsson 1995

The crown jewel of Swedish culinary fare is the "smörgåsbord." Even the word, smörgåsbord, conjures up warm thoughts of a wonderful Swedish eating experience.

The smörgåsbord, served buffet-style, is more than food. It is a feeling, an atmosphere, a visual delight, a cherished memory and a beloved tradition. Many Swedish-Americans don't realize that a smörgåsbord doesn't have to be elaborate!

The word, smörgåsbord, literally means "sandwich table" and can be traced back to Viking feast days.

At a smörgåsbord, custom calls for a clean plate for each course. In true style, the smörgåsbord begins with several kinds of herring. Next, a clean plate is needed for the second course which consists of various fish dishes. Then the cold dishes are served, followed by the hot foods, and finally, a dessert table is often presented. Beer, wine and coffee can all be served with the different foods. Of course, skoaling with "akvavit" is another tradition that often accompanies the smörgåsbord experience.

Like most traditions, today's smörgåsbord has evolved and changed over the years and may bear little resemblance to the original Viking feast. In America, the word, smörgåsbord, is sometimes even used to describe a "church basement potluck."

A smörgåsbord can be held in a small, intimate setting or for larger gatherings. Following are some suggested smörgåsbord menus and also recipes for some of the dishes which are often served at a smörgåsbord. Finally, there are recipes that have that larger gathering in mind — special dishes for a crowd.

SCANDINAVIAN DINNER PARTY MENU

Akvavit

Assorted Breads (Pumpernickel, *Limpa*, Rye, Breadsticks, Rye Wafers)

Cold Meat Slices (Ham, Bologna, Salami, Liverwurst)

Cold Canned Fish (Sardines, Anchovies, Herring, Salmon)

Relishes (Spiced Crab Apples, Watermelon Pickles, Carrot and Celery Sticks, Pickled Beets)

Salads (*Grönsallad*-Mixed Green Salad, *Sillsallad*-Herring Salad, *Hummersallad*-Lobster Salad, *Kycklingsallad*-Chicken Salad)

Köttbullar (Meatballs)

Kåldolmar (Stuffed Cabbage Rolls)

Assorted Cheeses

Butter

Beer

Immanuel Lutheran Church
Swea City, IA

"SMÖRGÅSBORD" MENU

Breads and Spreads:

White

Light and Dark Rye

Pumpernickel

Swedish Crisp Bread

Butter

Mayonnaise

Sour Cream

Mustard

Meats and Fish:

Roast Beef

Ham

Thuringer and Salami

Shrimp

Anchovies

Sardines

Herring

Meatballs

Pressylta

Kalvsylta

Jansson's Temptation

Lamb Roll

Vegetables:

Tomatoes

Cucumbers

Pickled Beets

Cucumber Salad

Radishes

Potatoes

Swedish Brown Beans

Immanuel Lutheran Church
Holden, MA

"SMÖRGÅSBORD" MENU

Herring Salad
Pickled Herring
Cold Veal Loaf
Pickled Beets
Liverwurst
Sardines
Caviar
Cold Roasted Meats
Cheese
Knäckebröd
Limpa
Butter
Omelet with Creamed Crab
Noodle Ring with Meatballs
Potato Balls
Pickles

Norden Women's Club
Jamestown, NY

"SMÖRGÅSBORD" MENU

Fresh Shrimp in Sauce
Tongue in Allspice
Anchovies
Sardines
Smoked Salmon
Pickled Eels
Stuffed Eggs
Spiced Pork Shoulder
Baked Ham
Brick Liverwurst
Caviar
Caraway Cheese
Pimento
Stuffed Celery
Beets in Vinegar
Crabmeat Omelet
Halibut Soufflé
Chicken Loaf
Creamed Mushroom Sauce
Biff á la Lindström
Small Meatballs
Potatoes in Cream
Baked *Knäckebröd*
Limpa
Butter
Pickles
Olives

Norden Women's Club
Jamestown, NY

APPETIZER PLATE

A Swedish appetizer plate might include:

Wedges of Apples and Pears
Colby Cheese
Olives
Herring
Assorted Crackers
Shrimp with Cocktail Sauce
Sardines
Anchovies
Smoked Salmon
Jellied Veal
Stuffed Celery
Tomato Aspic Ring

"It is customary to serve the fish in its original container. Just open a can or jar and place it on the appetizer tray."

North Central Svenska Klubben
North Central Iowa

SMÖRGÅS
Open-faced Sandwich

Small dark rye, *limpa* or other
 deli-style bread
Prepared mustard
Banana slices
Slices of Gruyère or other
 cheese
Curry powder, paprika and/or
 garlic powder

Heat the broiler or oven to 400°F. Spread the mustard on the bread slices. (Use a high quality mustard.) Place banana slices on the bread. Place cheese slices over the banana slices. Sprinkle with the spices. Broil or bake for several minutes until it is lightly browned and hot.

This makes five to six servings.

Swedish Cultural Heritage Society
Fargo, ND

SMÖRGÅSTÅRTA
Sandwich Torte

*"Make this one day before
serving. Put the decorations on
just before serving."*

2 loaves of white bread, sliced
   horizontally into 4 slices each

Filling #1:
1 /2 pound Danish blue cheese
   mixed together with 4 to
   5 tablespoons of cream or
   half and half.

Filling #2:
1 /2 pound cream cheese mixed
   with 1/2 pound small shrimp
   and 1/2 cup mayonnaise.

Filling #3:
1/2 pound liver sausage mixed
   with 4 to 5 tablespoons cream
   or half and half.

Cut the edges off the loaves and
put 2 slices of bread side by side
on a big plate. Spread filling
#1 on these slices. Take 2 more
slices of bread and spread them
with filling #2. Repeat with the
next layer.

Make sure there are 2 slices of
bread on top. Put plastic wrap
around them and leave them in
the refrigerator overnight.

Just before serving, spread a
thin layer of mayonnaise on the
top and sides.

**Suggested ingredients for
decorating:**
Mayonnaise on top and sides
5 slices of cucumber, on edge
3 hard-boiled eggs, sliced
Chopped radishes
Sliced green pepper
Very finely minced parsley
Pieces of tomato
Slices of lemon
1/2 pound shrimp

*Swedish Club of Metropolitan Detroit
Swedish Women's Organization
Farmington Hills, MI*

The following information on cheese making was submitted by Sonja Anderson of First Lutheran Church in Genesco, IL. She prepared this summary using information taken from a seventh grade cookbook which had been used in homemaking classes in Sweden 50 years ago.

CHEESE MAKING

"Cheese is made from the milk of various animals. Cows, goats, sheep and reindeer are the most common sources of the milk used in Scandinavian cheese making. There are many kinds of cheese. Variations in the texture and flavor of the cheese produced depend, in part, on the fat content of the milk which is used: whole milk, reduced fat, or skim milk. (Whole milk might sometimes have extra cream added. A reduced fat content is formed by using half whole milk and half skim milk.) Reduced fat and skim milk are often used in the production of cheeses that contain herbs, such as cumin.

"In past centuries and during the early part of the 20th Century, Swedish farmers often made their own cheese. According to the 50-year-old cookbook, the preparation of cheese went something like this:

> *"The milk was heated to 25 to 35 degrees Celsius depending upon the kind of cheese that was going to be prepared.*

> *"A few drops of 'controlled' resin was added to the milk which was slowly stirred to distribute the resin. The milk then stood until it started to curdle. The ripening of the cheese could be hastened by adding 1 liter of buttermilk to 10 liters of milk. Some people believed the addition of buttermilk also improved the cheese's flavor. Approximately 25 liters of milk was needed for about 2 kilos of cheese.*

> *"Different methods and different temperatures were used in making different kinds of cheese.*

> *"When the curds were forming, they were removed and*

placed in a special form usually made of wood and lined with clean muslin or linen. The form was usually made by a man skilled in carpentry work. The form had holes in the bottom for drainage. The mass of curds was pressed down and allowed to become firm before it was removed. Then the wet cloth was removed and replaced with a dry one. This process was then repeated once or twice a day until the cheese was dry.

"The cheese was also turned around each time. The herbs that were going to be used were added when the curds were placed in the form. Before the cheese was put away for ripening, it was usually placed in a specially prepared salt solution for a few hours. Longer ripening time made sharper cheese.

"The whey that was left was sometimes boiled down and placed in forms to become firm and then dried. This kind of cheese was called 'mesost.'"

First Lutheran Church
Genesco, IL

PRIMOST

"Bought by the 1-pound brick at Loranz' Gourmet Shop."

Melt and add cream until it is the consistency of soft peanut butter.

Evangelical Covenant Church
Helena, MT

SÖTOST

2 quarts buttermilk
1/2 cup brown sugar
4 tablespoons flour

Cook the buttermilk until it begins to curdle. Add the flour slowly to thicken, stirring constantly. Add the sugar and cook until it is thick and brown. Stir frequently.

"This is a brown cheese like 'primost.' It is delicious served on rye bread."

First Lutheran Church
Hector, MN

207

INLAGD SILL
Pickled Herring

14 to 15 salt herring fillets. *"You will get 7 to 8 pieces from each fillet."*

Leave the fish whole. Soak it overnight in cold water in a glass, porcelain or plastic container and cover.

Bring to a boil:
8 medium onions, sliced
2 cups cider vinegar
2 cups water
3 cups sugar
8 teaspoons whole allspice
Coarsely ground black pepper

Cut the fish into pieces. Layer the fish with the onions in a crock. When this mixture has cooled, pour it over *sill* and cover it with a lid. (Be sure the syrup mixture is cool before pouring it over the fish or the *sill* will be mushy.)

Put the covered crock in the refrigerator and leave it for about 2 weeks before eating.

Evangelical Lutheran Church
Tolley, ND

INLAGD SILL
Pickled Herring

2 large, or 3 small, salt herring soaked 10 to 12 hours
1 large onion
3/4 cup sugar
2 dozen whole allspice
Vinegar

Skin and bone the herring. Cut it into bite-sized pieces. Layer the fish with the sugar, some whole allspice and onion in a glass quart jar. Repeat until all of it is used.

When the quart jar is full, pour approximately 1 cup of vinegar into it. Screw the cap on tightly and refrigerate.

"This can be used in 24 hours, but the flavor improves if it is left longer.

"I like to store it at least a week for the best flavor. I turn the jars upside down and rotate them so the sugar dissolves quickly. This will keep for months."

Bethlehem Lutheran Church
Florence, WI

ROLLED HERRING

Soak salt herring in water overnight. Split the fish and remove the bones. Drain the fish on muslin and cover each half with a mixture of parsley, capers, onions, pickles, sugar and pepper. Roll the pieces up and fasten with a "*small stick.*" Season vinegar with pepper, sugar and a bay leaf. Pour this over the fish and let it stand for several days.

Slice thinly and serve.

Our Saviour's Lutheran Church
Hastings, MN

PICKLED HEART, TONGUE AND PORK HOCKS

Boil the heart, tongue and hocks from a pig for about 2 hours or until done. Peel and slice the tongue. (These are prepared separately, but the brine is the same for all three.)

Brine:
1 cup vinegar
3/4 cup water
1 onion, sliced
Salt and pepper "*to taste like Mother's.*"

Ada's Nostalgic Cookbook
Ada Hacke Martin

FYLLDA ÄGGHALVOR
Stuffed Eggs

4 hard-boiled eggs
Salt
Pepper
Celery salt
Mayonnaise

Cut the eggs in half lengthwise. Remove the yolks carefully. Place the whites on a serving platter lined with lettuce leaves. Mix the yolks with mayonnaise and season to taste. With a pastry tube or teaspoon, fill the hollowed out egg whites with the mayonnaise-yolk mixture.

Decorate them with a sprig of dill or parsley. Garnish them with thinly sliced tomatoes.

Immanuel Lutheran Church
Holden, MA

LEVERPASTEJ
Liver Pâté

1 pound veal liver
1/4 pound veal
1/2 pound pork fat
1 large onion
8 anchovy fillets
4 tablespoons flour
3 eggs
1 1/3 cups cream
1 tablespoon salt
1/2 teaspoon white pepper
3 to 4 chopped truffles

For Mold:
2/3 pound pork fat cut into thin
slices

Wash the liver and wipe it dry.
Cut the liver, veal and pork fat
into pieces and grind them
together with the onion and
anchovies 3 to 4 times. Force
this mixture through a sieve.
Beat the eggs, cream and flour
until they are well-blended.
Gradually add the egg mixture to
the meat mixture, stirring
thoroughly. Next add the
seasoning and truffles. Continue
to beat until it is well-blended.

Line an oblong mold or tin with
thin slices of fat pork. Fill it
3/4 full with the combined
mixture and tie waxed paper
over the top. Bake in a slow oven
at 250°F in a water bath for
1 1/2 hours. Keep it in the mold
until it is cold or until the
following day. Unmold.

Serve it sliced with cucumbers
and tomatoes.

First Lutheran Church
Genesco, IL

LIVER PÂTÉ
Poor Man's Pâté

1 pound smoked liver sausage or
  Braunschweiger
1 8-ounce package cream
  cheese, at room temperature
1 stick butter or margarine, at
  room temperature
1 small can mushrooms,
  chopped finely
1/2 teaspoon salt
1/2 teaspoon pepper

Blend all the ingredients with a
mixer. Shape into a mold on a
serving plate. Chill.

Decorate it with parsley. Serve
with crackers or party rye.

Swedish Club of Metropolitan Detroit
Swedish Women's Organization
Farmington Hills, MI

PICKLED BEETS WITH SAUCE

2 to 3 cans beets
3/4 cup sugar (more or less as
    desired)
2 tablespoons flour
1 teaspoon prepared mustard
1 cup vinegar

Drain the beets. Chop them finely and set them aside. Combine the sugar, flour, mustard and 1/2 cup vinegar. Cook over a medium heat.

Add the egg to the rest of the vinegar and whisk them together. Add the egg mixture to the sugar mixture and continue to stir until it is cooked. Mix 2 or 3 tablespoons of the sauce with the beets. Spread this in a shallow dish and spoon the rest of the sauce over the top of the beet mixture. Chill.

Richland Evangelical Covenant Church
Richland, MI

INLAGDA RÖDBETOR
Pickled Beets

4 quarts small beets
3 cups vinegar
2 cups water
2 1/2 cups sugar
1 teaspoon salt
2 teaspoons allspice
1 teaspoon whole cloves
1 3-inch stick cinnamon

Cook the beets until tender. Slip off the skins and set the beets aside. Combine all the other ingredients to make a syrup. Bring this to a boil. Simmer 15 minutes. Add the beets to the syrup and simmer for 5 minutes longer.

Strain and pack the beets into hot, sterilized jars. Bring the syrup to a boil again and pour it over the beets. Seal. (If there is not enough syrup to cover the beets, add hot vinegar.)

Makes about 8 pints.

North Crow River Lutheran Church
Cokato, MN

SWEDISH DILL PICKLES

Take medium-sized cucumbers and soak in salted water overnight. Drain. Arrange in layers: cucumbers, a layer of dill, and then a few pieces of horseradish to fill the crock.

Cover with the following:

Make a brine using *"10 cents worth of alum,"* 1/2 package of mixed spices, 1 cup of sugar and 1/2 gallon of vinegar.

Cover the container and place a weight on the cover.

"Make the brine strong enough to float an egg."

Norden Women's Club
Jamestown, NY

GREEN TOMATO PICKLES

7 pounds of green tomatoes
3 pounds sugar
1/2 cup vinegar
2 teaspoons ginger

Wash, peel and then chop or grind the tomatoes.

Combine all the ingredients and cook for 2 hours on a slow burner.

"Stir and watch closely as they burn very easily."

Red River Lutheran Church
Hallock, MN

SWEDISH CHRISTMAS RELISH

3 cups vinegar
3 cups sugar
1 dozen peppers, red or green
1 dozen onions
1 bunch celery
4 teaspoons salt

Heat together the vinegar and sugar until they boil. Set it aside. Chop the peppers, onions and celery. Add the salt, and cover all with the boiling water. Let it stand for 5 minutes. Drain well. Place these ingredients in a large kettle and add the vinegar-sugar mixture. Heat the combined mixture until it comes to a good boil. Pack the relish in pint jars and seal.

Makes 4 pints.

Bethel Lutheran Church
Willmar, MN

SPECIAL DISHES FOR A CROWD

BRUNA BÖNOR
Brown Beans

48 pounds pink beans
48 sticks cinnamon
20 "cubes" butter
12 tablespoons salt
16 packages brown sugar
4 cups light corn syrup
4 cups brown vinegar
10 cups peach-pickle juice*

Soak the beans overnight in plenty of water with cinnamon sticks. The next morning, drain and cover the beans with fresh water. Bring this to a boil and simmer until tender, but not mushy. Stir occasionally and keep the beans covered with water while cooking to keep from splitting. Do not add salt until the beans are tender.

When the beans are well Done, divide and place the beans into 4 (or more) roasters.

Add to each roaster:
5 cubes butter
3 tablespoons salt
4 packages brown sugar
1 cup light corn syrup
1 cup brown vinegar
2 1/2 cups peach-pickle juice

Simmer until absorbed well and heated through.

Put the beans in plastic 5-gallon buckets for refrigerator storage overnight. The next morning put half of the beans in 2 or 3 roasters and heat them until almost boiling. Stir until thickened. Add thickening by mixing 3/4 box of cornstarch with cold water into a thin paste.

(See page 215 in this chapter for Pickled Peach recipe.)

*Hilmar Covenant Church
Hilmar, CA*

MEATBALLS

15 cups milk
20 tablespoons salt
7 1/2 teaspoons pepper
3 1/2 cups onion, ground
60 eggs
16 ounces soy sauce
3 ounces Accent
15 cups bread crumbs
3 large jars beef bouillon cubes

Grind together:
45 pounds beef
15 pounds pork

Mix everything together except the beef bouillon cubes. Roll the mixture into balls and brown. This will make 3 roasters full. To each roaster add 1 large jar of beef bouillon cubes and water, using 1 bouillon cube per cup of water. Heat.

American Union of Swedish Singers
Norden Singers
Des Moines, IA

KORV
Potato Bologna

"37 pounds pork
22 1/2 pounds potatoes
2 1/2 pounds onions

1 cup salt
6 teaspoons pepper
3 tablespoons allspice

"Grind together and make into rings. 2 shanks beef casings. Add 1 cup salt to each pail.

"Makes 80 medium rings."

American Union of Swedish Singers
Norden Singers
Des Moines, IA

SALMON

45 to 50 pounds salmon
6 cups celery, chopped
1 1/2 cups onion, grated
2 cups parsley
2 pounds of butter

Cook the onion and celery together in butter until soft. Set it aside. Spread the inside and top of the salmon with the cooked celery and onion. Wrap the salmon in foil and bake in a 350°F oven for 3 to 3 1/2 hours.

Serves 300 to 325 people at a *smörgåsbord.*

American Union of Swedish Singers
Norden Singers
Des Moines, IA

PICKLED BEETS

12 1-gallon cans beets, drained
  (save 2 gallons of juice)
1 1/3 gallons cider vinegar
2 gallons beet juice
2 gallons sugar
1 1/3 boxes sliced cinnamon
  sticks
3/4 box whole cloves
1 tablespoon plus 1 teaspoon
  salt

Simmer the juice, vinegar, sugar
and spices for approximately
1 hour. Add the beets and heat
through.

Put this mixture in 5-gallon
buckets. Cover each top with a
plate to keep the beets under the
liquid.

Store the pickled beets in the
refrigerator when cooled.

Hilmar Covenant Church
Hilmar, CA

PICKLED PEACHES

9 gallons cling peach halves,
  each cut into 3 pieces
1 1/2 boxes pickling spice
3/4 box whole cloves
1 1/2 gallons peach syrup (from
  the 9 gallons)
3/4 gallon white vinegar
1 tablespoon plus
  1 1/2 teaspoons salt
3/4 gallon granulated sugar
3/4 box stick cinnamon

Drain the peaches and save
1 1/2 gallons of the syrup for
this recipe. (Keep the rest of the
syrup for making *"kräm"* or
large-quantity *"bruna bönor"*).

Tie the pickling spice and whole
cloves together in a small
cheesecloth bag. Simmer the
spices with the peach syrup,
vinegar, salt, sugar and
cinnamon for 1 hour or more.
Add the peaches gently and heat
through. Do not boil.

Put the peaches in 5-gallon
buckets. Store the pickled
peaches in the refrigerator when
cooled.

(See *"kräm"* recipe which follows, and
the recipe for *"bruna bönor"* found on
page 213 in this chapter.)

Hilmar Covenant Church
Hilmar, CA

KRÄM
(A Topping, Sauce or Thin Pudding)

6 quarts juice (grape, peach,
    plum, pomegranate,
    pineapple)*
2 1/2 cups sugar (or to taste)
1 2/3 cups potato starch
3 to 4 cups cold water

For *smörgåsbord:*
10 pounds sugar
60 quarts home-canned juice
5 cans pineapple juice
6 or 7 pounds potato starch

Mix the juices and the sugar and bring them almost to a boil. Use a large 8-quart aluminum kettle and a long wooden spoon. Mix the potato starch and water thoroughly. Keep mixing and add them to the hot juice. Stir rapidly and bring the mixture to a boil. Keep stirring and boil a few minutes.

"It will burn on the bottom if not carefully stirred."

*(See Pickled Peach recipe on previous page.)

Hilmar Covenant Church
Hilmar, CA

RICE PUDDING

1 gallon milk
2 cups rice, soaked overnight
4 teaspoons salt
16 eggs, separated
2 cups sugar
4 tablespoons butter
1 teaspoon vanilla

In a double boiler combine the milk, rice and salt. Cook until the rice is soft. Add the yolks and sugar to the rice mixture. Cook it until it thickens. Then add the butter and vanilla.

Meringue:
1 1/2 cups egg whites
1 1/4 cups powdered sugar
1/2 teaspoon vanilla

American Union of Swedish Singers
Norden Singers
Des Moines, IA

TRO

Faith

FAITH OF OUR FATHERS AND MOTHERS

In their efforts and struggles to create a new life for themselves in America, the Swedish immigrants not only relied on their own inner resources for strength and determination, but also upon their spiritual faith which had been imparted to them by their ancestors in Sweden. The Christian faith of our fathers and mothers can be traced back to the 9th Century when St. Ansgar brought the Christian Gospel to Sweden.

The Reformation, which was sweeping Europe came to Sweden in the 16th Century. The National Church, which was confessionally-grounded in Lutheranism and politically tied with the State, became the legal established church in Sweden.

In the 19th Century, religious revivalism swept throughout the countryside of Sweden. Many people, especially those in rural areas, became disillusioned with the National Church and chose to worship in their homes and villages without the mandates of the church and its clergy.

Concurrently, the opportunity for free land in the United States became a reality and a hope for many poor Swedish people, and the mass emigration of the Swedish people to the United States took place.

When the new Swedish immigrants came to this country, they did not have a legally-established National Church in America to join. Consequently, they joined religious groups and denominations that were already established. Many of them joined the Episcopalian, Methodist or the Baptist Churches. However, some of the immigrants chose to completely disassociate themselves from established religions and instead, joined various lodges and fraternal organizations for help and guidance. Yet, others wanted to transport the confessional faith and practices of the National Church in Sweden to their new homeland. Out of this group, the Augustana Lutheran Church was established in 1860 at Jefferson Prairie, WI. However, in 1885, many members of the Augustana Lutheran Church broke away and formed the Swedish Mission Covenant Church of America.

Through the religious conflicts and turmoil in the United States, the Swedish immigrants clung to their faith in God. Linnea Young, a member of The First Evangelical Lutheran Church of Oakland, NE, wrote:

> *"Churches were very helpful in this transition period. Swedish settlers coming to the Midwest brought their Swedish customs with them. Founded by the Swedes, for the Swedes, the churches gave them the strength and comfort they needed in this new and strange environment. The same liturgy, the hymns, and of course the same Bibles, were used as in Sweden."*

Many congregations wrote about the commitment the early pioneers had to their faith. Members of the East Sveadahl Lutheran Church of St. James, MN wrote:

> *"Saturday evening the bells, which could be heard across the prairie, would ring reminding the people of the Sabbath. In the homes there was the preparation of the Sunday School lessons, and the family preparation for the Sabbath."*

Trinity Lutheran Church of Benson, MN was organized in 1874 in a typical place – a sod house. Alphid Johnson of Trinity wrote:

> *"Before they had even built their own homes, the newly arrived immigrants were concerned about their spiritual life. The immigrant trunk became the altar covered with a white cloth. The Bible and hymn book became the basis for the worship services."*

Glorian Anderson of Spring Garden Lutheran Church of Cannon Falls, MN also wrote about the early settlers and how they found their way by following buffalo trails, staking out their claims and bringing their wives and women in by ox-carts. Many immigrants had to share the same small, humble homes. Glorian Anderson of Spring Garden Lutheran Church sent the following,   *"Mrs. Vanberg asked, 'How will we all get room in this house?' Mrs. Haggestrom answered, 'Where there is heart room there is house room.' "* They established their church in 1858, the same year Minnesota became a state.

Eric Norelius, a beloved pioneer in the Augustana Lutheran Church, first visited Goodhue County in Southern Minnesota in 1855. He immediately organized a church the same year, and he and his wife, Inga Charlotte, lived in a shanty until they could get better housing. Vasa Lutheran Church still honors his memory, and the members even sent us his wife's **Rennet Pudding** recipe:

> *"Stir together 2 or 3 eggs, 1/2 cup sugar, 1/2 cup flour and a pinch of salt. Mix in a little more than a quart of milk, 1 teaspoon of rennet in 1/2 cup of the milk. Pour into buttered dish and bake in a moderate oven. "*

Many other congregations wrote about their early beginnings. Augustana Evangelical Lutheran Church of Rockford, IL formed in 1854. Augustana Lutheran Church of Manson, Iowa dates back to 1868, but was formally organized in 1871. Their members first met in homes because they *"thirsted for the Word of God and felt a need of organized church work."* Immanuel Lutheran Church of Mediapolis, IA started the same year with 40 charter members.

In the 19th Century, the churches were being organized all over the nation, and many of them are still in existence today. Cambridge Lutheran Church of Cambridge, MN was the only Lutheran church organized in Minnesota during the Civil War. Braham Evangelical Lutheran Church of Braham, MN began in 1879 with 29 adults, 9 confirmed, and 39 baptized children. Augustana Lutheran Church of Sioux Falls, SD was started in 1882 by sixteen people. In 1887 their dues were $4.00 a year for each communicant. Three years later the Evangelical Lutheran Church of Tolley, ND was started by Scandinavians who settled around the Mouse River. The same year saw the start of Nathaniel Lutheran Church of Alcester, SD.

In 1889 with only 34 charter members, Zion Evangelical Lutheran Church of Neuman Grove, NE was organized, and four years later Zion Swedish Lutheran Church of Golden Valley, MN was formed. In 1907, the Evangelical Covenant Church of Kingsburg, CA was organized. This was a year before the little town of Kingsburg was incorporated.

Not only were immigrant churches organized and built in record time, but they also grew in membership. Calvary Lutheran Church of Rapid River, MI began with 12 members and has grown to 415, having been served in its early years almost entirely by student pastors. Mount Calvary Lutheran Church of Excelsior, MN organized in 1930 with 53 members and today the congregation numbers over 3,000. Under the capable direction of Pastor George Wold and his wife Ruth, the Evangelical Covenant Church of International Falls, MN went from 200 to 599 members between 1945 and 1974.

Many people and clergy sacrificed money, time and land in order to spread the Gospel in their new communities. Often pastors had to live in shacks or with other families. Many times they were paid in "chicken and eggs." When J.F. Fredrickson went to Helena, MT to attend school, his heart was set on going out to the mission fields of China; but while he was in Montana, he saw the need for mission work among the Scandinavians of the community and stayed to help them.

People donated land, material, money, time and talents to build their churches and parsonages. Most churches were built without architects or formal building committees. Members used the equipment from their farms to excavate the church basement. With sweat and toil, they volunteered their time and energy to build their spiritual homes.

Many congregations, however, saw their efforts go up in flames. Esther Lutheran Church of Parkers Prairie, MN was organized in 1893, and was struck by lightning and burned to the ground in 1919. Members of the First Evangelical Lutheran Church of Taylors Falls, MN saw their parsonage burn on Palm Sunday in 1930. Bethesda Lutheran Church of Chicago, IL burned in 1920. In 1987, Braham Evangelical Lutheran Church of Braham, MN was destroyed by fire, a devastating blow to the whole community. These are just a few of the Swedish-American congregations that suffered terrible losses due to fire.

Another painful problem for members of the Swedish immigrant churches was the switch from the Swedish language to English for worship services. Pioneer Lake Lutheran Church of Conover, WI first introduced English services in 1923, "*but only at the evening services.*" Bethany Lutheran Church of Wisconsin Rapids, WI went to all English services in 1932. Grace Lutheran Church, Rankin, IL changed from Swedish to English gradually between 1914 and 1920. In 1924, all services at Swedish Evangelical Lutheran Church in Crystal Lake, IL were to be conducted in English. They decided to only hold a Swedish service "*if necessary on a Sunday afternoon or at any other time desired.*" Swedish Evangelical Lutheran Church of Hector, MN – later named First Evangelical Lutheran Church – alternated between Swedish and English language services until the 1940's. First Evangelical Lutheran Church of Taylors Falls, MN held Swedish services until 1935-1936 "*in the months with five Sundays.*" Members of First Lutheran Church of El Campo TX wrote:

> "World War I caused the change to all English services. Cultural changes are always cruel, and many of the older members bitterly resented giving up their native language."

Many churches wouldn't have survived if it hadn't been for the women's organizations. The first women's organizations in the churches were called the *sföreningen* (sewing groups). Members of First Evangelical Lutheran Church in Taylors Falls, MN wrote:

> "In 1895 all women were automatically in the women's organization with the pastor as the chairman. They were in four units, each of the four units meeting on a different Wednesday so the pastor could be at all the meetings for Bible readings. Those present sang 'Hemland' songs. The dues were 10 cents each. Due to the lack of social events, many ladies came to several of the units each month, so the treasury grew in spite of the low rate of ten cents."

Elim Lutheran Church of Marquette, KS had a group called the "*Ten Cents Society*," and at Swedlanda Evangelical Lutheran Church of Hector, MN, dues were also ten cents. In Parkers Prairie, MN the women of Esther Lutheran Church met in the homes because "*it was too expensive to heat the church.*"

Members of the Lindsborg Kansas Mission Church of Lindsborg, KS wrote about the place that Ladies Aid held in the hearts of the women:

> "*Ladies Aid in Lindsborg was a great occasion. At 2:30 every other Wednesday it was a sacred hour when the women of the church came together to sing from 'Sions Basun', hear the exciting minutes of the last meeting, listen to the pastor's words of comfort and admonition, and indulge in some of the most delectable goodies (plus coffee –"King Oscar's") that our dear ladies could dream up. The farm cooks had an advantage over the city ladies because there were sufficient eggs available for the rural women to win prizes for the highest angel food cakes.*"

In 1910 , when Reverend J. H. Ford of Immanuel Lutheran Church of Dunnell, MN compiled a church history of the "Older Ladies Society", he wrote, "*. . . No one in our time can deny the good the ladies have done for the society . . . In every activity the ladies have done a blessed work.*"

The women's groups became important arms of the church providing offerings for the foreign missions as well as meeting the financial needs of the congregation. Pioneer Lake Lutheran Church members of Conover, WI wrote, "*Old timers said the church was built on cookies and coffee.*"

The women met and they organized, they worked and they improvised, they cooked and they cleaned, they prayed and they succeeded. People of the Mission Covenant Church of Foster City, MI wrote:

> "*Our first church was built at a cost of $800. The ladies sewing circle had given some money toward the building. They were called 'those always dependable ladies.'*"

In many churches "those always dependable ladies" made their money by serving *smörgåsbords*, holding auctions, setting up food stands at state fairs, and making handiwork. Grace Lutheran Church in Henning, MN served suppers to 200 people at 40 cents apiece – and their basement was little!

Augustana Lutheran Church in Grand Forks, ND rented Scandia Hall to serve dinners. They charged 45 cents for a meal of "banquet proportions." After their church was built in 1900, they still didn't have adequate facilities to serve their famous church suppers. They improvised by cooking in the church balcony and carried the water they needed for cooking from the lumberyard across the street.

In 1946, Wiley Heights Covenant Church of Yakima, WA held their first *smörgåsbord*. They baked for the servicemen, and canned hundreds and hundreds of quarts and gallons of fruit for the Union Gospel Mission.

Many churches still preserve their ethnic heritage by serving a Swedish *smörgåsbord*. Elim Lutheran Church in Marquette, KS, Trinity Lutheran Church in Boxholm, IA and Pioneer Lake Lutheran Church of Conover, WI all serve their Swedish *smörgåsbord* in December. First Lutheran Church of Genesco, IL always uses traditional Swedish copper coffee pots for its *smörgåsbord*, and Brantford Evangelical Covenant Church of Washington County, KS still cooks *"egg coffee"* for its special meals.

Salem Lutheran Church in Minneapolis, MN had a food stand at the Minnesota State Fair for over 40 years. Cambridge Lutheran Church in Cambridge, IL had a chicken pie stand and ice cream social at the Henry County Fairgrounds. Swedlanda Evangelical Lutheran Church of Hector, MN sold their handiwork at an auction on Midsummer's Day. At times, the money they made was loaned to the church, and often the loans were forgiven.

The congregation at Svea Lutheran Church of Hager City, WI made and sold cheese as a fundraiser for its church. Mary May Anderson of Svea Lutheran wrote:

> "The farmers milked early and brought their milk to the church. The ladies were at church to heat the milk on the wood stove in the kitchen. When the milk was the right temperature, they added rennet and stirred. The cheese curds were strained out and put in a steamer. The ladies pressed and worked the cheese with their hands. Then, the loaves of cheese were ready to be taken home. They washed the loaves every day with salt water, and cured them for about six weeks. The whey was divided and taken home to be boiled down for 'sandost.' Later, the church held an auction of fancy work, baked goodies, and all the cheese and 'sandost' was sold."

Bethesda Lutheran Church of Chicago, IL raised much-needed funds for their church by making potato sausages and Swedish coffee cakes. Evelyn Berg of Bethesda wrote:

> "We took orders first, and then sold them. Two women would arrive at church at 5 a.m., and set the first batch so it would be ready to bake when the others arrived. Sometimes, the two early-birds would go up to the sanctuary, lay down on the pews, and fall asleep."

Even though "those always dependable ladies" worked hard, they sometimes ran into opposition. Phyllis Nelson, a member of Alma Lutheran Church of Mead, NE, wrote:

> "For many years an auction was held in the church sanctuary. The first year Reverend Samuelson was at the church, he had no idea what was going on. The evening came and the church was filled. The ladies asked him to open with prayer. He refused. They pleaded with him. At last, he said he would if they wouldn't mind what he read. He read Mark 11: 15-19. Needless to say, that was the last auction held in the church. The ladies were criticized, but it was truly done in love for the church."

The women not only cooked and served and raised money, but they cleaned! Cleanliness was next to godliness. Evelyn Berg, Bethseda Lutheran Church of Chicago, IL wrote:

> *"The week prior to Confirmation, the same women who always cooked plus a few mothers of the Confirmands would get together and wash the pews, floors, and anything else that was washable. This included the gum from the bottom of the Choir seats."*

Phyllis Salberg of First Lutheran Church of Ault, CO wrote:

> *"The Ladies Aid cleaned the church. On cleaning days they would bring their used coffee grounds that they had saved, and these were moistened and scattered over the cement basement floor to keep the dust down as the floors were swept."*

Two churches even sent their recipes for soap. The recipe for soap from Salem Lutheran Church of Creston, IA is:

> *"5 pounds of melted and strained grease, 1 pound can lye dissolved in 3 pints of cold water, 1 1/2 tablespoons of borax, 1/2 cup of household ammonia.*
>
> *"When the lye and water mixture is cooled, add it to the fat and the other ingredients. Stir it until it is thick. The resultant soft soap is then poured into a paste board or wood box lined with oil paper and set away in a warm, dry place to harden."*

The soap recipe of Joyce Einorson of the Evangelical Covenant Church of International Falls, MN is as follows:

> *"Dissolve one can of Lewis Lye in one gallon of rainwater. Put 5 pounds of clear grease or 5 1/2 pounds of scraps, and one gallon of rainwater in a kettle and bring to a boil. Stir the lye and water and pour this into the grease and water. Let it boil for one hour. Add 1/4 pound or more of borax. Boil until the borax is dissolved. Put the mixture in molds or vessels to harden."*

Many Swedish-American church members were involved in the Temperance Unions because they were concerned with the evils of dancing, drinking and smoking. Members of the First Evangelical Lutheran Church of Taylors Falls, MN wrote:

"In the forties, Midsummer's Day was celebrated with refreshments and cigars for the men. That was until the pastor's wife bought all the cigars, and promptly crushed and burned them all."

However, smoking and chewing was common for many of the immigrant men, and Maria Lutheran Church of Kennedy, MN even sent us their recipe for snuff!

"Many of the old-timer preferred to make his own 'snus' and this is how he did it. In an old wooden coffee grinder (the kind with a little drawer that was kept especially for making snuff) he ground 'Old Tom Tobacco' and drip coffee beans. He used no exact measurement. A little salt was added. A few drops of flavoring (usually peppermint) came next. It was moistened with strong black coffee and well stirred. He tasted it and added more salt or flavoring to his taste. If satisfactory, it was sealed, usually in an earthen 'snus' jar and kept in a cool place. From this he filled his draw-pouch which he carried every day. He replenished his supply in his draw-pouch as needed."

Today, many of the Swedish-American churches and organizations celebrate the Swedish festival of Midsummer's Day, even if it is without cigars! Spring Garden Lutheran Church of Cannon Falls, MN has a Swedish *smörgåsbord* on Midsummer's Day, followed by a program. It was discontinued in 1938, but started up again in 1959.

Many churches and organizations also celebrate St. Lucia Festival. Thabor Lutheran Church of Wausa, NE, Zion Lutheran Church of Golden Valley, MN, Augustana Lutheran Church of St. James, MN, Evangelical Lutheran Church of Winthrop, MN, The Linneas of Texas and the American Swedish Institute (Bemidji Affiliate), Bemidji, MN are but a few that honor this most Swedish holiday.

226

Lloyd Johnson, President of The American Swedish Institute (Bemidji Affiliate), wrote:

> *"The day is December 13th, the hour is 6 a.m., 300 to 400 guests are seated in the darkened banquet hall waiting in silence for the arrival of the young maiden who has been selected to be the Lucia , her attendants and star boys. At the sound of the horn, the music begins and the procession, which is led by Lucia with a wreath of candles in her hair, begins to light the room. The candles throughout the room are lit, table by table, and soon the fully-lighted and beautifully-decorated banquet hall becomes the site in which one can truly sense the beginning of the Christmas season. A festive program that includes a choir of young children singing Swedish songs is followed by a traditional Swedish 'smörgåsbord' breakfast."*

Mary Lou Sather of Rochester Covenant Church also wrote about the significance of St. Lucia Day.

> *"All the cleaning, baking, letter-writing, gift-making, purchasing, wrapping and trimming, in short, all the arrangements for the holiday were to be finished by that date. The family was then free to contemplate the coming birth of Christ and his future Second Coming without the distractions of the household impinging on that special time. It's a wonderful tradition, one that truly frees one to anticipate the coming of 'Jul' with the kind of joy it deserves."*

Another Swedish festival celebrated by several churches and organizations is *Dopp i Grytan*. First Lutheran Church of Kensington, MN, Vasa Lutheran Church near Welch, MN and the families of Nathaniel Lutheran Church in Alcester, SD all wrote and described this special tradition of serving a simple meal around the stove on Christmas Eve Day to remind them of the starvation years.

227

The most beloved Swedish holiday celebrated by Swedish-Americans was, and still is, Christmas – especially *Julotta* Services. Hans Mattson who was born in Sweden and founded Vasa Village in Welch, MN published <u>The Story of an Emigrant</u> in 1891. In his book he described Christmas as he remembered it from Sweden. He said:

> *"Christmas has always been, and is yet, the greatest of all festivities or holidays among all the Scandinavian peoples. . . Christmas Day was considered a very holy day. There were no visits made, no work done except of the greatest necessity, such as feeding the animals and keeping up the fires; no cooking was done on that day, but meals were served mostly cold from the delicious head cheese, pork roast and other delicacies, which had been prepared beforehand. The greatest event of all the season, and in fact of the whole year, was the early service ('ottesång') in the parish church at five o'clock on Christmas morning. Hundreds of candles were lighted in chandeliers and candlesticks. The altar was covered with gold embroidered cloth; the floor was strewn with fresh twigs of juniper, and soon the people began to assemble. They came from every house and hamlet, in sleighs with tinkling bells, on horseback, and on foot along every road and winding pathway, usually in groups, swelling as the parties and the roads intersected, many carrying lanterns or burning pine-knots to light the way. Everywhere the greeting, 'Happy Christmas' was heard, but all with joyful solemnity. Outside the church the burning torches were thrown in a pile which formed a blaze that could be seen a long distance off. The church was soon crowded; then the solemn tones of the organ burst forth; the organist led in the beautiful hymn, 'Var Hälsad Sköna Morgonstund', in which every member of the congregation joined, until the temple was filled with their united voices so that the walls almost shook. And when the minister ascended the pulpit, clad in his surplice and black cape, he had before him a most devout congregation. Of course the sermon was about the Messiah, who was born in the stable, and placed in the manger at Bethlehem.*

The next service was at ten o'clock, and the rest of the day was spent quietly at home by everybody."

Many of you wrote of your fond remembrances of this Holy Day. Members of Alma Lutheran Church of Mead, NE wrote:

"The first 'Julotta' service was held in a sod house. An altar was a box decorated with a black calico dress that had been torn apart. Some flowers from old hats were pinned on to make it more festive."

Glorian Anderson of Spring Garden Lutheran Church of Cannon Falls, MN wrote:

"Today this service includes communion and candle-lighting to commemorate the birth of Jesus, the light of the world. This service ends with the singing of 'Lotom Oss Pa Barnavis' or 'Hosianna' as it is commonly called."

Members of New Gottland Evangelical Covenant Church of McPherson, KS wrote, *"We still celebrate 'Julotta' very early on Christmas Day morning, and the choir sings 'Lyssna, Lyssna'."*

Mildred Carlson of Augustana Lutheran Church of Comstock, WI wrote:

"Fortified against sub-zero temperatures with heavy quilts and robes and heated bricks and flat-irons, we snuggled together with friends and neighbors for the six-mile trek to Cumberland, gliding into the frosty night to the accompaniment of sleigh bells. Any misgivings we may have had about being routed out of bed at such an atrocious hour were soon dismissed by the sight of an enormous, candle-lit evergreen tree in the front of the church, and musical strains of the reed organ playing 'Var Hälsad Sköna Morgonstund' (All Hail to Thee, O Blessed Morn)."

Phyllis Wahlstrom of Grace Lutheran Church of Sheyenne, ND wrote:

> *"The family would stay up on Christmas Eve and at 4 o'clock in the morning hitched up the horses and went by bob sled five miles across the frozen prairie, often in 30 degree below zero weather, to church and to early morning services. They covered themselves with buffalo robes and to keep their feet warm, they would heat flat-irons and a soap stone. These were wrapped in newspapers and put in the hay. Grandpa had Swedish bells on his horses that made a beautiful sound as the bobsled glided across the snow."*

The members of Evangelical Covenant Church of International Falls, MN wrote, *"It was only fitting that the first service held at the new Holler Mission Church be the 5 a.m. Julotta Service, 1926."* Dolores Taylor of Christ the King Lutheran Church in New Brighton, MN summed it up by writing:

> *"'Julotta' Service started at 5 a.m. with the ringing of the church bells across the countryside as the congregation gathered. Young and old came. No one missed 'Julotta' Service. It was about as close to heaven as one could get on earth . . . What a blessing those 'Julotta' Services were. All these years later, I can still experience the exuberance, warmth, and love that I felt in the House of God those early Christmas mornings."*

Along with special meals and holiday celebrations, congregations are keeping their Swedish heritage alive in other ways too. The Evangelical Covenant Church in Clay Center, KS devotes one week in January to prayer. Stockholm Lutheran Church of Shickley, NE flies the Swedish flag in their cemetery on the day of their church picnic.

Many congregations are trying to preserve their church buildings which are no longer used for church services. Vasa Lutheran Congregation of Welch, MN has turned its old church building into a museum. Augustana Lutheran Church in Andover, IL has preserved its church building as a national, historic shrine. They have renamed it the "Jenny Lind Chapel" in honor of Jenny Lind who gave the congregation $1,500

to build the church. Mamrelund Lutheran Church of Pennock, MN is beautifully preserved and uses the third Sundays of June, July and August and Christmas Eve for special services.

In addition to churches, many descendants of the immigrants also belong to a variety of Swedish-American organizations to learn more about the Swedish culture and their Swedish-American heritage. Lloyd Johnson, President of the American Swedish Institute (Bemidji Affiliate), wrote:

> "To sing in a 'Tomte' Choir; to dance around a maypole on a sunny afternnon in June; to bring light into the darkness on a cold December morning; or to share in some other special Swedish experience, will help future generations to keep alive an interest in their heritage and the celebration of these traditions."

Even though many congregations have worked hard to preserve their Swedish-American heritage, Swedish-American church members believe their main mission is "to bring the Good News to the people." Salem Evangelical Lutheran Church of Dalbo, MN has a strong Swedish heritage. However, their congregation believes – like so many congregations do – that "their church is open to everyone, no matter what the background, age or color."

Many of the rural churches are now struggling with declining memberships. Hazel Wiese, a member of Balsamlund Lutheran church of Verndale, MN summed up the problems of the rural churches beautifully. She wrote:

> "We are a country church in a two-point parish that is small enough to help one another. By the grace of God, and remembering the faith of the first 17 members, we want to continue to serve the Lord. We are only 8 active members in Ladies Aid. All the other women work out, but they help with church activities. We older one have to pray for the younger ones that are so busy. We have the time."

Many congregations founded by Swedish immigrants are optimistic about their future. Mrs. Arnie Kivioja, a member of Swedlanda Lutheran Church of Hector, MN wrote, *"Looking to the future, our prayer is to keep on doing the Lord's work and preach the Gospel to future generations."*

Marian Pearson, a member of North Crow River Lutheran Church of Cokato, MN wrote, *"God has blessed us with many years of serving a community in many ways. God's Work and Word will always prevail."*

Asta Ostlind Chase, a member of New Gottland Lutheran Church of McPherson, KS echoed the sentiments of all the immigrant church members when she wrote,

> *"No one knows how long these traditions will continue. Our prayer is that our church will always bring glory to God, by pointing folks to the Lord Jesus Christ."*

LANDSKAPSBLOMMOR

Provincial Flowers

EK

"Oak"

Quercus robur

A deciduous tree growing to heights of 45 mm: They are very long-lived, with some lasting 600 years and more. The oak produces flowers for the first time at the age of 50. The blooms (both male and female) appear alongside of the new leaves.

The acorns of the oak are spread by birds and squirrels who proceed to bury an excess amount every fall, most of which are forgotten.

The leaves are oblong, having 3 to 7 lobes.

BLEKINGE

VILDKAPRIFOL

"Honeysuckle"

Lonicera periclymenum

A tall, climbing and sprawling bush with twining woody stems: The leaves are oval shaped. The flowers' heads are long-tubed (to 50 mm) and all the flowers are on one plane. They thrive along steep mountain paths, woods, scrub, and hedges. They're planted around summer homes for decoration and their sweet fragrance.

BOHUSLÄN

ÄNGSKLOCKA

"Spreading Bellflower"

Campanula patula

A mid-height plant with rough, angled stems: The flowers are bell-shaped and grow in a loose, much-branched cluster. They bloom from June to August. Bees are attracted to their wonderful blue color. In the time of Karl von Linné, these plants were unknown in Sweden, but have since invaded the country, perhaps coming from Finland. People in *Dalarna* say they are "in a war" with *Ängsklocka.*

DALARNA

ÄKTA FÖRGÄTMIGEJ

"Forget-Me-Not"

Myosotis scorpioides

A short to mid-height plant with creeping stems that turn upward: These heavenly blue flowers, usually with 5 petals, are 5 to 10 mm. The fruit is black.

Habitat: Acidic soil, water-damp with mid-shade to none.

The forget-me-not is a symbol of loyal friendship. One of many legends about this flower tells of an angel whose punishment was to sow forget-me-not seeds over the whole earth because he loved an earthling.

DALSLAND

MURGRÖNA

"Ivy"

Hedera helix

Creeping or climbing, its woody stems are covered with glossy evergreen leaves that have yellowish-green flowers 3 to 6 mm appearing in September and October. Only the nonflowering shoots are lobed. A long, hardy perennial having rooting nodes, it can grow into massive thickets climbing as high as 20 m up trees, brick walls, etc. It spreads by dark blue berries that ripen in the spring and are eaten by birds.

Habitat: Woods, hedges, walls and rocks in moist-dry, acidic soil. They can stand heavy shade or little shade.

GOTLAND

LILJEKONVALJ

"Lily-of-the-Valley"

Convallaria majalis

A low patch-forming, poisonous plant that has pairs of oval leaves opposite each other protecting stalks of bell-shaped, nodding white flowers: Even the water they sit in can become poisonous. The flowers are very aromatic and are a favorite in wedding bouquets.

This is a very hardy perennial growing from rhizomes.

Habitat: Non-acidic dry soil in light to heavy shade.

GÄSTRIKLAND

HÄRGINST

"Hairy Greenweed"

Genista pilosa

A short creeping bush that has spineless, ridged stems supporting oval, blunt leaves: The undersides of the leaves are covered with silky hairs. The flowers are 10 mm long. These are very hardy and grow in heaths, grasslands and cliffs. They like acidic dry soil with no shade.

In *Halland* this plant grows very close to the ground. It is often called *knutginst* or *krypginst*.

HALLAND

LIN

"Flax"

Linum usitatissimum

Blue as the summer's heavens, this plant has been cultivated so long for its flax and oil that one forgets it is really a wildflower. A few flowers can be white, blooming from June until August. They grow to a height of 30 to 80 cm and produce high-quality fiber for the best linens. Oils from its seeds are used for linseed oil, cooking oil, and in the manufacture of varnish, paint and artists' oil paints.

HÄLSINGLAND

MOSIPPA

"Pale Pasque Flower"

Pulsatilla vernalis

A low plant with less feathery leaves and stems than its relative, the pasque flower. Its leaves are hairy on the outside and grow in a rosette around the base of the stem. The flowers are buttercup-like with a creamy-white inside and violet outside. Many Swedes say the *mosippa* is the most beautiful of all the springtime flowers. They are slightly toxic and shunned by livestock. They are also a hardy perennial, growing from root stock.

Habitat: Heaths, open woods, and mountain meadows in damp soil that is deficient in lime. They grow at altitudes from sea level to 3000 m.

HÄRJEDALEN

BRUNKULLA

"Black Vanilla Orchid"

Nigritella nigra

A rare flower growing on varied grassy alpine meadows and on unfertilized pastures found at altitudes of 1700 to 2500 m. Its height is low to short with narrow oblong leaves up the stem. The flowers are dark purple, spurred, and vanilla-scented. They grow in a dense spike. Some flowers are white, but they are rare. The flower blooms in June. Pollination is carried out by a vast array of insects attracted to the flower's unique fragance.

The soil should be moist, but not acidic.

The saying goes that cows that have eaten *brunkulla* will give purple milk and vanilla-tasting butter.

JÄMTLAND

FJÄLLSIPPA

"Mountain Avens"

Dryas octopetala

A low-creeping under-shrub plant: The leaves are oblong with rounded teeth and are silver on the underside. The flowers are 25 to 40 mm and have 8 or more petals. They grow one per stem sticking up over the mats of the green leaves. Many people call this flower simply *dryas*, which means wood nymph. The seeds are spread by the wind.

Habitat: Mountain rocks in moist to dry calcium soil with no shade.

LAPPLAND

GRAN

"Norway Spruce"

Picia abies

An evergreen tree producing soft wood, without much odor: It grows in Central and Northern Europe and is easy to work with. Its height can reach to 50 m and its life span is 400 years or more. The cones are cylindrical, averaging 10 to 15 cm long. One tree can spread an immense amount of pollen. Wood from the tree is used in general carpentry, for packing cases and sounding boards, and for stringed instruments. Its timber is turned into pulp for paper and rayon, and its resin is purified to yield turpentine.

MEDELPAD

ÅKERBÄR

"Artic Bramble or Raspberry"

Rubus arcticus

Sometimes it is called the "Raspberry of Northern Sweden." Its flowers are a most beautiful red-rose, blooming in June and July. It grows abundantly along the coasts of *Norrbotten* and *Västerbotten* in damp, lime-deficient meadows, grassy glades and ditch banks. The fruit appears in August. The berries are dark and defy description because, depending on the light, they seem to be a mixture of red, green, brown and violet with hints of grayish-rose. They are extremely aromatic and produce wonderful preserves and liqueurs.

NORRBOTTEN

245

GULLVIVA

"Cowslip"

Primula veris

A low to short plant with downy leaves growing in rosettes. Its flowers are orange yellow and are 10 to 15 mm in size. Each flower grows on its own short stalk in a cluster on top of a common stalk. The story goes that since the flower cluster resembles a bunch of keys, it can be used to break spells.

Habitat: Grassland, scrub, dry, non-acidic soil with no shade.

NÄRKE

PRÄSTKRAGE

"Oxeye Daisy"

Leucanthemum vulgare

Named because it reminds one of the *prästernas rundkragar,* (the priest's round ruffled collar), which was worn in times past: This is the flower that originated the game "She Loves Me, She Loves Me Not". The outer petals are picked one at a time while repeating "She Loves Me, She Loves Me Not". The last remaing petal determines the fate of one's love life.

SKANE

LINNEA

"Twinflower"

Linnaea borealis

A low creeping, mat-forming perennial with rounded leaves growing opposite each other. The flowers are bell-shaped, nodding in groups of two which grow opposite each other on long upright stalks. They are a very delicate pink in color and they are named for Karl von Linne, the famed Swedish botanist. Today, they seem to be the flower most identified with Sweden, appearing on fine china and many art objects.

Habitat: Confer woods, moist acidic soil and light to heavy shade.

SMÅLAND

VIT NÄCKROS

"White Water Lily"

Nymphaea alba

A floating plant with circular leaves less than 30 cm across: The leaves are green on top and reddish-brown on the underside. Some young plants have reddish-brown leaves on both the top and the bottom. The flowers have 20 to 25 petals and are up to 200 mm wide, and are held flush with the surface of the water. The blooms are the largest of all of Sweden's wild flowers. They open with the sun around 7:00 each morning and close at 4:00 in the afternoon. Long ago children were forbidden to swim near them or pick the flowers because they were thought to be dangerous.

SÖDERMANLAND

KUNGSÄNGSLILJA

"Fritillary"

Fritillaria meleagris

A short plant with very narrow leaves on its stem: The flowers are bell-shaped, 30 to 50 mm, solitary, nodding and checkered. It is a perennial growing from a bulb. The blood-red and white checkered colors are so unusual that they have become a symbol of friend and foe, war and peace. The seeds spread with the wind.

Habitat: Grasslands in damp, moist, non-acidic soil.

UPPLAND

SKOGGSSTJÄRNA

"Chickweed or Wintergreen"

Trientalis europaea

A low woodland flower that grows in conifer woods in moist, acidic soil. Its leaves grow in a whorl of 5 to 6, while it also has a few small leaves on the stem. White flowers rise from the whorl on long narrow stems and have from 5 to 9 petals, usually 7. More than any other flower in Sweden, this one has inspired poets, songwriters and philosophers. Such small stars in such large woods cause much inspiration. It produces a seed pad which is gray-blue in color, with markings like that of a soccer ball.

Habitat: Conifer woods, moors, in moist acidic soil.

VÄRMLAND

KUNG KARLS SPIRA

"Moor King" or "Lousewort"

Pedicularis sceptrum-carolinae

A mid-tall, thick-stemmed, unbranched, half-parasite: It is a hardy perennial growing from root stock. The leaves are pinnately lobed. The flowers grow in dense spikes and are 30 to 35 mm in length. They are gold with reddish-violet on the inside as well as on the tips of the petals. The sepals are reddish-brown. They bloom in July and August. Because it has a weak root system, it takes nourishment from surrounding plants.

Habitat: Grasslands and moors in damp soil.

VÄSTERBOTTEN

LJUNG

"Heather"

Calluna vulgaris

A woody evergreen with its habitat being the heaths, moors, bogs and pine woods: This plant likes wet to dry acidic soil with little to no shade. The leaves are very narrow, appearing in dense rows up the stems. The flowers are bell-shaped and hang along the stems. Its sepals are longer than, but the same color as, the petals. The blooms sometimes linger until the next year's blossoming. They destroy and sour the soil, and have been called the "Gray hair of Sweden."

VÄSTERGÖTLAND

MISTEL

"Mistletoe"

Viscum album

A parasite anchored to host by suckers: The leaves are usually evergreen in color, leathery in texture, are oblong and grow opposite each other. The four-petaled flowers are small and green and form a white, sticky berry. This sticky viscin clings to the beaks of birds that feed on the berries. The economic value of this plant is small, but it does provide a traditional holiday decoration. If one is kissed while standing under a spray from this plant, one is assured of luck and fertility."

VÄSTMANLAND

STYVMORSVIOL

"Wild Pansy"

Viola tricolor

A low to the ground, short, variable branching plant: The leaves are oval and toothed. The flowers are 10 to 25 mm, flat, and often blue and yellow. This is a persistent annual or short-lived perennial that blooms from April to September.

Habitat: Disturbed and grassy places and sand dunes; moist to dry and acidic soil; light shade to none.

ÅNGERMANLAND

254

ÖLANDSSOLVÄNDA

"Hoary Rockrose"

Helianthemum oelandicum

A half bush blooming during the day with a most glorious gold color: Its blooms follow the sun as it moves across the sky thus getting its name. (*Sol* meaning sun and *vända* meaning to wander). It thrives best in open places on the Island of *Öland*. The flowers have much pollen, but little nectar.

ÖLAND

BLÅKLINT

"Cornflower"

Centaurea cyanus

In 1638, these were called Blue Cornflowers or Blue Buttons. In America, they are called either Bachelor Buttons or Cornflowers. Almost every area in Sweden has a different name for them such as Bluecorn, Blue Lily, Boatman's Hat, and *blågubba*r or old man.

These are medium tall annuals with pinnately-lobed leaves. The upper leaves are unlobed. The flowerets are 15 to 30 mm, with the outer florets much enlarged.

ÖSTERGÖTLAND
Sketches and text by Avis Johnson

FESTIVALER

Festivals

Many of Sweden's beloved festivals and celebrations are steeped in religious tradition. Some, like Walpurgis Night, have elements of superstition and date back to pagan times. Others like Ascension Day and Whit Sunday (Pentecost) are based on Christianity. Some, like the St. Lucia Fest, have roots in other countries, and others such as "Midsommar" are secular holidays.

Along with birthday celebrations, Swedish families celebrate name days, baptisms, confirmations and weddings.

Mother's Day, Father's Day, Flag Day and All Saint's Day are all more recent celebrations and have been established in the twentieth century.

In Sweden, celebrations vary from one locale to another in both importance and customs.

WALPURGIS NIGHT, APRIL 30

The Swedish people strive to take leave of winter by welcoming Spring with public and private festivities. Friends and relatives get together to celebrate the end of a long winter with good food and perhaps dancing. Bonfires are lit all over the country, and people gather to watch the fires and to welcome spring with singing and speeches. Even students at some universities join in the festivities by donning white caps to celebrate spring. Typically the main dish is *gravad lax* served with a special mustard sauce.

EASTER, "GLAD PÅSK!"

As Lent draws to an end and the bleak grayness of winter subsides, Easter comes to Sweden bursting out in colors of green, pink and yellow. These colors are reflected in the colors of chicks and dyed Easter eggs. The markets are full of birch twigs that are wrapped with bundles of colored feathers set in a vase so that the twigs can start to sprout their bright new spring leaves or feathers. The most common decoration is the bright yellow daffodil found in people's homes.

On Easter Eve, young girls dress up like "kitchen witches" and go from house to house begging for sweets, much as children do in the United States on Halloween. The high point of Easter Eve is eating eggs. The children compete to see who can eat the most eggs. Even those who never eat eggs try to manage at least one. The dyed eggs have had onion peel, corn and leaves tied on them while cooking which makes wonderful patterns on the eggshell.

The following foods make a good Easter dinner:

    Bread, Butter and Cheese
    Herring and Anchovies
    Liver Pâté and Cucumbers
    Leg of Lamb and Boiled Potatoes
    Eggs with Mayonnaise and Shrimp
    Stuffed or Deviled Eggs
    Boiled and Dyed Eggs
    Omelets with Creamed Lobster Sauce
    Fried Sweetbreads and Peas
    Coffee

MIDSUMMER FESTIVAL

This festival is celebrated during the weekend closest to the 24th of June. A Midsummer pole or Maypole that has been generously decorated with flowers, leaves and ribbons is raised into place by several strong, young men. People join hands to sing and to circle-dance around the pole. Fresh birch branches are cut and placed at doorway entrances.

With everyone in a festive mood, games and dancing delight the young while plenty of coffee is consumed by the adults. Women are dressed in their finest costumes and have circles of flowers and ribbons in their hair.

Even though this festival is enthusiastically celebrated all over Sweden, it is commonly associated with the Province of Dalarna.

The following is a traditional *Midsommar* menu:

> Boiled New Potatoes with Fresh Dill
> Pickled Herring
> Bread, Butter and Cheese
> Hardtack
> Cucumbers in Sour Cream and Dill
> Tomatoes, Radishes and Celery
> Fresh Strawberries served on Ice Cream or Rice Pudding
>   topped with Whipped Cream
> Beer, Schnapps and Coffee

CRAYFISH PARTIES IN AUGUST

The crayfish season opens in Sweden in August. This also marks the first crayfish parties of the year, a uniquely Swedish celebration. Recently, the numbers of crayfish in many of Sweden's lakes are decreasing (due to a parasite) so crayfish have been imported from Turkey, Spain and the United States. Sweden is now the world's largest importer of crayfish!

For a crayfish party, the gardens are decorated with large, colored paper lanterns in the shape of a full moon. It is especially nice if there is also a full moon on the evening of the party.

The following is a simple menu to use if hosting a crayfish party:

> Butter, Toast and Cheese
> A large platter of Crayfish with Fresh Dill
> Green Salad and Apple Sauce
> Torte with Raspberries or Vanilla Cream Filling
> Fruit
> Beer and Coffee

"SURSTRÖMMING" PARTIES IN NORTHERN SWEDEN

In the north of Sweden another fish festival called *Surströmming*, (soured Baltic herring), is celebrated in the early days of Autumn.

This celebration revolves around eating canned, fermented Baltic herring which has been ripening for about a year. When the cans of herring are bulging, they are opened releasing a foul, repugnant smell into the air. The herring is "washed down" with beer or schnapps. New yellow potatoes and thin bread are often eaten with the fermented fish.

The tradition of eating fermented herring dates back to the time when fish was preserved by salting it. However, because salt was expensive, only enough salt was used on the fish so it wouldn't rot; it would only ferment.

EEL PARTIES IN THE PROVINCE OF "SKÅNE"

When the nights grow darker in Southern Sweden, eels—on their way to the Sargasso Sea—are unable to see nets and are easily trapped. Thus begins the season where up to a dozen varieties of eel, prepared in many different ways, are served. The fat eel needs to be helped to the stomach of the party-goer with a few drops of schnapps.

ST. MARTIN'S EVE, NOVEMBER 10

In St. Martin's native France, November was the month for testing the new vintage wines. The Saint had to be fed a good meal so the combination of goose and good wine began in France, spread to Germany, and in the 16th Century, arrived in Sweden. The history of geese in Sweden goes back to the Stone Age, and today geese are mainly found in the Province of Skåne.

On November 10, St. Martin's Eve parties are held in homes and in eating establishments. The menu begins with a heavily spiced sweet and sour Black Soup which is made from goose or pig blood. (It is understandable why there is usually an alternative soup available for the less hardy.)

The following is a sample menu served at a St. Martin's Eve Party.

> Black Soup and Goose Liver Sausage
> Bread, Butter and Cheese
> Roast Goose and Red Cabbage, Apples and Prunes
> Fruit Salad
> Apple Pie or Apple Cake or *Spettkaka*, a 3-foot high
>   creation made from hundreds of egg yolks and sugar.
>   It is baked on a skewer over an open fire. It melts in
>   your mouth!

ST. LUCIA DAY, DECEMBER 13

Many legends surround the origin of St. Lucia Day, but in all of the legends, it signals the beginning of the Christmas season. In Sweden, the season will last from December 13 until January 13 of the new year.

Since medieval times, it has been the custom of Swedes to eat up to seven breakfasts on December 13 to prepare themselves for the Christmas Fast. In Swedish homes, a young female member of the family portrays Lucia. Very early in the morning she and her older brothers and sisters, along with their mother, prepare a tray of freshly-baked flat saffron rolls with a currant in each of the four rounded corners. These rolls are called *Lussekatter* or Lucia Cats. They are served with *pepparkakor* and steaming coffee. The *pepparkakors* are made in the shapes of hearts and stars.

Mother helps to dress one of her daughters in a long white robe with a red sash, and a crown of lighted candles. Her sisters wear coronets of silver tinsel and her brothers wear tall, white, conical hats.

Father is in bed pretending to be fast asleep. As the procession enters the bedroom, it seems he wakes up in heaven surrounded by white-robed figures, one of them an angel with a halo on her head. The song **Sankta Lucia**, is sung and the candles are blown out. Rolls and cookies are served to the whole family.

CHRISTMAS EVE, DECEMBER 24

On Christmas Eve, homes are decorated with candles or lights in every window. Wonderful table runners, wall-hangings, and folded paper *tomten* are everywhere. Straw goats, the oldest Swedish Christmas symbol, stand guard by the tree, on the tree, and in the corner. Pine boughs are made into garlands and hung over doors and fireplaces. Poinsettia, red tulips, and hyacinth are on the tables, and the beloved pine tree is decked out in homemade ornaments that have been in the family for years. Each one brings back special memories. Another special decoration is the manger scene with fresh straw.

When the *smörgåsbord* has been topped off with coffee and Christmas cookies, a knock will be heard at the door. Father Christmas enters with a full sack of presents on his back. He asks, "Are there any good children in this house?" The father, brother or uncle try to disguise their voices while handing out presents. Then they leave to go to the next house.

At noon, breads are dipped in a large kettle of pot liquor, the liquid that remains after cooking Swedish Potato Sausage and Ham. This is called *Dopp i Grytan* or "Dip in the Kettle". Christmas Eve supper begins with Christmas breads, hardtack and rye bread, butter and cheese. This is followed by a Christmas *smörgåsbord*.

The following is a *smörgåsbord* menu for the evening of December 24, and often served on New Year's Eve.:

Pickled Herring and Anchovies
Beet and Herring Salad and Lingonberries
Head Cheese or *Sylte,* with vinegar on the side
Sausages, boiled and smoked, hot or cold
Pickled Pigs Feet and Cold, Sliced Tongue
Salmon in Aspic, Meatballs, Christmas Ham
Janssons Frestelse, Brussels Sprouts, Carrots and Peas
Lutfisk with melted Butter, Cream Sauce or Mustard Sauce
Boiled Potatoes with Salt and Pepper
Boiled Rice Pudding with Milk, Cinnamon and a hidden Almond
Coffee with a plate of assorted Christmas Cookies
Schnapps and Beer

"JULOTTA", DECEMBER 25

Julotta is an early morning service on Christmas Day that dates back to the Christmas devotions of the Middle Ages. While it formerly was held in the very early morning, 7:00 a.m. is now considered a normal time to begin.

Traditionally, father and the children went to the service while mother stayed home to watch the candles that burned in all the windows of the homes on Christmas Day. The rest of the family arrived at a Swedish country church which had been lit with candles held in shining brass holders which were magnificent amongst the Christmas greenery placed throughout the church. When the family returned home, mother had the breakfast ready.

Food served throughout the day varied from home to home. It did not always include a full *smörgåsbord*. A typical dinner menu could include the following:

> Consommé with Asparagus Tips
> Rolled Fish Fillets with Lobster Sauce
> Roasted Spareribs and Browned Potatoes
> Apple Sauce and Prunes
> String Beans
> Radishes and Tomatoes
> Lemon *Fromage*
> Coffee

For some, Christmas festivities end on the Twelfth Night or Epiphany. For others, it is stretched out another week until Knut's Day.

This section was researched and compiled by Ann L. Nilsson.

APPENDICES

ACKNOWLEDGEMENTS   **APPENDIX A**

We want to thank the individuals and the members of the following churches and organizations who submitted recipes, traditions and histories, or helped in any way to make this book a success. Some of the recipes submitted are family recipes and others are recipes from departed friends and relatives. Hopefully we have credited the recipes properly.

ADULLAM LUTHERAN CHURCH ELCA
OVERTON, NE
Hildur Gardine
Elsie Carlson
Connie Vaugh from Corinne Johnson
Zeadelle Matson
Florence Carlson
Lisa Tagge
Roger Matson
Betty Matson

ALL SAINTS LUTHERAN CHURCH
DARWIN, MN
Blanche Slaughter

ALMA LUTHERAN CHURCH
MEAD, NE
Inez Barrett
Phyllis Nelson

AMANA LUTHERAN CHURCH
SCANDIA, KS
Mrs. Delbert Aspegren
Mrs. George Larson
Max Berry
Esther Hammer
Mrs. C. P. Rydell (Deceased)
Mrs. Algot Anderson
Mary Larson
Arlene Stephenson
Alice Greenslode
Minnie Cardwell
Mrs. Earl Melby
Iona Tuley
Ruby Berry smith
Ellen Hammer

AMERICAN SWEDISH HISTORICAL MUSEUM
PHILADELPHIA, PA

AMERICAN SWEDISH INSTITUTE
BEMIDJI AFFILIATE
BEMIDJI, MN

AMERICAN SWEDISH INSTITUTE
MINNEAPOLIS, MN

AMERCIAN UNION OF SWEDISH SINGERS
NORDEN SINGERS
DES MOINES, IA
Mary Dickey

AMERICAN UNION OF SWEDISH SINGERS
SUNCOAST SWEDISH VETERANS CHORUS
FLORIDA
Betty Rundquist
Kay Sawdey
Dorothy Johnson
Doris Gullborg
Lucille Severson
June Carlson
Harriet Bolling
Dorothy Blom

ANDOVER LUTHERAN CHURCH
WINDOM, KS
Inez Olson

ARLINGTON HILLS LUTHERAN CHURCH
ST. PAUL, MN
Cookbook

ASCENSION LUTHERAN CHURCH
SAN DIEGO, CA
Kathy Hass
Greta Sandberg

THE AUDUBON PARK COVENANT CHURCH
ORLANDO, FL
Selma Olson
Helen Linden
Ruth Carlson
Carolyn Linden
Louise Worden
Anita Thorin

AUGUSTANA EVANGELICAL LUTHERAN CHURCH
COMSTOCK, (CUMBERLAND) WI
Rod Voshell
Corrine Thoe
Esther Berg
Losi Odden
Grace Ericson
Lena Erickson
Mildred Carlson

AUGUSTANA LUTHERAN CHURCH
ANDOVER, IL
Doris Brodd

AUGUSTANA LUTHERAN CHURCH
GRAND FORKS, ND
Mrs. Annie Espeland
Mrs. Arne Brekke
Mrs. Carl Thurn
Ida Thovson
Mrs. Hilda Lee
Mrs. Einar Swanson
Circle One
Mrs. Ray Anderson
Mrs. Howard Glehm
Mrs. Hilda Lee
Mrs. Peter Nelson
Mrs. Mandus Swenson
Miss Marjorie Nelson
Mrs. Leo Colson
Mrs. Fred Benson
Mrs. M. H. Overland
Mrs. Einar Swanson
Mrs. Arlo Pearson
Mrs. Roger Johnson
Mrs. Robert Wedin
Mrs. Oscar Johnson
Mrs. Ronald Lee
Mrs. John Booty
Mrs. Oscar Lund
Mrs. Alfred Jacobson
Mrs. Agnes Hadland
Mrs. Kenneth Waddell
Miss Hulda Edman
Mrs. Laurence Sjolinder
Mrs. John Neville
Mrs. Leonard Lunde
Mrs. A. W. Erickson

AUGUSTANA LUTHERAN CHURCH
MANSON, IA

AUGUSTANA LUTHERAN CHURCH
ST. JAMES, MN
Marcia Kunze
Aurora Kading
Helen Erickson
Dorothy Olson
Janae Anderson
Marilyn Hedlund
Hazel Weisbrod
Viola Allen
Val Anderson
Beth Rettke
Diane Missling
Mabel Nordby
Marcella Sorensen
Judy Anderson
Frances Jensen
Arline Warner
Irene Anderson
Edith Seal
Austrid Bakke
Mrs. Emmett Olson
Marlyn Gilbertson
Jeanne Miest
Ann Kintzi
Pat (Johnson) Hall
Hazel Weisbrod
Mercedes Wolner

Audrey Swanson
Dagny Petersen
Marge Jenkins
Shirley Moody
Selma Johnson
Mrs. Ruth Anderson
Lucia Breakfast Committee
Chris & Orma Hansen

AUGUSTANA LUTHERAN CHURCH
SIOUX FALLS, SD
Betty Bundine
Clarine Lange

AUGUSTANA LUTHERAN CHURCH
TUSTIN, MI
Shelby Plyler
Mabel Nelson
Margaret Hammar

AXTELL MISSION COVENANT CHURCH
GRESHAM , OR
Marilyn Nelson Wenzl

BALSAM LUTHERAN CHURCH
AMERY, WI
Margaret Carlson

BALSAMLUND LUTHERAN CHURCH
VERNDALE, MN
Orivne Werhan
Marian Fuller
Anna-Lisa Lindberg
Hazel Wiese
Cora Anderson
Janice Walkup
Ruby Walkup
Miriam Loo
Jill Walkup
Carrie Lindblom
Mary Salter
Margaret Hanson
Janice (Hanson) Ihoke
Joann (Hanson) Lee
Judy (Hanson) Maivum

BENSONVALE COVENANT CHURCH
OMAHA, NE
Georgia McCurdy

BETHANY LUTHERAN CHURCH
CRYSTAL LAKE, IL
Linnea Swenson
Jackie Johnson
Lucy Tietz
E. Provo
Elmer Benson
Mary Eckstrom
Laurel Kloepfer

BETHANY LUTHERAN CHURCH
NEGAUNEE, MI
Jean Mitchell

BETHANY LUTHERAN CHURCH
SIREN, WI
Katie Johnson Hedlund

BETHANY LUTHERAN CHURCH
WISCONSIN RAPIDS, WI
Sue Worlund
Ellen Kronstedt

BETHEL LUTHERAN CHURCH
ATKINSON, MN
Helen Drelow
June Benson

BETHEL LUTHERAN CHURCH
DANVILLE, IL
Barkman Family
Nelle Lind
Leisa Erickson Julian
Mary Lou Klage
Gladys Conrad

BETHEL LUTHERAN CHURCH
OMAHA, NE
Marilyn Thiesfeld
Vicky Shalberg
Dorothy Nimrod

BETHEL LUTHERAN CHURCH
SPICER, MN
Betty Rule

BETHEL LUTHERAN CHURCH
WILLMAR, MN
Cookbook

BETHESDA LUTHERAN CHURCH
CHICAGO, IL
Evelyn Berg
Eleanore Berg

BETHESDA LUTHERAN CHURCH
MORRISON, IL
Shirley Kelly

BETHESDA LUTHERAN CHURCH
NEW HAVEN, CT
Sonia Krummrey

BETHLEHEM LUTHERAN CHURCH
CHEROKEE, IA
In memory of Mrs. Albert Peterson
In memory of Mrs. Ellen Johnson
Mrs. Marie Nelson
Nancy Petersson
In memory of Astrid Bengston
Mrs. Eric Gustafson
In memory of Linnea Gustafson
In memory of Mrs. Klaus Magnusson
Mrs. C. J. Johnson
In memory of Mrs. Olivia
Halstrom
Mrs. Alex Petersson
Mildred Mortenson
Women of Bethlehem Lutheran

BETHLEHEM LUTHERAN CHURCH
FLORENCE, WI
Susan Van Marter
Inga Linnea Fleming

BIG LAKE EVANGELICAL COVENANT CHURCH
CLOQUET, MN
Irene Carlson
Ethel Skarp
Joanne Anderson
Vi Lee

BRAHAM COVENANT WOMEN
BRAHAM, MN
Winnie Groth Johnson

BRAHAM EVANGELICAL LUTHERAN CHURCH
BRAHAM, MN
Myrtle Telstad
Rosella Olson Brown
Aileen Anderson
Lorraine Holmberg

BRANTFORD EVANGELICAL COVENANT CHURCH
BRANTFORD TWP,
WASHINGTON CO, KANSAS
Venita Nelson
Lucille Ostlund
Alice Carlson
Mrs. Astrid Kisby

CADILLAC AREA SCANDINAVIAN SOCIETY
CADILLAC, MI
Ida Saari
Eleanor Nelson
Mary Norkoli
Mrs. Willard Wilcox
Alice Best
Lillian Fredin
Naomi Keller
Ellen Krauss

CALVARY LUTHERAN CHURCH
RAPID RIVER, MI
Norma Weberg
Alice Lundberg
LaVerne Brannstrom

CAMBRIDGE LUTHERAN CHURCH
CAMBRIDGE, IL
Trudy Johnson
Marjorie Gustafson
Ruth Munson (Deceased)
Dorothy Johnson

**CAMBRIDGE LUTHERAN CHURCH
CAMBRIDGE, MN**
Chris Misewich
Shirley Gebrielson
Mrs. Dudley Hanson
Valborg Ellingson
Mrs. Erben Norman
Carol A. Erickson
Hazel Samuelson
Bessie Bertelson
Marian Kluck
Berit Hauge
Ethel Stake
Jean Melius
Sally Johnson
Laura Ristow
Mrs. Reuben Wing
Lois Tureen
Merle Hendrickson
Slyvia Babb
Clint Moline
Mrs. Erben Norman
Evelyn Anderson
Blenda Holmstrom
Maude Tureen

**CAPRON LUTHERAN CHURCH
CAPRON, IL**
Alma Bue

**CHRIST THE KING LUTHERAN CHURCH
NEW BRIGHTON, MN**
Levonne Larson
Dolores Taylor
Ruby Carlson
Marilyn Carlson

**CONCORDIA LUTHERAN CHURCH
KINGSBURG, CA**
Evelyn Ericson
Juli Olson
Hannah Holmberg
Esther Condray
Mabel Munson
Muriel Peterson
Inez Knutson
Sally Haggmark
Gunborg Moore
Sally Steffens
Joanne Bennett
Eleanora Widmark
Lisa Moore
Elizabeth Moore Karby
Hildegarde Bolinder
Lorraine Mellstrom
Ruth Croft
Marion Hillblom
Bernice Woods

**DALA HERITAGE SOCIETY
MORA, MN**
Emmy Eklund
Doris Jensen
Joanne Olen
Ardis Hallstrom
Margaret C. Nelson
Dee Salmonson

**DALESBURG LUTHERAN CHURCH
BERESFORD, (VERMILLION) SD**
Grace Lind
Opal Dahlberg
Lennea Peterson
Virginia Johnson
Ron Johnson

**EAST SVEADAHL LUTHERAN CHURCH
ST JAMES, MN**
Mrs. Earl L. Olson
Austrid Noren

**EBENEZER LUTHERAN CHURCH
WILLIMANTIC, CT**
Wendy Clifton

**ELIM COVENANT CHURCH
STOCKHOLM, SD**
Phyllis Evjen

**ELIM LUTHERAN CHURCH
MARQUETTE, KS**
Linda Johnson

**EMANUEL LUTHERAN CHURCH
BLACKFOOT, ID**
Beulah Jenson
Evelyn Neff

**EMANUEL LUTHERAN CHURCH
BRADFORD, PA**
Cindy Edel
Evelyn Rishell
Naomi Carlson
Sara Swanson

**ESTHER LUTHERAN CHURCH PARKERS
PRAIRIE, MN**
Stella Nelson Berg
Doris Arvidson
Ethel Hedlund
Eleanor Thompson
Gertrude Hanson
Eldora Hanson
Doris Paulson

**EVANGELICAL COVENANT CHURCH
CLAY CENTER, KS**
Arlene M. Anderson

**EVANGELICAL COVENANT CHURCH
HELENA, MT**
Myrtle Klos
Ida Lundberg
Judy Golob
Hilma Johnson

**EVANGELICAL COVENANT CHURCH
INTERNATIONAL FALLS, MN**
Joyce Einarson
Violet Johnson
Grace (Johnson) Earnist
Bernice Englund

**EVANGELICAL COVENANT CHURCH
KINGSBURG, CA**
Alice Ostrom

EVANGELICAL COVENANT CHURCH
MILWAUKEE, WI
Marcy Minix
Jean Olson

EVANGELICAL COVENANT CHURCH
STANTON, IA
Harriet Olson
Frances Hogberg
Jean Palmquist
Dorothy Rossander
Kay Slump
Frances Berglund
Phyllis Lindstrom
Eloise Palmquist
Mergeline Olson
Helga Urn
June Palmquist
Linda Strickland
Linda Palmquist Stanek
Florence Requist
Charlotte Palmquist
Bev Palmquist
Helen Anderson
Laura Bergstrom

EVANGELICAL COVENANT CHURCH
WARREN, MN
Mille Engstrom

EVANGELICAL LUTHERAN CHURCH
TOLLEY, ND
Helen Peterson
Theoda Johnson
Dagney Siebert
Marilyn Froberg

FAITH LUTHERAN CHURCH
BALSAM LAKE, WI
Lorine Hendrickson

FAITH LUTHERAN CHURCH
FOREST LAKE, MN
Dorothy Grandstrand
Cookbook

FAITH LUTHERAN CHURCH
ODEBOLT, IA
Phrona Johnson
Hazel Sommers
John Noyd
Lois E Johnson
Arlene Sundell
Gladys Johnson

FIRST COVENANT CHURCH
MINNEAPOLIS, MN
Cookbook
Helen Olfelt

FIRST COVENANT CHURCH
OAKLAND, CA
Alice Norman
Alma Edwardson
Gunvor Peterson
Julia Norman
Vi Martinson
Martha Carlsen
Evelyn Stenstrom

Esther Berg
Elinor Bergen
nna Eliason
Vicki Johnson
Esther Peterson
Barbara Ayer
Liz Hultgren
Ted Martinson

FIRST EVANGELICAL LUTHERAN CHURCH
OAKLAND, NE
Lucille Linden
Elsie Sebberson
Karen Dismer
Linnea Young

FIRST EVANGELICAL LUTHERAN CHURCH
ROCKFORD, IL
Raye Stone
Dorothy Stone
Helene Laurson
Vi Johnson
Charlotte Erickson
H. Nordstrom
Mary Wilson (From Edna Johnson)
Edith Forberg
Edla Engberg
Selma Carlson
Marie Samuelson
Helga Johnson

FIRST EVANGELICAL LUTHERAN CHURCH
TAYLORS FALLS, MN
Helen Anderson

FIRST EVANGELICAL LUTHERAN CHURCH
WINTHROP, MN
Gertrude M. Olson

FIRST LUTHERAN CHURCH
AULT, CO

FIRST LUTHERAN CHURCH
BISMARCK, ND
Muriel Seidel
Ruth Miller

FIRST LUTHERAN CHURCH
EL CAMPO, TX
Marilyn Kight
Luella Eide

FIRST LUTHERAN CHURCH
GARDNER, MA
Grethe Anderholm
Joan Paul
Catherine Opgenorth
Selma Olson
Gunhild Anderson
Dottie Swenson

FIRST LUTHERAN CHURCH
GENESEO, IL
Donna Doubler by Joyce Rickmos
Sonja Anderson
Joyce Rickmos
Elly Flagberg
Keith Nordling
Mildred Lundin
Emy Kopp
Frances Wiedenkoeft
Juanita Terpening
Ingrid Hook
Joyce Rickman
Merle Swanson
Winifred Ward
Gladys Meier
Anna Berglund
Mrs. Ellen Benson
Ruth Bengtson
Margaret Weisser
Arne Lindeberg
Frank Andersen
Teppa Korpela
Lillian Bartlett
Vera Nissen
Jill Rimington
Gladys Swanson
Desyl Thornbloom
Teresa Jacobsen
Dorothy Anderson
Sherry Erickson
Marie Hulting
Birgit Spang Andersen
Ruth Drehman
Betty Kipp
Janice Nelson
Donna Doubler
Hilma Hagelin
Elly Flagbert
Tyra Parson
Ruth Hagelin
Dorothy Nelson
E. J. Carlson

FIRST LUTHERAN CHURCH
GRANVILLE, IL
Eleanor Birgerson
Evelyn Jeppson
Ruth Franceway
Ellowyn Kaletka

FIRST LUTHERAN CHURCH
HECTOR, MN
Elaine Radloff

FIRST LUTHERAN CHURCH
KENSINGTON, MN
Eleanor Gunderson

FIRST LUTHERAN CHURCH
LINCOLN, NE
Mildred Wilson
Leone Hagstrom

FIRST LUTHERAN CHURCH
OTTUMWA, IA

FREMONT LUTHERAN CHURCH
ESSEX, IA
Dorothy Olson
Maxine Johnson
Evelyn Anderson
Maxine Chastain
Lenore Freed
Lillian Johnson
Laverna M. Larson
Elroy Blomberg
Shelene Carlson
Berneice Carlson
Norma Kampe
Eleanor Freed
Louise Bergren

FRIDHEM LUTHERAN CHURCH
HORDVILLE, NE
Mrs. Delores Viburg

GETHSEMANE LUTHERAN CHURCH
UPSALA , MN
Anna Smedman
Marlee Holmen
Marlys Juhnke
Margaret Johnson
Frances Groth
Betty Staricka
Lorraine Lovain

GLORIA DEI LUTHERAN CHURCH
HUNTINGTON STATION, NY
Ruth Clement

GRACE LUTHERAN CHURCH
AURORA, IL
Emily Ostergren
Rae Jean Hultgren

GRACE LUTHERAN CHURCH
HENNING, MN
Hazel Rodman

GRACE LUTHERAN CHURCH
MANKATO, MN
Emelyn Larson

GRACE LUTHERAN CHURCH
MARATHON, IA
Esther Okerberg
Mrs. Mildred Fredricks
Lorraine Anderson
Mrs. Clarence Larson
Ruth Burns
Mrs. Martin Johnson

GRACE LUTHERAN CHURCH
RANKIN, IL
Mildred Andree Holmes
Dorothy Seidel

GRACE LUTHERAN CHURCH
SHEYENNE, ND
Ida Phyllis Wahlstrom
Astrid Anderson
Aileen Berglund

GRACE COVENANT CHURCH
STAMBAUGH, MI
Florence Piflce

GAMMELGÅRDEN VOLUNTEERS'
SCANDIA, MN

GUSTAFSON REDEEMER COVENANT CHURCH
BELOIT, WI
Julie Gustafson

HEBRON LUTHERAN CHURCH
BURDICK, KS
Alvida Larson
Inez Schild
Maj Britt Hawk
Nancy Hanson

HIGHLAND GROVE LUTHERAN CHURCH
HITTERDAL, MN
Mamie Peterson
Gale Iverson
Shirley Iverson
Laurie Rian
Thelma Ulven
Beverly Wibe
Mable Johnson
Nora Wibe
Ella Malakowsky
Mary Anderson
Beverly Anderson
Alice Anderson
Sarah Lofgren
Hannah Nord by Joanne Hitterdahl
Violet Anderson
Devaughn Meyer
Esther Luthi
Juanita Leno
Beverly Iverson
Mrs. Alfred Anderson
Mrs. Albin Anderson

HIGHLANDA LUTHERAN CHURCH
LANGFORD, SD
Mrs. Ehlert Ogren
Mrs. Ralph Ogren
Mrs. Edith Palm
Gay Ogren

HILMAR COVENANT CHURCH
HILMAR, CA
Susie Van Foeken

HOPE LUTHERAN CHURCH
MINNEAPOLIS, MN
Helen Everett

IMMANUEL AND UNION CREEK LUTHERAN
CHURCH
AKRON, IA
Hulda Johnson
Fern Roy
Anna Frisk
Phyllic Frisk

IMMANUEL LUTHERAN CHURCH
ATWATER, MN
Leone Hedlund
Amanda Monson

Russell Olson
Shirley Walsh
Marion Kingery

IMMANUEL LUTHERAN CHURCH
CLARISSA, MN
Sadie Hokanson

IMMANUEL LUTHERAN CHURCH
DUNNELL, MN
Florence Peterson
Myrtle Peterson
Mrs. A. M. Hall
Mrs. J. Walter Nelson
Mrs. A. H. Lyon
Ferne Nelson

IMMANUEL LUTHERAN CHURCH
EAST MOLINE, IL
Margaret Peterson
Virginia Johnson

IMMANUEL LUTHERAN CHURCH
GREELY, CO
Marie Lindeen Mosbo
Estella Stroberg
Ruth Swanson
Mrs. G. M Christensen
Mrs. Esther Benson
Shirley Uhrich
Helen Elgsten

IMMANUEL LUTHERAN CHURCH
HOLDEN, MA
Lilian Hudson by Valeda Schmuchi

IMMANUEL LUTHERAN CHURCH
MEDIAPOLIS, IA
Judy Thomas
Greta Cling
Violet Amenell
Peggy Hansen
Karen Hedges
Joyce Bloomberg Brackman
Trude Campbell

IMANUEL LUTHERAN CHURCH
OMAHA, NE
Ida Tucker
Irene Barswell
Virginia Williams

IMMANUEL LUTHERAN CHURCH
SWEA CITY, IA
Clara Thorson

INTERBAY COVENANT CHURCH
SEATTLE, WA
Gladys Gerdin
Alice Dodds
Marie-Ann Swanstrom

LINDSBORG COMMUNITY LIBRARY
Lindsborg, KS
Karen J. Olson

LINDSBORG KANSAS MISSION CHURCH
LINDSBORG, KS
Virginia Brunsell
Nora Winblad
Ida Lindberg

THE LINNEAS OF TEXAS
Dorothy Mckenzie
Rainie Johanson
Jeanette Leavens
Helen Almquist
Ingrid Werler
Pat Fisher
Harry Maurine Swenson
Gudrun Merrill
Lois Jordan
Alice Dodd
Eileen Fowler
Vivian Frisk
Kerstin Ruud
Brite-Marie Bodorff

MAC ARTHUR PARK LUTHERAN CHURCH
SAN ANTONIO, TX
Kathryn Schwanenberg Carter
Martha Mueller
Shari Dybdahl
Gloria Schwanenberg
Carol Benson
Betty Spickler
Lillian Young
Pastor G. W. Schwanenberg
Forence Fahlberg
Ruth Faubion
Nancy Kusenberger
Melanie Mayfield
Birgit Suaning Olsen
Cheryl Johnson
Pomykal Family
Cyndi Smykay
Leslie P. Marsh

MAGNOLIA LUTHERAN CHURCH
SEATTLE, WA
Anna Kellison
A. G. Fjellman
Lisa Lethenstrom
Stina Johanson
Chris Backstrom

MAMRELUND LUTHERAN CHURCH
PENNOCK (WILLMAR), MN
Helen Tosso
Franny Yule

MARIA LUTHERAN CHURCH
KENNEDY, MN
Lue Mattson
Nancy Lundberg
Mrs. C. E. Johnson
LaDonna Truedson
Jeanette Spilde
Bonnie Johnson
Martha Nelson
Corrine Gunnarson
Edna Lundberg
Julie Larson
Dorothy Orsund

Frank & Ethel Larson
Ellkay Larson
Marion Mattson
Erlyce Larson

MESSIAH EVANGELICAL LUTHERAN CHURCH
BAY CITY, MI
Elva Wahlstrom

MESSIAH LUTHERAN CHURCH
BURLINGTON, IA
Jane Dallin Stallsworth

MISSION COVENANT CHURCH
FOSTER CITY, MI
Cookbook
Esther Dawe
Janet Nelson
Joanne Stenfors
Lucille Kling
Verna Peterson

MORIAH LUTHERAN CHURCH
LUDLOW, PA
Grace Mattison

MOUNT CALVARY LUTHERAN CHURCH
EXCELSIOR, MN
Jeannette Cummings

MOUNT OLIVE LUTHERAN CHURCH
ROCHESTER, MN
Bonnie Wingert
Lucy DeRenee

MOUNT ZION LUTHERAN CHURCH
HUDSON, WI
Lawrence O. Anderson
Carol Kreigl

NATHANAEL LUTHERAN CHURCH
ALCESTER, SD
Eleanor M. Anderson
Marion Sternquist

NEW GOTTLAND EVANGELICAL COVENANT
CHURCH MCPHERSON, KS
Asta Ostlind Chase

NORDENS WOMEN CLUB
JAMESTOWN, NY
Cookbook

NORMANDALE LUTHERAN CHURCH OF EDINA
EDINA, MN
Bonnie Wingert

NORTH CENTRAL SVENSKA KLUBBEN
NORTH CENTRAL IOWA
Edith Isaacson
Myrtle Erickson
Ruth Kling
Martha Fesler
Carol Castenson
Lorraine Young
Audrey Carlson
Eileen Samuelson
Myrtle Anderson

Ingrid Hunter
Helen Nelson
Katheryn Burkgren
Carol Castenson
Alice Fardal
Cleo Swanson
Dorothy Carlon
Sadie Mossberg

NORTH CROW RIVER LUTHERAN CHURCH
COKATO, MN
Vernette Heidenreich
Jeanette Johnson
Margaret Lundeen
Lila Carlen
Florence Sunblad
Hazel Benson
Marian Pearson
Adelyne Lankki
Carole Semke
Edith Nelson
Irene Ekstrand
Beatrice Johnson
Marie Anderson
Mrs. Walter Anderson

NORTH PARK COVENANT CHURCH
CHICAGO, IL
Mrs. Walter Gobel
Eleanor Hedstrom
Florence Hogfeldt
Mrs. Otto S Carlson
Mrs. Otto F Ohlson
Mrs. Signe M Carlson
Mrs. Eric G Hawkinson
Essther M Carlson

NORTHWEST IOWA CHAPTER
AMERICAN-SCANDINAVIAN FOUNDATION
Ione Johnson

OLANDSKLUBBEN
NEW YORK AREA
Stella Swanson
Vicki Bender

OUR SAVIOURS LUTHERAN CHURCH
HASTINGS, MN
Darlene Myers
Janet Martin
Ilene Lorenz
Cookbook

OUR SAVIOURS LUTHERAN CHURCH
LANSING, IL
Margaret Johnson

PILGRIM LUTHERAN CHURCH
FREDERIC, WI
Carol Thompson

PIONEER LAKE LUTHERAN CHURCH
CONOVER, WI
Frieda Jefferson
Margaret Johnson
Roger Jensen
Florence & Ed Hedberg
Peggy Waldron
Irene Johnson

Elsie Lindberg
Thelma Larsen

POWELL VALLEY COVENANT CHURCH
GRESHAM, OR
Ruth Gustafson

PRINCE OF PEACE EVANGELICAL LUTHERAN
CHURCH
GRANDVIEW, MO
Hazel Berglund
Lorene Hope
Norma Sandvig
Betty Stenstrom
Alpha Lundquist
Lois Moeller
John Sandvig

PROVIDENCE VALLEY LUTHERAN CHURCH
DAWSON, MN
Mildred Miller
Lois Swenson
Sari Kilheffer
Mrs. Merill Lund
Audrey Bengtson

RED RIVER LUTHERAN CHURCH
HALLOCK, MN
Mrs. Wilbur Lindgren
Elsie Johnson
Mrs. Wallace Nelson

RICHLAND EVANGELICAL COVENANT CHURCH
RICHLAND, MI

ROCHESTER COVENANT CHURCH
ROCHESTER, MN
Mary Lou Sather
Bonnie Fenton
Carolyn Cedarleaf
Evie Hedstrum
Juanita Griffin
Elsie Westphal
Helen Kennedy
Sue Larson
Arleen Johnson
Evie Hedstrum
Marian Fladeland

ST. ANSGARS LUTHERAN CHURCH
CANNON FALLS, MN
Lois Nelson

ST. PAUL'S LUTHERAN CHURCH
GALETON, PA
Edna Greene
Ruth Leach
Elsie Verbjar

ST. PAUL LUTHERAN CHURCH
OAKLAND, CA
Karin Mai

ST. PHILIP'S LUTHERAN CHURCH
HASTINGS, MN

ST PETERS LUTHERAN CHURCH
CANYON, MN
Doris Swanson

SALEM EVANGELICAL LUTHERAN CHURCH
DULUTH, MN
Helen Bergh

SALEM LUTHERAN CHURCH
CRESTON, IA
Linda Kilgore
Lila (Anderson) Monday
Mrs. C. E. Youngquist (Deceased)
Joyce Anderson

SALEM LUTHERAN CHURCH
DALBO, MN
Helen Johnson

SALEM LUTHERAN CHURCH
MINNEAPOLIS, MN
Bonnie Sandgren

SALEM LUTHERAN CHURCH
ROCK ISLAND, IL
Audrey Larsen

SILLERUD LUTHERAN CHURCH
BALATON, MN
Fern Nelson
Anna Swan

SILOA LUTHERAN CHURCH
MORRIS RUN, PA
Velma Johnson
Mertella Smith
Faye Davies
Teresa Morris
Viola Bombaski
Gerda Isaacson

SOUTHERN FLORIDA ASSOCIATES OF
AMERICAN-SCANDINAVIAN FOUNDATION INC
FLORIDA

SPRING GARDEN LUTHERAN CHURCH
CANNON FALLS, MN
Stella Swanson
Vicki Bender
Marjorie Pagel
Pastor Heidi Kvanli
Evelyn Challis
Betty Sjoquist
Gerry Haggstrom
Mrs. Ralph Haggstrom
Lyla Swanson
Lois Slades
Idella Clauson
Lydia Martenson
Milton Swenson Family
Magnus Edstrom Family from Jeanne Lindell
Kvittem
Mrs. Eldon Anderson

STOCKHOLM LUTHERAN CHURCH
SHICKLEY, NE
In memory of Mrs. Albert Hendrickson
Melba Replogle
Norma Hendrickson
Mabel Berquist
Sheila Hendrickson
In memory of Evelyn Thurin
In memory of Esther Wongdahl
Euhla Sharp
In memory of Emma Baker
Joan Hendrickson
In memory of Effie Johnson

STRATFORD LUTHERAN CHURCH
STRATFORD, IA
Marilyn Berglund

SVEA LUTHERAN CHURCH
HAGER CITY, WI
Mary May Anderson

SVENSKA VÄNNER
JAMESTOWN, ND
June Lundgren
Winifred Townsend
Ted Voigt
Christine Lee
Bill Soper

SVENSKA VÄNNERNA, INC
SOUTH CENTRAL, MN
Elsie Westphal
Stella Carlson
Magie Carlson

SWEA (BOSTON CHAPTER)
SWEDISH WOMENS EDUCATIONAL
ASSOCIATION INTERNATIONAL
WEST CONCORD MA
Eva Gitta Habih

SWEDISH CLUB OF METROPOLITIAN DETROIT
SWEDISH WOMEN'S ORGANIZATION
FARMINGTON HILLS, MI
Astrid Stadler
Emmy Holmberg
Gunilla skogfeldt
Winnie Cramton
Greta Nilsson
Eric Johnson

SWEDISH COUNCIL OF AMERICA
MINNEAPOLSI, MN
Eja Nilsson

SWEDISH COUNCIL OF ST LOUIS
ST. LOUIS, MO
Lilian Morath
Doris Martin
Dorothy Hill
Ruth Goeglein
Astrid Tucker
June Nystrom
Walter Peterson
Diane Peterson Zimmer
Jean Pierson

Millie Anderson Lammi
Charles Anderson
Joyce Johnson Sauer
Warene Anderson
Ruth Ericson
Delpha Swanson
Evelyn Fagerberg
Avis Dickey
Maude Weston
Florence Selvig
Mrs. J. A. Jacobson

THE SWEDISH CULTURAL HERITAGE SOCIETY
FARGO, ND
Ann Zavoral
Phyllis Paulson

SWEDLANDA EVANGELICAL LUTHERAN
CHURCH
HECTOR, MN
Mrs. Arne Kivioja

THABOR LUTHERAN CHURCH
WAUSA, NE

TRE KRONOR SCANDINAVIAN SOCIETY
HOLDREGE, NE
Margaret Hodge
Mrs. Oscar Brown (Deceased)
Arleen Brown
Nadine Brown
Margaret David
Nancy Tiderman Osborne

TRINITY LUTHERAN CHURCH
AXTELL, NE
Clara Olson

TRINITY LUTHERAN CHURCH
BENSON, MN
Mildred Johnson
Alphild Johnson

TRINITY LUTHERAN CHURCH
BOXHOLM, IA

TRINITY LUTHERAN CHURCH
CARTHAGE, SD
Elleda Magnuson

TRINITY LUTHERAN CHURCH
GRESHAM, OR
Lou Bohn
Juliette Lundquist
Anna Kallman
Violet Ayres
Trudy Runnels
June Kramer

TRINITY LUTHERAN CHURCH
LINDSTROM, MN

TRINITY LUTHERAN OF MINNEHAHA FALLS
CHURCH
MINNEAPOLIS, MN
Norma Hall
Edith Rosdahl

VALLEY EVANGELICAL COVENANT CHURCH
STILLMAN VALLEY, IL
Charlotte Carlson

VASA LUTHERAN CHURCH
VASA VILLAGE (WELCH), MN
Mrs. Eric Norelius
Eleanore Miller

WALNUT HILL LUTHERAN CHURCH
DALLAS, TX
Mrs. J. Elof Johnson
Avis Evenson
Mrs. Robert Cunningham
Elaine Clayton

WALSBURG LUTHERAN CHURCH
LEONARDVILLE, KS
Lilyan Oman
Beverly Sundgren
Elsie Oman
Jeanette Alstatt

WILEY HEIGHTS COVENANT CHURCH
YAKIMA, WA
Lucille Johnson

ZION EVANGELICAL LUTHERAN CHURCH
MINNEAPOLIS, MN
Rose Molacek

ZION EVANGELICAL LUTHERAN CHURCH
NEWMAN GROVE, NE
Violet Anderson
Edith Pearson
Myrtle Long
Elvera Carlson
Phyllis Anderson

ZION LUTHERAN CHURCH
GOWRIE, IA
Phyllis Rasmussen
Ingrid Hunter
Frances Brown
Belle Srand
Dorothy Carlon
Sadie Mossberg
Mabel Carlson

ZION LUTHERAN CHURCH
MARINETTE, WI
Carol Holstrom

ZION LUTHERAN CHURCH
ORTONVILLE, MN
Arlene Larson
Evelyn Brolin
Anna Johnson
Olga Brolin in memory of Mrs. Oscar Johnson
Bette Mattson

ZION LUTHERAN CHURCH
ROCKFORD, IL
Mrs. Lorin Beegbee
Mrs. M L Kjellstrom
Mrs. G H Ekstrom
Mrs. Nels Holm
Mrs. Martin Rosen
Mrs. Frank Nelson
Mrs. R skog
Mrs. Willie Anderson
Mrs. F P Eldredge
Mrs. P C Howland
Jane LaBrande
Sally MacCallum

ZION SWEDISH LUTHERAN CHURCH
GOLDEN VALLEY, MN
Martha Norrgard

OTHER CONTRIBUTORS:

Ada's Nostalgic Cookbook
Virginia Johnson
Doris Martin

Marian Anderson
Ft. Montgomery, NY

Butterfield Books
Egg Gravy
Linda K. Hubalek
Aurora, CO

Inger Karlsson
Lima, Sweden

Elsa Larson
Shrewsbury, MA

Ann Nielson, Dala Painter
Edina, MN

Pennfield Press
Superbly Swedish
Iowa City, IA

Catharine Tenebäck
Rock Hill, SC

SWEDISH DALMÅLNING

One of the unique features of Swedish folk culture is Dala painting which developed during the 18th and 19th Centuries by self-taught painters from the Province of Dalarna. Dala painting is a naive narrative, a fantasy picture, created with simplicity and playfulness of color and forms, a mix of prehistoric and present times. This style developed about 1780 and continued for about 100 years. Huge floral motifs characterized the paintings. Painting styles varied between the Northern and Southern Provinces of Sweden. The rich paintings reflect the artists' knowledge of the Bible. The main source of inspiration for peasant painters were the illustrations in the "Picture Bibles": the Gustavus Adolphus Bible of 1618 and Hubner's Biblical Stories.

Dala painting is often referred to as kurbits painting. The kurbit or gourd plant was written about in the Book of Jonah. God caused a kurbit to grow and shade Jonah while he sat in the desert, thus saving his life. The kurbit became an important part of the paintings. In fact, at times, the kurbit became as important as the story that was depicted in the painting.

The use of elaborate borders, including a type of painted folded ribbon, was also popular among the peasant painters. Svante Svärdström, a noted Swedish author and painter, said, *"Dala painting is one of the most extraordinary things that has happened in the history of Swedish art."*

In the United States, interest in Swedish Dala painting is growing rapidly. *A Swedish Dalmålning Society* and a newsletter for artists of this craft was founded in 1993. Membership information may be directed to:

Swedish Dalmålning Society International
14817 North Court
Clackamas, OR 97015
USA

This information on Dala painting was written by Ann L. Nilsson.

DALA PAINTERS OF THE SECTION DIVIDERS

DARLENE PETERSON BUCHANAN of Kirkland, WA is of Swedish descent. Along with her business of custom painting porcelain, she is also an antique dealer. Her collection of Swedish decorations, accessories and custom-painted wall cabinets were pictured in the February, 1994 issue of *"Country Living Magazine."* Darlene hand-painted a ceiling border in the IKEA store in the Puget Sound area of Washington. She also creates designs for Bergquist Importers of Cloquet, MN and has designed and built custom cabinets for the Seattle and Bellevue, WA Nordstrom stores. Public showings of her works include: Panacea Gallery, Bellevue Square; Nordic Heritage Museum, Seattle WA; *Gammelgården* Museum, Scandia, MN and Pacific Lutheran University, Tacoma, WA.

Her painting can be found at the front of the Beverages Section.

NANCY MORGAN of West Des Moines, IA is of Swedish descent on her father's side. She has been a *rosemaler* for many years, but became interested in Swedish Dala painting in 1984 after she toured the *Nordiska* Museum in Stockholm, Sweden. She has taken painting classes from Sallie DeReus in Decorah, IA.

Her painting is found at the front of the Desserts and Sweets Section. It was inspired by the works of Johannes Nilsson (1757-1827) from southern Sweden.

LISA DAHLFJORD-NELSON of Clackamas, OR was born in Göteborg, Sweden. She came to America as a young bride in 1967. She has been painting for over 16 years and teaches *Dalmålning* and tole painting in her home. She founded the *Dalmålning* Society in 1993 and publishes a newsletter three times a year. Every Christmas she sells her paintings and dolls at the Scandinavian Celebration in Portland, OR. She also paints consignment work and stays active in the Scandinavian community in Portland.

Her painting can be found at the front of the Appendix Section.

ANN L. NILSSON of Edina, MN is of Swedish descent. Her husband, Bengt-Eric, grew up in Sweden. Ann teaches both Swedish Dala painting and Norwegian *rosemaling.* She also demonstrates Scandinavian painting and is the co-chair for the International Dala Painting Exhibit and Competition held each year at *Gammelgården,* a Swedish Historical Museum in Scandia, MN. She recently was awarded a Folk Art Grant from the Minnesota State Board of Arts for further study of Swedish painting. She is a member of the *Dalmålning* Society, the American Swedish Institute, *Gammelgården,* the Norwegian-American Museum of Decorah, IA and Western *Rosemalers* of Seattle WA.

Her paintings can be found on the cover of this book, and in the front of the Breads and 'Smörgåsbord' Sections.

BOBBIE PETERSON of Minneapolis, MN has made numerous journeys to Sweden to research the folk arts. She has studied with many famous Dala painters such as: Hans Prins, Bengt Engman and Birgitta Hedengren. She has written two books: <u>A Gnome's Christmas,</u> and <u>A Folk Art Journey</u>. She also illustrates the beautiful Swedish heritage calendars published by Paulstad Communications of Minneapolis. She has designed several Christmas card lines and has been a contributing editor to several national magazines. She teaches Dala painting classes at the American Swedish Institute in Minneapolis and European folk art classes in the Minneapolis/St. Paul area. She recently painted a 20-foot clock for the town square at Mora, MN.

Her paintings can be found at the front of the Salads, Vegetables and Soups Section as well as the front of the Festivals Section.

ADDIE PITTELKOW of St. Paul, MN has been a serious student of Scandinavian folk art for over 20 years. She has studied with such outstanding foreign artists as: Sigmund Aarseth, Bergliot Lunde, Nils Ellingsgaard, Knut Andersen, Birgitta Hedengren, Hans Prins and Bengt Engman. In 1970 she was awarded the coveted Gold Medal of Honor for her *rosemaling* expertise. She teaches extensively throughout the Upper-Midwest and has demonstrated Dala painting at many cultural events. Her paintings appear in churches and public buildings, as well as in private collections.

Her painting can be found at the front of the Faith Section.

GAIL SANDEEN of St. Paul, MN started painting as a child with her well-known grandfather, C. O. Christiansen – the famous Danish landscape and portrait artist. She has studied *rosemaling at* the Norwegian-American Museum in Decorah, IA under Sigmund Aarseth, Nils Ellingsgaard and Knut Andersen. She has studied Dala painting at the American Swedish Institute in Minneapolis, MN under Hans Prins and Bengt Engman. She has also made several trips to Norway and Sweden to study folk art painting. She has taught *rosemaling* classes for over 40 years. She owns a Scandinavian gift shop in St. Paul and still "paints for fun and/or commission."

Her painting can be found at the front of the Provinicial Flowers Section.

RITA SHARPE lives in the Swedish-American community of Lindsborg, KS. She started *rosemaling* in the mid-70's and painted with Pat Virch of Marquette, MI. In 1987 Rita "discovered" Swedish Dala painting. She has been Dala painting for over 15 years, and loves the story-telling aspect of it.

Her painting can be found at the front of the Meats and Main Dishes Section.

PROVINCIAL FLOWER SKETCHES

Avis Johnson was brought up on a farm in Taylor, WI. Her favorite haunt was an old apple tree which, in effect, became her first studio. It was there that she spent many hours drawing and sketching. Wild flowers have always been a passion of hers. In high school she transplanted flowers from the marsh and woods to her own private wild flower garden. She has since moved several of them to her yard in Minneapolis.

Basically a self-taught artist, she attended classes at the University of Minnesota and the American Swedish Institute and has studied with Leif Holgersson and Fred Somers on location in Sweden. Among her works are illustrations in books and corporate publications. The artist's paintings can be found in private collections in several nations. Watercolors of Scandinavian churches, flowers, log cabins and boats are her most popular paintings.

SAFFRON BREAD SKETCH

Barb Pinc is the owner of Studio 61 Art Gallery, Hastings, MN.

METRIC CONVERSION CHART

Approximate Liquid and Dry Measure Equivalencies

Customary	Metric
1/4 teaspoon	1.25 milliliters
1/2 teaspoon	2.5 milliliters
1 teaspoon	5 milliliters
1 tablespoon	15 milliliters
1 fluid ounce	30 milliters
1/4 cup	60 milliliters
1/3 cup	80 milliliters
1/2 cup	120 milliliters
1 cup	240 milliters
1 pint (2 cups)	480 milliliters
1 quart (4 cups)	960 milliliters
1 quart (32 ounces)	0.96 liters
1 gallon (4 quarts)	3.84 liters
1 ounce (by weight)	28 grams
1/4 pound (4 ounces)	114 grams
1 pound (16 ounces)	454 grams
2.2 pounds	1 kilogram (1000 grams)

==

2 tablespoons = 1 ounce
4 tablespoons = 1/4 cup
16 tablespoons = 1 cup
1 pint = 16 ounces
1 pint = 2 cups
1 quart = 2 pints

1 Swedish *"Kkp"* is = about
   1/2 cup

1 Swedish *matsked* =
   1 Tablespoon

1 Swedish *tesked* = 1 rounded
   1/2 teaspoon

1 kilogram = 10 hectograms
1 hectogram = 100 grams
1 kilogram = 1000 grams
1 liter = 10 deciliters
1 1/2 deciliters = 1 regular
"coffee cup"
1 quart = 9.5 deciliters
1 pint = 4.75 deciliters
1 cup = 2.4 deciliters
1 liter = 3 3/4 cups

1 cube of butter = 1 inch by 1
   inch by 1 inch or 1/4 cup

Swedish Women's Educational Association International, Inc
Boston Chapter

When you know:	Multiply by:	To find:
Grams	0.035	ounces
Kilograms	2.2	pounds
Milliliters	0.03	fluid ounces
Liters	2.1	pints
Liters	1.06	quarts
Liters	0.26	gallons
Teaspoons	5	millilters
Tablespoons	15	millilters
Ounces	30 m	milliliters
Cups	0.24	liters
Pints	0.47	liters
Quarts	0.95	liters
Gallons	3.8	liters
Ounces	28	grams
Pounds	0.45	kilograms

Oven Temperature Equivalencies

Description	Fahrenheit (°F)	Celsius (°C)
Cool	200	90
Very slow	250	120
Slow	300-325	150-160
Moderately slow	325-350	160-180
Moderate	350-375	180-190
Moderately hot	375-400	190-200
Hot	400-450	200-230
Very hot	450-500	230-260

U.S. Department of Commerce
Technology Administration
Metric Program
Gaithersburg, MD

SVERIGE *APPENDIX D*

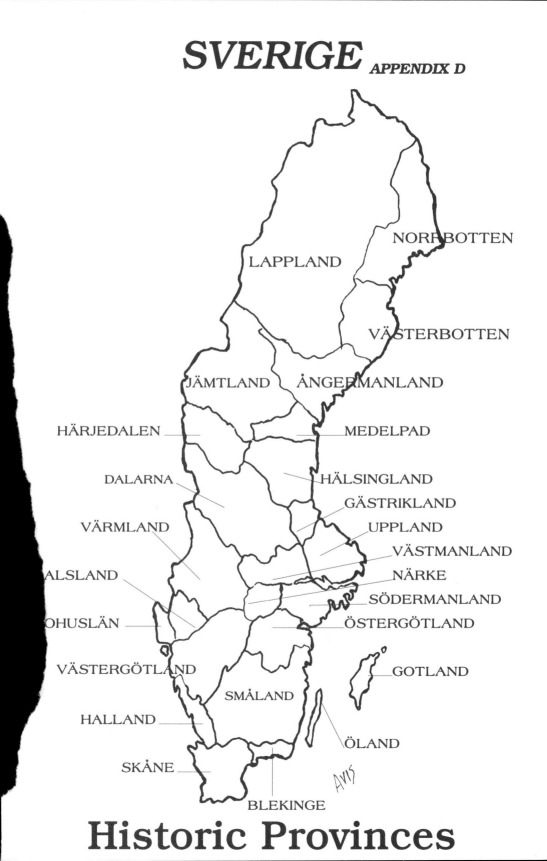

NORRBOTTEN

LAPPLAND

VÄSTERBOTTEN

JÄMTLAND   ÅNGERMANLAND

HÄRJEDALEN   MEDELPAD

DALARNA   HÄLSINGLAND

GÄSTRIKLAND

VÄRMLAND   UPPLAND

VÄSTMANLAND

ALSLAND   NÄRKE

SÖDERMANLAND

OHUSLÄN   ÖSTERGÖTLAND

VÄSTERGÖTLAND   GOTLAND

SMÅLAND

HALLAND

ÖLAND

SKÅNE

BLEKINGE

Historic Provinces